Building the Space Infrastructure and Developing the Cis-Lunar Neighborhood

By

ALASTAIR STORM BROWNE

Co-author of Cosmic Careers

ISBN: 979-8-89694-155-2 Paperback
ISBN: 979-8-89694-154-5 eBook
ISBN: 979-8-89694-156-9 Hardcover

Printed in the United States of America

To my parents:

Howard Storm Browne Jr., M.D.

and

Doris Mae Cox Browne

"Any society, if it is to flourish instead of merely survive, must strive to transcend its own limits."

-ANDREW CHAIKIN

CONTENTS

ACKNOWLEDGEMENTS

This book is my life's work, of which *Cosmic Careers* was spawned, though it came out first. This book is the core of everything I've always written about space development.

I would like to thank the following people who contributed to the publishing of this book, for believing in me though at times I didn't, and in my writing career in general:

Ali Murtaza Shaikh and Hussain Syed Mohammed, two illustrators that I have hired. You will see a lot of their illustrations in this book.

Charlie Shaw and Chad Glass, whose illustrations you will also see in this book.

Elizabeth Ribera, who took three photos of a NASA 747 jet carrying the Space Shuttle *Endeavour,* flying over the San Francisco area to show to the public on its way to Los Angeles. Her father, Salvatore Ribera, emailed them to me, one of which I used in this book.

Sally Jacobson, of the Christus Rex Lutheran Center at UND, who went out of her way to take pictures of the UND campus and the CAS building for me to publish in this book, because I mentioned this university because of its discipline in Space Studies. I also wrote the original manuscript of this book at the Rex, back in 1990.

The University of North Dakota for granting me permission to use a full color photo of the UND Archway/campus from their website, und.com. Photo taken by Shawna Schill.

Alison Tugwell, who was my mentor in publishing this book, and gave me lots of good advice; and I followed it!

Katelynn Koontz, Dandy Anwuacha, TJ Marquis, Uti Peace, Ciara Meija, of the Selfpublishing.com Editing Department who all edited this book.

Chad A. Aleo, publishing and marketing strategist of selfpublishing.com.

Matthew E. Emmorey, Author Resource Team, selfpublishing.com.

The University of North Dakota, and the Department of Space Studies, which educated me on space development before I started to write this book, and I began after receiving my M.S. Degree. I would like to acknowledge Jim Vedda, also a member of the faculty and later head of the department. His name was accidentally left out of the acknowledgements in my previous book (*Cosmic Careers*) when I mentioned this department, so I want to include him here. Of course, I also acknowledge my three closest teachers/friends in the department, Joanne Irene Gabrynowicz, John Graham, and the late David Webb.

Veronica Chiaravalli, my mentor for two years, who recommended me to self-publish this book, and also recommended the company in which for me to do so. Ms. Chiaravalli also designed my web page, helped me to do podcasts, created a logo for my company, among other works she has accomplished for me.

The National Space Society, by hosting the International Space Development Conference, many of which I have attended and have done presentations of this very book, as I was working on it through the years. My first book was advertised in *Ad Astra,* also.

Debra Billieux Hawkins, whose encouragement kept me at work on this book until it was finished.

Catharine Browne, who helped me market my first book overseas.

Mary Kathleen Alberter, who continues to encourage and inspire me.

Karen Edwards, Deborah Herz, Patricia McMahon, and William A. Petit, Jr., who never lost faith in me for what I was doing.

Maryann Karinch and Tim Burgard, who gave me much needed advice in publishing this book.

Boleyn Willis and all her staff, who helped me sell my first book by advertising it in her school, The Durham School for Ballet and the Performing Arts, and in the programs for her dance performances.

Last, but certainly not least, Chandler Bolt and all the staff and editors at selfpublishing.com, whose names I am unable to mention but still played a vital role in the creation of this book, I thank you all! I would not have done it without you.

Many not mentioned here are noted in the acknowledgements of my first book, *Cosmic Careers*, and they are all equally important in this book as well. If there are some people who were not mentioned in either book, my apologies. I'll get you all next time. For all of you involved in both my first and second book, mentioned or not, you were all equally important in the production of both books, and I thank you all.

LIST OF ILLUSTRATIONS

Most of these illustrations are produced from A.I. Other photos come from NASA, which are in the public domain, along with photos taken before 1922. Four illustrations were purchased from Stock Adobe (stock. adobe.com) under Extended License, which, in accordance with their agreements, grants the author the right to publish these illustrations.

In addition, four diagrams (three really, one is used twice) are reprinted from *Cosmic Careers*, co-written by myself and Maryann Karinch, published by HarperCollins Leadership, 2021. These diagrams are, by number, 4.2, 5.13, 7.6, and 7.8. Permission has been granted to me by the editor to use these diagrams for the purpose of this book. Each diagram will be noted in their captions with the label "Reprinted from *Cosmic Careers*, used with permission."

ALL photos and illustrations are in accordance with copyright laws, and either have been printed with the permission of the owners, are owned by the author, produced by AI giving the author ownership, purchased from hired illustrators, or are in the public domain.

Introduction

Diagram, "We Have a Choice," drawn by Alastair Browne.

Chapter 1: The Coming of Private Enterprise

1.1A. Photo of Buzz Aldrin on the Moon taken by Neil Armstrong, Apollo 11. NASA photo in the Public Domain.

1.1B. Photo of Earthrise taken by William Anders on Apollo 8. NASA Photo in the Public Domain.

1.2A. Photo of Space Shuttle *Endeavour* on NASA 747 jet taken by Elizabeth Ribera. Used with Permission.

1.2B. Photo of ISS taken by NASA, in the Public Domain.

1.3A. Image of Blue Origin New Glenn rocket by ChatGPT, by Alastair Browne.

1.3B Image of SpaceX Falcon 9 by ChatGPT/Alastair Browne.

1.4 Photo of BEAM for ISS; NASA photo in the Public Domain.

1.5A. Lunar Habitat in a Unique Earth Style Environment by Ali Murtaz Shaikh. This and subsequent drawings/AI illustrations by Ali Murtaza Shaikh hired by the author via Upwork. All Illustrations by Ali Murtaza Sheikh Used with Permission.

1.5B. Space Factory by Ali Murtaza Shaikh.

1.5C. Building an SPS on a near Earth Asteroid (NEA) by Ali Murtaza Shaikh.

1.6. Lunar City by Hussain Syed Mohammed. This and subsequent drawings/AI illustrations by Hussain Syed Mohammed hired by the author via Upwork. All Illustrations by Hussain Syed Mohammed Used with Permission.

1.7A. Photo of Student Union at UND taken by Sally Jacobson. Used with Permission.

1.7B. Photo of UND Archway/Campus courtesy of the University of North Dakota. Photo taken by Shawna Schill. Used by Permission.

1.7C. & 1.7D. Photos of the Center for Aerospace Sciences at UND taken by Sally Jacobson. Both photos Used with Permission.

1.8. Photo of Ariane 5 before a launch in French Guiana. ESA photo, Used by Permission.

Chapter 3: The New Role of NASA, the Government, and a Proposed Department of Space

3.1A. Various NASA Satellites; Public Domain.

3.1B. Communication Satellite in GEO - NASA Photo. Public Domain.

3.1C. Communications/Navigation Satellite by Hussein Syed Mohammed.

3.1D. Hurricane Lee in the Atlantic Ocean, NASA Photo, Public Domain.

3.2A Transcontinental Railroad East meets west. 1869 Photo. Public Domain.

3.2B Pedro Miguel Locks, Panama Canal. Photo in the Public Domain.

Chapter 4: Space Infrastructure

4.1 International Space Station. NASA Photo. Public Domain.

4.2 Earth-Moon LaGrange Libration Points. Diagram by Alastair Browne. Reprinted from *Cosmic Careers*, used with permission from HarperCollins.

4.3A. Passenger Way Station, by Ali Murtaza Shaikh.

4.3B. Way Station created by Alastair Browne (ChatGPT). Edited by Ali Murtaza Sheikh.

4.4 Earth Orbiting Fuel Depot Station by Ali Murtaza Shaikh.

4.5A OMV Transferring Space Station to higher, safer orbit by Alastair Browne (ChatGPT).

Chapter 5: Building a Lunar Civilization

Chapter 7: Near Earth Asteroids

Chapter 8: Energy and the Space Infrastructure

8.7. Helium-3/Tritium Reaction (Stock Adobe. Extended License. Used by Permission).

8.8. Helium-3/Deuterium Reaction (Stock Adobe. Extended License. Used by Permission).

8.9. Helium-3/Lithium Reaction (Stock Adobe. Extended License. Used by Permission).

8.10. Helium-3/Helium-3 Reaction (Stock Adobe. Extended License. Used by Permission).

8.11 Diagram of Fuel Cell drawn by Alastair Browne.

Chapter 9: O'Neill Space Habitats

9.1A. A cutaway view of a space-colony by Rick Guidice. Image in the Public Domain.

9.1B. Agricultural Modules for Farming. Can be on any space colony. Illustration by Rick Guidice. Image in the Public Domain.

9.2. Outside of an O'Neill space colony, surrounded by industries (Not Drawn to Scale) by Alastair Browne via ChatGPT.

9.3 Construction of the inside of a space habitat (Bernal sphere) by Hussain Syed Mohammed.

9.4A. & 9.4B. Two Illustrations of a Mass Driver by Alastair Browne via ChatGPT.

9.5 Construction of the Stanford Torus - The soil/ground will come from the Moon or an asteroid - Donald Davis, NASA, Public Domain.

9.6A. & 9.6B. Two illustrations of the exterior of the Stanford Torus, by Hussain Syed Mohammed.

9.6C. Stanford Torus Interior by Donald Davis, NASA, Public Domain.

Chapter 10: Conclusion: The Final Infrastructure

Appendix B: Zero Gravity and the Physically Disabled

Appendix C: Space and Earth's Environment - A Collaborative Solution

The Past

Throughout history, whenever there is a major threat to humanity, there was also a major discovery that held great promise for all humankind.

At the end of the Medieval era, there were still plagues, fighting amongst small kingdoms in Europe, religions vying for dominance, abject poverty, and many other ills. The world as they knew it was at a crossroads, and the wrong choice could have ended in utter destruction for all of Europe.

Then came Columbus, who, with the support of King Ferdinand and Queen Isabella of Spain, discovered a New World. Soon after, there was colonization and exploitation, fortunes were made, and in a few hundred years, new nation-states rose up in the New World, including the United States. The rest is history.

The Present

We have reached a crossroads again, this time involving the entire world, with a threat of destruction greater than anyone could have imagined.

We are on the brink of world disaster, with war, climate change, destruction of the environment and our food supply, depletion of our natural resources, overpopulation, and refugees migrating to places whose residents cannot support and do not desire them. There are also pandemics— pick your disease, there are plenty of choices.

We are now at a Crossroads, and we have to make a Choice

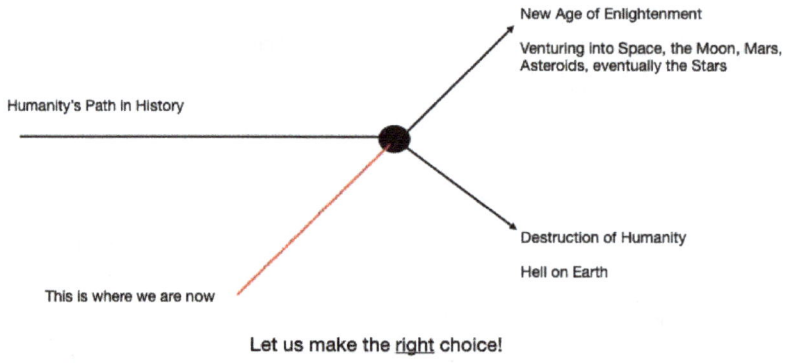

New Age of Enlightenment

Venturing into Space, the Moon, Mars, Asteroids, eventually the Stars

Humanity's Path in History

Destruction of Humanity

Hell on Earth

This is where we are now

Let us make the right choice!

Diagram: "We Have a Choice." Self Explanatory

There is also hope. We are progressing on many fronts, especially in the realm of science.

We are now advancing into space, slowly but surely. This is our New World. Rocket launch companies have gone private, the ISS (International Space Station) is carrying on with experiments in the Life Sciences and Materials Processing. There is the problem of space junk in Earth orbit, but companies are devising ways to clean that up too. It will not be easy.

New space companies are rising. Some will succeed, and some will fail.

There are now plans to settle the Moon and mine Near-Earth asteroids (NEAs).

This movement will grow as people recognize its economic potential. That is a major factor that will propel us upward.

There is much economic potential in space. Space manufacturing is a prime example. There are many chemicals and medicines that can mix in the zero gravity of space that cannot be mixed in Earth's gravity, thus never allowing one chemical to mix with another due to their mass. This process can lead to treatments and cures for previously incurable diseases. There are also crystals that can be formed with greater purity, and alloys that can mix to form harder metals, perhaps leading to the manufacture of superconductors. All of this is presently being experimented on the International Space Station. There is also space construction of new habitats and industries, and mining of minerals from the Moon and Near-Earth asteroids, the cleaning up and salvaging of space junk in Earth orbit for used but still valuable precious metals, and of course, more advanced satellites, of all kinds. This is just the tip of the iceberg. Most of this will be covered in this book.

The "why" of space has already been answered. For decades, people have asked why we are going into space when we have so many problems here on Earth. The answer is in the question. There are resources in space that can provide for the growing population on Earth, and Earth alone cannot support this growing population. Many resources on Earth that are badly needed by the growing population are becoming scarce. For example, metals from Earth's asteroids, such as platinum group metals vital for electronics, will be needed as we advance into this technology. We are also running out of iron for construction. Energy is a major factor, as we keep burning fossil fuels, which are not only hard to obtain, but pollute the environment and the air, leading to extreme climate change. If we were to harness the sun by building Solar Power Satellites, or use Helium-3 mined from the Moon for fusion (when it is perfected), we could have almost unlimited energy for the Earth, not pollute the environment, and even reverse the damage we have done to this planet using these fossil fuels.

With the scarcity of resources on Earth, and a huge bounty of these same resources on the Moon and asteroids, many times the amount on Earth, there would be enough to provide for the entire human race, and then some. Imagine a pie, and imagine the Earth's people all wanting a piece of it. Instead of giving everyone a tiny sliver of pie, which will satisfy no one, we make the pie bigger, much bigger, so everyone can be satisfied.

There it is in a nutshell. There are many other reasons to exploit space, and they will be covered as you read this book.

It's ironic that our best hopes occur during some of our most turbulent times in history.

How I Wrote This Book

In 1990, inspired by President George H.W. Bush's Space Exploration Initiative (SEI), I developed a comprehensive proposal which I titled *A Permanent Moon Base and a Mission to Mars.* The proposal detailed a space transportation system utilizing hypersonic vehicles to Low Earth Orbit (LEO), modular way stations, and lunar and asteroid mining to sustain and finance the initiative. It emphasized a collaboration between governments and private industries to create self-sufficient lunar and Mars settlements, covering life support, manufacturing, and resource utilization.

The proposal was submitted to The Synthesis Group, a government organization dedicated to writing the proposal for the SEI. My own proposal was partly included in the government publication *America at the Threshold*. Though SEI was canceled, I expanded and updated the manuscript over the years, eventually publishing *Cosmic Careers* (co-written by Maryann Karinch) in 2021 with HarperCollins. Now I am planning to self-publish the remaining material as a guide to space infrastructure in the Cis-Lunar orbit. That's the book you are holding.

This body of work highlights a visionary framework for sustainable space exploration and settlement.

The Purpose of This Book

The purpose of this book is to encourage industries, nations, individuals, anyone and everyone, to look at what space has to offer, and take advantage of it, by way of settling and industrializing it. Building the infrastructure lays the groundwork for setting up industries, settlements, and civilizations both on the Moon and in Earth orbit, and everything in between. This will then serve as a base, a back-up and support system, a springboard to then journey outward to Mars, the Asteroid belt, then to Jupiter, Saturn, and eventually, the stars themselves. It's a long reach, but in this book, I will cover space from Earth to the Moon and everything in-between—there is a lot to build up just in this area alone.

I will discuss the space infrastructure, from its beginning to its use as humans migrate into space. We need to have a support system as we journey out into the solar system. We need to have a transportation system, a police force, order and safety as we settle and industrialize the Moon and mine the asteroids, and then set up more business and industry.

Our infrastructure in space would be just like the highways, bridges, rest stops, and gas stations on Earth, with police to enforce traffic laws and watch for criminal activity. The difference here is that this space/cis-lunar infrastructure would provide easy and convenient transport from one place to another, be it the Moon, an asteroid, a space factory, or a space habitat.

We will focus on the development of Cis-Lunar Space, from Low Earth Orbit (LEO) to the Lunar surface, and everywhere in-between.

By this, I mean near-Earth asteroids. There are tens of thousands of them between the Earth and the Moon. Imagine planet Earth being in the middle of a shooting gallery. Between Earth and the Moon will be space factories and space habitats, hundreds, possibly thousands of them orbiting in Cis-lunar space, and transportation between them, like a major highway on Earth, with Way Stations and refueling stations, the space police directing traffic and looking out for traffic violators for speeding, piloting recklessly, smugglers, space pirates, and other scofflaws. Yes, this will all be real, I'm not making this up. On the surface of the Moon, we hope to develop bases, habitats, mining bases, manufacturing bases, and cities.

We will need advanced transportation systems, and a lot can be covered here by itself—solar power satellites to provide energy for Earth, asteroid mining, and orbital space factories of all kinds.

As stated, law enforcement will be an absolute necessity because we cannot run wild in space, get in everyone's way, and kill each other. There must be some kind of order, and this will be prevalent as the space population increases.

In this book, the first chapter will cover NASA, private industry, space transportation from Earth to LEO, and the view of the infrastructure itself, including law enforcement and the proposed Congressional Space Act, i.e. land grants on the Moon. The next seven chapters will go into more detail about settling the Moon, mining the asteroids, and energy from space.

I will then go into O'Neill space habitats, followed by the conclusion, with four appendices.

I will *not* go into landing on Mars, because I feel that in order to do so, we must have a solid base in space to back up these Mars missions. I will mention Mars as an afterthought in these chapters, but I feel we must build the infrastructure and settle the Moon first, before going to Mars. I don't object to NASA or a private entity venturing there, but that will be separate from this proposed infrastructure.

This is my second book. My first is *Cosmic Careers*, which was written with the help of Maryann Karinch, who is not only the co-author, and did a lot of research on this herself, but also my agent, who helped to place that book with a prominent publisher.

Cosmic Careers is about space development, how it can appeal to ordinary people with everyday skills on Earth, and how they can be applied to space. It provides these very people with information about space related careers.

As we develop and settle space, we will want to have a good quality of life. We will want to live in comfort, and this will require sewers, tailors for clothes, spacesuits, interior decorators for habitats, gardeners for farms in space and on the Moon (we will need a food supply), unusual professions like bear biologists for studying hibernation, to apply to astronauts put into suspended animation for long term space voyages.

Of course, this also includes scientists, engineers, and construction workers, but I think you get the point.

Cosmic Careers also includes the history of space development, why we didn't take some of the opportunities that were available (often for good reasons), and anecdotes about certain subjects, so none of that will be covered here.

Why are we doing all this? So all of humanity will advance on these platforms in space (the infrastructure) so as to expand to the stars. The Earth is overpopulated, running out of resources, and the quality of life we are pursuing will be gone, unless we take full advantage of the resources in space. There are an almost infinite amount of resources out there to provide for every living being, comfortably. All we have to do is go out there, settle and industrialize space, open space up to the whole world, and opportunities will abound for everyone. It won't be easy, and it will take time, money, and work, but the rewards are exponential.

There is one advantage I especially like. The amount of resources out there on the Moon, Mars, and Near-Earth asteroids are so vast that they would practically make wars for resources unnecessary.

As stated, there are resources like Helium-3 on the Moon for energy and other uses, ice in the form of asteroids—more than what the Earth contains—precious metals like platinum and other related metals, and common metals like nickel and iron. Sourcing these in space will preserve the environment on Earth. All these are useful in space just as much as on Earth, as we shall see.

That said, I would also like to point out that I do not want war or conflicts of any kind in space. This proposed space infrastructure will be international and open to any and all countries, friends or not.

I do support the Outer Space Treaty forbidding weapons of mass destruction and any other weapon, including sidearms.

There are spy satellites in Earth orbit, but strange as it may sound, they help keep the peace. They warn the rest of the world about what is happening in the countries being spied on, so everyone can be aware.

This is the best way to create an interplanetary civilization. Read on!

1

The Coming of Private Enterprise

I would like to tell you a little bit about myself in relation to the space program. I was born in 1957 and grew up watching the race to the Moon. The very first rocket launch I saw on television, live, was Gemini 5, carrying Gordon Cooper and Charles "Pete" Conrad, on August 21, 1965. Upon seeing it lift-off, I was thrilled at seeing a rocket launch for the first time in my life, knowing that it was going to space, with two astronauts aboard, and seeing the astronaut's wives give their spiel on seeing their husbands on that rocket. I remember seeing Mrs. Conrad, wife of Charles "Pete" Conrad, talking excitedly about the rocket launch and the astronauts on board. It was a very exciting day for everyone at Cape Kennedy in Florida. Being the eight-year-old that I was, I went around describing what I saw to everyone I encountered that day in my own hometown.

Even before seeing these launches, I always had a fascination with space, seeing pictures of rockets in storybooks and on cartoons on TV. My siblings would tell me about how we would all go up there to visit someday, perhaps even live. It was left up to my imagination to envision how. It was seeing the real thing that solidified my fascination for space travel. Later on, shows like "Lost in Space" and "Star Trek" also contributed to it, along with the movie "2001, A Space Odyssey." I also read a lot of science fiction novels, my four favorite authors being Heinlein, Bradbury, Clarke, and Asimov.

Growing up, I saw other launches, up to Apollo 11. I watched astronauts walk on the Moon, and then saw on television the flights of Skylab and the space shuttles.

1.1A: On July 20, 1969, Apollo 11 landed on the Moon, the first spacecraft to do so. This was a historical moment for the entire world, and the entire world watched. Here is Buzz Aldrin, the second human being to walk on the Moon. Photo was taken by Neil Armstrong, the first Man on the Moon.

This will never occur again, the live launches of spacecraft on television with the American public, and the world, watching in awe. Why? Launches have become routine, almost like planes taking off and landing at any airport. Like these airlines, many launches are now done by private companies. There are so many of them that it's no longer news to launch a rocket. The government is also slowly fading out of the launch business.

Does this mean that this is the end of the space program?

No, it is only the end of the first space program...and the beginning of a new space movement.

The Apollo Moon program is no doubt one of our greatest accomplishments, and it served us well. The Apollo program's benefits extend far beyond the historic lunar landings. Among its most enduring impacts is the shift in environmental consciousness it inspired. The Earthrise photo, captured by Apollo 8 astronauts as they orbited the Moon, showed our planet as a fragile, luminous sphere floating in the vast darkness of space. This image galvanized global awareness of Earth's vulnerability and the need to preserve its resources, catalyzing the modern environmental movement.

1.1B Earthrise photo taken by Apollo 8 astronaut William Anders. Little did he know the impact that photo would have.

Technologically, Apollo accelerated innovation at an unprecedented rate, with estimates suggesting it doubled the pace of technological advancement. The race to meet President Kennedy's "within the decade" challenge drove breakthroughs in electronics, computing, and miniaturization. These advancements laid the foundation for numerous modern industries, including medical technology, aeronautics, and remote sensing. The resulting economic ripple effects were profound, with every dollar invested in Apollo returning an estimated five to fourteen dollars in return, in the form of new industries, new products, new processes and new jobs. Many of these benefits include advancement in technologies, including computer technology (hand held calculators, for example), aircraft, fireproof attire for fighting fires, weather satellites to warn of coming hurricanes, and many others. These are a few of the many technical spinoffs we received from the Apollo program that benefited humanity.

Apollo's scientific contributions are equally significant. By bringing back lunar samples and conducting experiments, the program revealed critical insights about the Moon's age, structure, and composition, shedding light on the origins of Earth and the solar system. Beyond geology, Apollo fostered advancements in fields such as astronomy, physics, and biology, expanding our understanding of the universe and our place within it.

The program also played a pivotal role in restoring national confidence and bolstering international relations. In the context of the Cold War, Apollo was a decisive response to the Soviet Union's space achievements. Its success demonstrated the capabilities of democratic free-enterprise systems, inspiring pride and optimism in the United States. On the global stage, Apollo united humanity in awe of its shared potential. The images of astronauts on the Moon and the collaborative study of lunar samples fostered international goodwill and cooperation.

Economically, scientifically, and culturally, Apollo's legacy is unparalleled. It proved that with resolve, resources, and collaboration, humanity could achieve the seemingly impossible. More than a historical milestone, Apollo continues to remind us of what is possible when we aim for the stars. As we carry these lessons into the 21st century, the Apollo program stands not only as a testament to past achievements but a beacon for future exploration and innovation.

The mission of Project Apollo was never to colonize space or establish settlements on the Moon. It was to simply send a man to the Moon and return him safely back to Earth. This was in response to Sputnik's launch in 1957, and later Vostok, where the Soviets sent Yuri Gagarin into Earth's orbit, making him the first man in space. America was so shocked, and fearful of Soviet missiles being fired on the U.S., that we had to have a response. So, in addition to the arms race, we felt we also had to catch up with the Soviets in space. After some launch failures, we finally were able to send astronauts up to orbit via the Mercury and Gemini flights.

We climaxed with the Apollo flights, where, with Apollo 11, we finally landed a man on the Moon, and we, being the U.S., were the first, and so far, the only country to do it. We then sent up five more flights (Apollo 13 had a malfunction in lunar orbit, but the astronauts did come back alive, though there was no lunar landing). After Apollo 17, we moved on to Skylab, the space shuttle, and the ISS. There were no more Apollo Moon landings.

Quite simply, the goal was to "beat the Russians," and show the world how great American technology was. In a way, it was a circus, but it was also one of humanity's greatest achievements nonetheless.

Regardless, the Apollo program did blaze the trail for space. Had this not occurred, private enterprise would not be pursuing this venture today.

Unfortunately, the program wasn't built to last. Like it or not, it was a show—a show telling the world that we, the United States, can beat the Soviets, and that we can do anything we set our minds to. After we landed on the Moon, other programs were proposed but were rejected. The reason we couldn't remain on the Moon was simple; we couldn't afford it. Huge amounts of tax money would have kept on being spent, with little to show for it, even without the Vietnam war.

It was inevitable that this excitement and enthusiasm would wane after the initial mission was accomplished, along with the passage of time. This is a law of nature, and it applies the world over, even in countries like Russia and China.

Why the Government Alone Cannot Continue to Pay for a Space Program

The Space Shuttle and the ISS were not originally planned to be as they are, or to cost so much as they did. The shuttle was meant to be more of an airplane, to be used in space, refurbished after landing, and launched two weeks later. It turned out to take six months to be refurbished at many times the expected cost.

The International Space Station was meant to cost $8 billion, back in 1984, but constant changes and cost overruns ballooned it to over $100 billion.

1.2A. Space Shuttle Endeavour on its final mission to Los Angeles (Photo taken by Elizabeth Ribera).

1.2B. The International Space Station (NASA Photo).

Even if we had a bigger space station holding fifty people, and a shuttle twice the size of what we had, and both were proposed by appointed space commissions, there still would have been cost overruns, but on a much grander scale, many times as much as the actual shuttle and the ISS.

Remember, the U.S. space program was completely paid for with taxpayer's money, nothing else. Does that matter? Yes it does!

In the original version of this proposal, as described in the Introduction, I intended for the government to continue to blaze this trail. In other words, it would have continued to be funded by the taxpayer: space transportation, space stations, the Moon base, asteroid mining, all of it, with private enterprise following. There would have been profits to be made, but only after all this was built.

What many people don't realize is that any long-term space endeavor that requires the constant infusion of tax money will not last. That's all there is to it. Historically, governments have initiated bold, groundbreaking projects like the Apollo program, but these efforts often lose momentum once their primary objectives are met. When public interest wanes, and competing terrestrial priorities take precedence, sustained funding becomes difficult to justify. Colonization efforts on Earth have followed a similar pattern, transitioning from government-sponsored exploration to private investment for long-term viability. This same principle applies to space colonization.

The cost of maintaining a space colony—whether small or large—is immense. Even a small colony supporting a handful of people would require significant resources for life support, resupply, and infrastructure. Scaling up to a larger colony would multiply these costs exponentially, further straining government budgets. The government, and the taxpayer, will eventually ask, "What are we getting from all this? How are these space settlements benefitting us on Earth?" Meanwhile, these expenditures would compete with pressing needs on Earth, such as healthcare, education, infrastructure, and climate change mitigation, making it harder for any political system to sustain public support for such initiatives over time. The governments, and the taxpayer, would no longer tolerate it.

For colonies to thrive, they must turn a profit and eventually achieve economic self-sufficiency. This could be accomplished by utilizing local resources—such as mining lunar regolith for helium-3, extracting water for fuel, or manufacturing goods in situ—and developing a robust space economy centered on tourism, research, manufacturing, and logistics. The goods manufactured from these resources must be useful to the people back on Earth, earning a profit.

International collaboration could also play a role, with multiple countries sharing the costs and benefits of space colonization, although this would require extensive coordination and agreements.

Ultimately, government-led space colonies face a high risk of abandonment due to shifting political priorities and the unsustainable nature of tax-funded ventures. To avoid this fate, a hybrid model is essential, with private industry leading the way and governments acting as facilitators. Governments could focus on research, development, and creating regulatory frameworks, while private companies take on the challenges of innovation and commercialization. This approach offers the best chance of building enduring and economically viable colonies in space.

Private Enterprise in the Launch Business, After the Space Shuttle

When the space shuttle was retired in 2011, there was no form of space transportation in the U.S. to transport astronauts to the International Space Station. NASA had to rely on the Russian Soyuz to ferry these astronauts to the ISS, but for a price.

According to *Forbes* magazine, the Russians charged the astronauts up to $90 million per seat. But then SpaceX and Boeing came along, and NASA's Inspector General estimated the cost per seat for SpaceX's *Crew Dragon* at $55M and Boeing's *Starliner* at $90M in 2019, the same as Soyuz. Subsequent contract extensions have increased *Crew Dragon*'s cost per seat due to inflation and SpaceX's increased leverage. The Crew-7 through Crew-9 extension raised the cost to $65M per seat, and the Crew-10 through Crew-14 extension further increased it to $72M per seat. Boeing faced some difficulties with Starliner, as shown in 2024 when Starliner malfunctioned in orbit and the crew was left stranded on the ISS. Boeing brought the capsule back, uncrewed, and SpaceX had to plan on bringing Boeing's crew back. Boeing then delayed their future crew missions until further notice.

These two companies, SpaceX and Boeing, were chosen by NASA to come up with a space taxi to replace Soyuz. Although Boeing faced difficulties, SpaceX ended up not only sending up astronauts but also resupplying the ISS with food and other supplies, and bringing back finished experiments, along with garbage, at a fraction of the cost of the shuttle. Each shuttle launch cost $1.5 billion. Other private companies will soon follow.

1.3A Blue Origin, a private space taxi sending astronauts to the ISS.

*1.3B SpaceX, another space taxi replacing NASA's and
Russia's rockets at a much cheaper rate.*

Sierra Nevada was a candidate for NASA, but lost out to SpaceX and Boeing. Nevertheless, Sierra Nevada will continue to build and test their Dream Chaser, which resembles a miniature shuttle. NASA has renewed interest in this.

More competing companies will enter the race, with different models, demonstrating who can offer the best and/or most inexpensive transport.

Among them are Blue Origin and Virgin Galactic. Blue Origin recently proposed a new heavy lift launch vehicle, and that has received a lot of press.

SpaceX now has Starship. Work still needs to be done to be efficient, but it's getting there. This vehicle has nearly twice the power of the heaviest SLS (Space Launch System).

All of these companies have their own unique launch systems, all very different from one another, and all for different purposes. The list will get longer, and some of these companies will fold, others will merge, and new ones will emerge altogether.

LEO will be handed over to private industry in the end. Bigelow Aerospace has recently added an inflatable compartment to the ISS for experimental purposes. It is known as the Bigelow Expandable Activity Module (BEAM). The new technology here is that it is an inflatable module, the first of its kind. Bigelow has ambitious plans for bigger space stations for bigger functions, whether it be a hospital, a hotel, or anything else the customer might desire, all from inflatable modules.

1.4 Photo of BEAM on the ISS.

Other private research companies are also eyeing ISS for the manufacture of their goods in near zero gravity.

Companies are gearing up to deal with orbiting space debris (space junk) and a profit is expected, along with making LEO safer for new satellites and other space systems.

From there, Near-Earth Asteroids are being targeted to mine.

As these asteroids are being mined, there will be resources to take back to the Earth for processing, and later to orbiting facilities, opening up a whole new industry. These resources are listed in Chapter 7, Near-Earth Asteroids, but some examples are the water in these asteroids that will be used for both fuel and life support, and the minerals for space manufacturing such as iron, nickel, and platinum group metals.

As space facilities and foundries are first launched into orbit, new goods will be produced for profit. Building materials will be manufactured, to build the first factories and habitats entirely in space, from mining the metal to completion of the space facility. Other orbiting stations, such as solar power satellites and space habitats needed to house these workers will be needed as the demand for space workers grows, along with robotics. Robotics will be used extensively, but they will rarely be mentioned in this book.

Could space factories and other facilities eliminate resource shortages on Earth? Yes they can, because most resources used on Earth are also found in space and on the Moon, even some rare metals like Platinum Group Metals. For space factories, we will only be able to use minerals from the Moon and Near-Earth Asteroids because it is too expensive to launch them from Earth. The products made can be sent to Earth, and be of better quality, as well as conserving such resources Earth-side.

As the settlements grow and profits are made, new space facilities will be relocated at the Lunar L4 and L5 sites, along with L1, in front of the Moon from Earth's view, and L2, in back of the Moon. What function these stations will have remains to be seen. See Chapter 4, Space Infrastructure, for a Diagram and Explanation of LaGrange (L4, L5) Points.

There will then be a return to the Moon, with mining, manufacturing, and living quarters set up, along with long-term habitats.

1.5A. An Advanced Lunar Habitat, with shelter, water source, air filter in the form of trees, and a glass dome to protect against the vacuum and radiation.

1.5B. A space factory Orbiting Earth.

1.5C. Mining a Near Earth Asteroid, using the minerals to build a Solar Power Satellite.

New wealth will be created, products will be shipped back to Earth, and other space settlements. Private space merchants will create livelihoods shipping goods from one space settlement to another, and there will be a large variety of spaceships and space stations, more than you can count.

There will be refueling stations and supply stations for these ships as they travel among the Near-Earth asteroids. These have already been proposed, but the problem is transporting fuel from Earth. The solution is to use water from the asteroids themselves.

Colonies will grow into settlements, all manufacturing different products depending on the materials available around that settlement. Depending on what is in demand, settlements will grow into cities. Scientists of all disciplines will study the properties of the Moon, asteroids, and the cosmos.

We will then have the first extraterrestrial civilization, and soon people will set their eyes on Mars.

1.6 City on the Moon Drawing is not done to scale, but it covers a lot of ground, and it shows advanced dwellings, in the form of towers, with food sources such as farms and parks. This could be spread out more, but is an excellent model.

This whole process may begin and proceed sooner than you think. In fact, it's starting right now. We all know of SpaceX and its competing launch companies.

Virgin Galactic, winner of the first X-Prize, are presently taking reservations for sub-orbital, near-zero gravity tours, and other space tourism companies are offering their own unique space tours. Bigelow Aerospace has proposed an inflatable, orbiting space hotel. Other tourism companies, such as Zero Gravity Corporation and Space Adventures, are already on the books.

The International Space University, located in France, exists for educating space enthusiasts and offering degrees. There is also the Space Studies program at the University of North Dakota, located in Grand Forks. I myself earned a Master of Science degree from that university.

1.7A. & 1.7B The University of North Dakota, located in Grand Forks.

1.7C & 1.7D. UND has a well known Space Studies program that has advanced over the years, keeping up with new space technologies. Here are two photos of the CAS Buildings, the Center for Aerospace Sciences, in which the Space Studies department plays a major role. They also train airline pilots.

Even if some of the businesses listed here go defunct, others will come in to take their place. No matter what, the profiteers are coming into space, and as long as there is money to be made, nothing will stop the Spaceports being built. At the time of this writing, there are twenty licensed spaceports in the U.S., with thirteen of them licensed by the F.A.A. They are located in Alabama, Alaska, California, Colorado, Florida, Georgia, New Mexico, Oklahoma, Texas, and Virginia.

I should mention that Texas, with SpaceX, launches their own rockets on the coast of the Gulf of Mexico, along with Florida at Kennedy Space Center, launching rockets from the Atlantic Coast, as they always have.

Don't forget other spaceports around the world, with their own rockets and launch systems. Among these are England, Scotland, Norway, Russia, India, Brazil, French Guiana (Ariane, the European Space Agency), Australia, China, and Japan.

1.8 There are many spaceports and space programs worldwide. Here is the first, outside of the United States and Russia, the Guiana Space Centre, located in Kourou, French Guiana run by the European Space Agency, known as Europe's Spaceport. Here we have Ariane 5 before launch.

Humanity's journey from the first daring steps into space to the current surge of private industry involvement has been extraordinary. What began as a race between nations has evolved into a realm of expanded interests and boundless opportunities, paving the way for lucrative prospects that were once the stuff of science fiction. As a space researcher and advocate, I am dedicated to ensuring that this future materializes faster than we ever imagined. By pushing the boundaries of innovation and fostering collaboration across sectors, we are shaping a spacefaring society poised to thrive among the stars.

2

A Call for Private Leadership in Space Development

One of the most important pieces of legislation that would benefit the space movement is "The Space Settlement Act." The Act simply states that "it is the right of the first permanent settlers on the Moon or Mars to claim and trade private ownership of the real estate around them. This would create an incentive 'prize' for the private entrepreneurs of Earth to risk their lives and fortunes developing affordable space travel for all, and transporting the settlers to their new home, at zero cost to US taxpayers."

The act itself is straightforward and easy to read, and quite simply states that the goal of the United States should be to settle space, period. This especially includes private industry, because they are going to be the real strength behind all of this.

The act has recently been proposed before Congress for the second time. The first time it was proposed was in 1988, and it passed, but nothing came of it, so it is being proposed again. Hopefully, it will be taken a lot more seriously this time. A copy of this act is included in Appendix A at the end of this book.

NASA and the government, however, will play a major role in this new movement. It will not be as showy as the Apollo and Shuttle Programs—they will be in the background—but they will have a large part nonetheless. In this chapter, we will explore the roles of NASA and other government agencies in actualizing the goal of colonizing outer space.

NASA After Apollo, and How it Should Be Restructured

NASA was at its best in the Apollo years, with everyone working together to achieve the goal of landing on the Moon. New technologies were developed within a period of two to four years, because scientists and engineers worked with each other around the clock, and had the cooperation of the government, companies and corporations, colleges and universities, and space centers, with almost unlimited funding.

However, from the glory days of Apollo, NASA has since become a fractious, bureaucratic monopoly, roiling with politics and infighting, thick with red tape and self-interest. I have stated earlier that the demise of the space program wasn't NASA's fault. NASA only acts on orders from the President and Congress, and with the cutbacks due to Johnson's Great Society Program, the Vietnam War, and later Watergate, NASA came out with the space shuttle and the ISS.

There have been times, however, when NASA abused its position.

Flying and maintaining the space shuttle became an end in itself. Originally intended to replace all Expendable Launch Vehicles (ELVs) and save money, it became one of the most expensive spacecraft in which to do business, with disastrous results. Within a span of seventeen years, two shuttles were destroyed in flight, killing a total of fourteen astronauts.

The *Challenger* was the first shuttle to be destroyed. The Challenger disaster on January 28, 1986, occurred due to the failure of rubber O-Rings in the rocket boosters, which were compromised by unusually cold weather, allowing hot gases to escape and cause an explosion. Despite engineers warning of the risks, NASA deemed the O-Rings an "acceptable risk" based on past performance and adherence to established protocols. Sociologists attributed the disaster to organizational behaviors like "groupthink" and Diane Vaughan's "normalization of deviance," where repeated minor failures were accepted as normal over time. Ultimately, the tragedy was rooted in a cultural belief that following established rules guaranteed safety, despite underlying systemic flaws.

In other words, too much was taken for granted, and even though NASA was warned not to launch that day, they proceeded to do so anyway, resulting in the disaster.

The *Columbia* was the second shuttle disaster, which occurred seventeen years later, on February 1, 2003. After spending seventeen days on the ISS, the shuttle departed for home. Upon entering the Earth's atmosphere, it disintegrated during re-entry, killing all seven astronauts onboard. Investigations revealed that the disaster was caused by a breach in the shuttle's left wing, created during launch when insulation foam from an external tank struck the wing. The superheated plasma encountered during re-entry compromised the wing's structure, leading to the shuttle's destruction. This incident was not just a technical failure, but also a failure of organizational culture.

Physically, the disaster underscored the underestimated risks of foam debris impacts, which had occurred in previous missions without catastrophic consequences. This "normalization of deviation" became a central issue. Engineers assumed the lightweight foam could not cause operational damage, a belief that proved tragically false. Organizationally, NASA's culture at the time encouraged procedural shortcuts, driven by pressure to meet deadlines. Safety concerns were often dismissed, and dissenting opinions were sidelined, leading to mischaracterization of risks.

Like the *Challenger*, where the officials took the O-Rings for granted, thinking they could never fail regardless, the same pattern of thought was with the foam on the space shuttle, where even if it broke off and hit the wing of the shuttle, nothing could happen, just like many times before. Both situations were taken for granted, and both situations had their days of reckoning.

The *Columbia* disaster, as with the *Challenger*, remains a somber reminder of the cost of complacency in high-stakes endeavors. It highlighted the necessity of addressing both technical and cultural challenges to prevent future tragedies. While both losses were devastating, the lessons learned continue to shape NASA's approach to safety and risk management, ensuring that the sacrifices of both the *Columbia* and *Challenger* crews were not in vain.

The International Space Station has become another example of NASA's bureaucratic monopoly. From the proposal in 1984 to first assembly in 2000, costs increased from $8 billion to over $100 billion and counting, the design went through several reconfigurations (on paper), other countries contributed to the funding, and through it all, there was no concrete goal. No one knew what the ISS was for, aside from a few scientific experiments. It has evolved into a station for astronomy, materials processing, life sciences, and the testing of new technologies for advanced human exploration for Mars and to other parts of the solar system.

Bigelow Aerospace has added a new extension onto the ISS, its first by a private company, and other private companies have expressed interest in doing the same.

The cost of maintaining the station is over $3 billion per year. Of that, $1.7 billion goes toward transportation of cargo and crews to and from the station, $1 billion for operations, and $700 million to $800 million for research (Space News, March 27, 2017, "The Long Goodbye: Transitioning from the ISS to Commercial Space Stations will take time," by Jeff Foust, p. 14). The station is due to run until 2032, when one could either privatize it and make it into an industrial park, adding modules from private companies to it, if one could maintain or reduce the cost, or the ISS could be decommissioned. Privately owned stations would be launched in LEO to take its place.

I would simply hate to see the ISS thrown into the Earth's atmosphere and burn, especially when it can be put to further use.

I have stated that NASA has abused its position at times. I'll give you one example. Russia's *Mir*, old as it was, held promise to complement the ISS and to help humanity advance in space. There were potential customers interested in *Mir*, for testing new materials in zero gravity, imaging Earth, assembling and deploying small satellites, and even space tourism. NASA, however, saw *Mir* as a threat to the existence of the ISS, and pressured the Russians to bring it down, on the assumption that it was too dangerous to use, though clearly *Mir* could have been renovated.

NASA even warned anyone wanting to do business on *Mir* not to do so, or else be denied access to the shuttle, the ISS, or any ELV from Boeing and Lockheed anytime in the future.

Russia complied and in 2000, *Mir* came down, burning through the Earth's atmosphere, crashing in the Pacific Ocean, and resulting in a waste of prime real estate and an opportunity for true advancement in space.

NASA felt that only through them could human space flight move forward. In reality, NASA had mortgaged its vision for the most basic of ambitions, survival. NASA works against change and can no longer see the vision of space flight.

NASA needs reform, and needs it badly. One solution to this problem is to take certain activities of NASA and reassign them to other organizations dealing with that particular activity. For example, the Earth Observation System should be transferred to the National Oceanic and Atmospheric Administration (NOAA). Basic research and development unrelated to the space program should go to the National Science Foundation (NSF). The government-industry-academic complex should be managed under the Centers for Commercial Development of Space.

A competitive enterprise has finally been introduced in NASA's culture. The shuttle failed, and the ISS, although being used, faces an uncertain future. Rather than being a monopolist, NASA should be a buyer for competitive services, a customer.

Government should develop laws and tax incentives that encourage investment in space infrastructure, and otherwise get out of the way. As an example, with launch vehicles, the U.S. Government should stop owning and operating a national fleet of vehicles for civilian purposes.

The Space Launch System (SLS) is a good example. It is a new heavy lift launch vehicle, but it's being built for the wrong reason. They say it will be available when needed for deep space missions and lifting heavy payloads, but it has no present purpose. The real reason is that the senators endorsing this are simply trying to provide jobs in their own states where the SLS is being built, no more. The SLS is expensive, has no goal, and should be canceled.

SpaceX is developing a Heavy Lift Launch Vehicle (HLLV) called Starship, and when it is perfected, it will be able to lift heavier loads than the SLS. So why not get Starship to do the job?

Blue Origin has also announced plans for their own, privately built, Heavy Lift Launch Vehicle. With this and Starship, we can cancel the Space Launch System altogether.

NASA, and the government, must get out of the launch business completely.

One bold suggestion is after the ISS is retired, it should be turned over to a commercial enterprise.

According to The Planetary Society, 50 percent of NASA's annual budget was spent on human space activity, meaning the shuttle and the ISS, both of which turned out to be insufficient for the job of space development.

NASA can have private launch companies compete for its needs, and have the space station leased, or even sold, to potential clients. The government and NASA can then buy data and services from these private enterprises. The government simply cannot be the dominant, all-controlling party in the business.

The agency should focus on science and technology advancement. Again, NASA should be just one of many customers purchasing goods and services in a competitive marketplace.

NASA needs to form a partnership between the public and private sector. In this partnership, NASA should play the following roles:

1. The primary activity of NASA should be to explore, survey, and expand our knowledge of the space frontier. They should leave LEO, and most of the Moon and Near-Earth asteroids to the private sector, and focus on deep space missions, Mars and beyond.

2. NASA should support research beyond the scope and affordability of the private sector, along with non-profit research. This means new technologies presently beyond the affordability of the private sector, such as advanced propulsions systems.

3. NASA should seek to support the private sector in space; for example, buying data from both scientific and settlement oriented exploration from private firms, or providing grants to support mixed private and public sector missions.

NASA did this successfully with COTS, the Commercial Orbital Transport Services. After the shuttle program was terminated in 2011, *Soyuz* was the only service provider to the ISS. NASA needed a new launch service, and they turned to private companies.

COTS was a NASA funded program with the purpose of funding and stimulating the development of commercial launch vehicles, for both cargo and personnel, by private launch companies.

Two companies were selected by NASA to accelerate development. The first was SpaceX, which succeeded and is providing launch services for NASA today, among many other services for other entities, such as the military and private companies.

The second was Rocketplane Kistler. They were terminated due to insufficient progress, so Orbital Sciences Corporation replaced them in 2008.

Orbital Sciences Corporation now delivers cargo to the ISS. In 2018, it was acquired by Northrop Grumman, who took over services delivering cargo.

 These cargo vehicles commenced operations in 2012, a year after the shuttle was retired. SpaceX commenced delivering astronauts in their space taxi, the Falcon 9, in 2020, replacing the Russian *Soyuz*. The COTS program ended in 2013, but was a big success while it ran.

Private companies are funded to develop, or help develop, their own space vehicles for the purpose of transporting cargo and crew to the ISS, or anywhere else in LEO. Extending this, they would also launch any and all satellites in LEO, and NASA would no longer have any vehicles to do so, but would have to purchase all needed launch services to LEO, the ISS, and possibly all other levels of Earth orbit, from these private companies.

In the past, NASA's relationship with the commercial space sector has been disastrous, mainly because NASA insisted on remaining in the launch business. With NASA's subsidies from the government, private launch companies could not compete. As a result, the cost of launching anything remained high.

In the present circumstance, it is recommended that NASA turn over all transportation services flying to LEO to the private sector. NASA should only operate launch vehicles where the private sector cannot venture, or where it is too risky, be it the Moon, Mars, the asteroids, or the outer planets.

There are other launch companies to consider. Blue Origin came into the picture at their own expense, but were very successful. Already they have launched tourists for short, sub-orbital flights.

Among the passengers was William Shatner, who played Captain Kirk in the original *Star Trek* series. He went into space on October 13, 2021, along with three other passengers.

The Polaris Dawn mission on September 10, 2024, however, represents a milestone in private space exploration, showing how commercial initiatives are expanding humanity's reach beyond Earth's atmosphere. Funded by Jared Isaacman, a serial entrepreneur with a passion for space, the mission demonstrated the increasing viability and ambition of privately funded missions.

Reaching an impressive 1,400 kilometers in Earth orbit, Polaris Dawn pushed beyond typical low-Earth orbit, approaching altitudes not seen since the Apollo era. By traveling through the Van Allen radiation belt, the mission enabled studies on how such intense radiation affects the human body—a critical inquiry for future deep-space endeavors.

The mission's most notable achievement was the first commercial spacewalk, undertaken by Isaacman himself, along with SpaceX engineer Sarah Gillis. They ventured outside the spacecraft for about fifteen minutes. Their excursion symbolizes the practical steps being taken toward normalizing human activity in space, outside governmental programs. Meanwhile, the remaining crew, Scott Poteet and Anna Menon, were safely exposed to the experience of space while remaining within the craft.

As space tourism and private missions continue to evolve, these ventures promise to play a transformative role in extending humanity's presence in space. This milestone, like others on the horizon, points to an era where private industry will lead the journey to new frontiers.

If the Polaris Dawn had been handled by NASA, it would have been just as successful, but it would have cost a lot more money. Remember, a shuttle launch cost $1.5 billion, and it is estimated that an SLS launch would have cost as much or more due to inflation, and because the rocket is manufactured by several companies, which in itself raises the cost by tens of millions of dollars. Polaris Dawn only cost a few hundred million dollars, a fraction of what NASA would have charged, and Isaacman paid for it all himself, though he won't reveal the exact cost.

Looking at the examples of SpaceX and Blue Origin, NASA now has an abundant choice of space vehicles, depending on what sort of cargo or personnel they need to launch. With competition between the firms, costs could be kept at a decent level, but remain high enough to make a profit to justify their existence.

Note that non-U.S. groups are also developing transportation systems for ISS cargo. Two examples are Europe's Automated Transfer Vehicle (ATV) and Japan's HII Transfer Vehicle (HTV). The ATV delivers cargo and supplies to the ISS, and then is loaded with garbage and deployed back into the Earth's atmosphere, where it is burned.

U.S. companies are developing cargo and crew launch vehicles, and they will have international competitors. NASA's role should be to fund the U.S. companies as they develop their own space vehicles, and then guarantee purchases of these services upon development.

The only role NASA should now play is to develop the advanced launch vehicle technology that private industry cannot afford to develop, turn this new technology over to any and all private launch industries, and then get out of the way.

The New Role of NASA, the Government, and a Proposed Department of Space

The Artemis program, NASA's flagship effort to return humans to the Moon, is a landmark initiative with ambitious goals. However, its execution has drawn significant criticism due to reliance on the Space Launch System (SLS) and Lunar Gateway. Its design choices and reliance on government-led infrastructure raise serious questions about efficiency and long-term viability.

The SLS is an expendable system, and each launch requires the construction of an entirely new rocket. This approach stands in stark contrast to reusable systems like SpaceX's Starship. SLS is also more costly to launch and utilize, both as a cargo carrier and a transport for astronauts. SpaceX, Blue Origin, and other private launch companies have been proven to be cheaper and better alternatives to SLS.

The Lunar Gateway is a proposed platform orbiting the Moon. It's an intriguing idea, but adds complexity and cost without clear justification. Envisioned as a waystation for lunar operations, utility pales in comparison to direct surface missions. The same experiments and infrastructure could be deployed directly on the Moon, reducing mission durations and costs. The Gateway is redundant in comparison to other modern craft, with capable reusable systems on the rise.

Artemis has experienced significant timeline shifts, with the first crewed landing now several years behind schedule. These delays hinder progress toward establishing a lunar presence, raising doubts about whether the program can deliver. Meanwhile, private companies operate with a sense of urgency driven by competition and market incentives. SpaceX has demonstrated an ability to rapidly iterate, test, and deploy groundbreaking technologies like Starship.

SpaceX and Blue Origin have achieved milestones once thought exclusive to government programs. They bring to the field not only innovation, but also cost efficiency and operational flexibility. With streamlined development processes, reusability, and modularity, they are better equipped to lead the charge in building lunar infrastructure. The Artemis program represents an outdated model that may struggle to keep pace with the rapidly evolving capabilities of private-sector players.

As governments pivot to a supporting role, public funds could be directed toward grants and partnerships with private industry, encouraging innovation while avoiding the inefficiencies of bureaucracy. Government leadership remains essential, for policy, safety standards, and international collaboration, but everything else about lunar development would benefit from the agility of the market.

Private industry is not merely a complement to government efforts but a viable alternative for leading the next chapter of lunar exploration. Allowing companies like SpaceX and Blue Origin to take the lead, while governments provide the necessary support, could dramatically accelerate progress toward a permanent lunar presence.

A Department of Space

NASA should basically be involved with research into new space technology that no one else can afford to do alone, deep space exploration in places where humans have not yet ventured, non-profit research, development of advanced space technologies, and scientific research such as astronomy and astrophysics, using space telescopes and deep space probes.

Launching rockets is now up to private launch industries.

There are many other activities NASA no longer needs to do, because other government and private organizations are able to do the technologies and research that NASA no longer needs to do. They should drop these efforts completely and save themselves, and the taxpayer, lots of money.

Now that private companies are coming in, there is and will continue to be conflict between NASA and these entities. On top of that, NASA is asked to do too many things with too small a budget.

There is the problem of NASA pride, red tape, or the "not invented here" syndrome, meaning any space proposal not involving NASA will be killed for that reason alone. There will also be the necessary regulations for private spacecraft, commerce, compliance with space laws, and NASA will be given more than they will have the ability to handle.

Since NASA will have to get back to research and development, i.e. developing new space technology, turning it over to private industry, then proceeding to the next project, we will need a bigger entity, an entire department in the U.S. government, to cover the commerce, international affairs of space, the politics, economics, settlement dispute between companies, building and running space infrastructure, and application of laws already on the books, even working with other departments and countries.

In *Space News* (July 2, 2012, pp. 19, 21), Madhu Thangavelu proposed a U.S. Department of Space to be added to the presidential cabinet. Actually, it's been proposed for decades, but this is an idea whose time has come. Its tasks, besides those already mentioned, would be to:

1. Build up space infrastructure and make it available to all, meaning the transportation systems, fuel depots, solar power satellites (can later be privatized), space debris mitigation (the complete cleanup of space debris, something that needs to be done), and possibly a system to protect Earth from asteroid strikes.

2. Align the projects and goals of various spacefaring nations and assist in global projects such as international crewed missions (i.e. to Mars).

3. Help coordinate the activities of fledgling private space companies.

4. Establish a rule of law, with proper law enforcement activity. This is simply to bring order to the space environment, not chaos, ensure that human life and property is respected and protected, and to enforce the laws already on the books.

5. Lease space, not control. This means a parceling of land, filing claims, and financial protection.

This is vital because in the past, private space companies have proposed projects that have been squashed by NASA to protect its charter and monopoly. MirCorp is the classic example. With a Department of Space, future proposals like this could be supported, but with NASA having little or no say in the matter.

The DoSp (my abbreviation) would not threaten NASA in any way, shape, or form. NASA, returning to its original charter of Research and Development (R&D), would be a branch of this department.

According to Dr. Thangavelu, a University of Southern California team researching this project stated that a DoSp would, and should, have an annual funding of $60 billion a year (2020 dollars, could be higher by now), consistent with the funding of other departments.

NASA would receive $20 billion of this funding for all their research projects. The remaining $40 billion would be for the department to handle all coordinating functions among large global infrastructure development projects, NASA (in the event NASA needs more funding), other partner agencies, and the private sector (COTS, for example).

Note that this would be different, and much more influential than a National Space Council (NSC), revived by the Trump Administration in 2017. While the NSC speaks of proposals for space exploration, the DoSp would involve all aspects of space development and include all entities, public and private. The DoSp would have more influence on space development.

Providing Incentives for Space Development

Space commercialization will be a wave to last throughout the 21st century. In order to encourage commercialization, tax incentives and regulatory relief should be applied to encourage the investment community to provide capital needed by those trying to build new space businesses. This includes:

1. New launch services
2. Space tourism
3. Space manufacturing
4. New mining operations, once we return to the Moon and reach Near-Earth Asteroids
5. Space related engineering and technology, e.g. computers, guidance systems, propulsion systems, energy.

The new space movement must have the full commitment of the government, dedicated to consistently subsidizing the program over a period of two to four decades. This does not have to be an extraordinary commitment, like the Apollo project back in 1961, but the program cannot be funded in fits and starts.

There are three key contributions of the Federal Government:

1. Providing experience for human activities in space
2. Along with human activity in space, establish a rule of law, with proper law enforcement activity.
3. Building the infrastructure, just as they built the Interstate Highway system in the 1950s.

The government sector of the space program should derive the following benefits:

1. Economic - through taxes, to help pay for other government programs and not get into debt.
2. Political - as prestige, to gain the respect of the rest of the world, and to have the world's cooperation.

3. Scientific - advancement in technologies derived by the space movement, such as computers, communications, and many others.

4. Defense - To defend their own country, their allies, and space itself as we advance up there.

Benefits have already included:

- Surveillance for treaty verification - Many treaties have been made, especially in arms control, and the surveillance by spy satellites and other forms have successfully ensured that the countries with which we made our treaties are keeping their part by not creating any new weapons of mass destruction. Surveillance can ensure this.

- Remote sensing for finding resources - Remote sensing satellites can detect crucial and valuable minerals for use in important programs and industries.

- Navigation for ships at sea - to locate lost ships, and prevent ships from getting lost.

- Weather reporting - such as hurricane warnings, via satellite, to warn people to evacuate areas in the hurricane's path, saving tens of thousands of lives.

- Communications satellite business - For rapid advancement in communications, which is progressing at breakneck speed, and to market these advancements in business and defense.

3.1A Various types of satellites, from weather to remote sensing to spy satellites, and everything in between.

3.1B Communications Satellite.

3.1C Artist's rendering of a Navigation Satellite, helping to guide ships at sea, or in space on the way to the Moon. Could also be weather satellite.

3.1D A Hurricane in the Atlantic. This is why weather satellites are so vital. They can track storms and the direction these storms take, and then we can warn people in these storm's paths to evacuate, thereby saving tens of thousands of lives.

These have shown three categories of benefits. The fourth, political, means national prestige, international respect, and having other nations join us on cooperative ventures.

When a country returns to the Moon and develops their means for survival, they can slowly start building plants to process the mineral resources they obtain. These resources could be precious metals, even Helium-3. Even though it is not used for energy yet, it is used in security, by detecting small nuclear devices at airports, and in surgery. Other minerals, such as platinum, can be used in energy related devices, such as fuel cells or computer technology. They can be brought back to Earth in special cargo ships and be processed at a nation's facilities, and then be sold as a finished product. Here, they would sell for a lot of money.

The economic development of lunar and asteroidal resources will contribute taxes to the treasury and help tilt the balance of payments (i.e. the ratio between imports and exports) toward something more favorable to the U.S. That is, we could eliminate the trade deficit and create a trade surplus. This, in addition to eliminating the national debt.

When lunar and asteroidal resources are developed for industrial use, the economy will expand very rapidly, with many industries investing. The payback will be substantial.

One benefit, rarely mentioned, is political. There have been cases where countries hostile to the U.S. and other countries have a mineral that is badly needed, in such technologies as computers, energy, and space. This can result in either kowtowing to the hostile country to get the resource, or going to war, and I am opposed to resource wars, of any kind. An alternative would be to simply bypass that country and simply go to the Moon or an asteroid to obtain the mineral, and our problems would be solved. We would also benefit greatly technologically and economically.

To have a strong economy, we must maintain a technological lead. Investing in a space-based system leads to advanced technologies for life support systems, computer systems, and all forms of engineering. This is also an incentive to improve our educational system. This in turn will lead to:

- A stronger industrial base
- A stronger economy
- Higher employment
- Better standards of living
- Better quality of life

Infrastructure

Building space infrastructure will be different from building anything on Earth. There has to be means of survival, shelter from the hostile elements of space: the vacuum, radiation, both solar and cosmic, extreme temperatures, and space debris, both natural and man-made. Each space vehicle, station, and port, must carry its own atmosphere, shielding, and, in many cases, be able to produce its own gravity. In docking, there must be seals between the ship and the port. This applies in space, on the Moon, and on asteroids.

In space, there must be ports, space factories, space stations, and habitats. On the Moon, there must be structures for habitats, laboratories, mining and processing plants, ground transport, and factories and farms. On asteroids, there must be methods of dealing with extremely low gravity to prevent objects or personnel from flying off into the infinite void of space.

Of course, there must be food and energy production for all, everywhere.

Any space infrastructure needs to have universal availability.

This infrastructure would include:

1. Way Stations
2. Fuel Depots
3. Support Systems for Interplanetary Missions
4. Space Solar Power (with a possibility of privatization in the future)
5. Orbital Debris Mitigation, or Cleanup
6. Deflection system for Earth Threatening Asteroids. (Rare as this occurrence may be, the threat does exist and we must have the ability to deal with the threat.)
7. Law Enforcement. Keeping law and order in the new space environment, and preventing any conflicts between any entities, be they countries, private business, or individuals. This would be done by international agreement.

These would remain the domain of NASA and the government.

Large space infrastructure projects cannot be built by private investors alone, and shouldn't be done anyway, for they would be restricted to their own companies.

Further details of this will be covered in Chapter 4, The Space Infrastructure.

Models

As explained, there is a proper role for the government to foster, facilitate, and provide incentives, such as research and development of transportation systems, space stations, and lunar habitation, to enable private enterprise to open up space for development.

This has been done in the past in a major way, with the building of the transcontinental railroad in the 1800s, the building of the Panama Canal in the early 1900s, development of air transportation, and the building of the Interstate Highway System. In all four of these projects, the government paid for the building or development of these systems. After they were done, the government got out of the way and let private enterprise use these systems for their own benefit, and the benefit of the people.

The railroads, after they were developed, brought people and commerce out west, building up our quality of life, industry, and the nation. The Panama Canal saved the shipping industry over 12,000 miles on shipping between the Atlantic and Pacific Oceans, meaning lots of time and money. The air transportation system opened up the skies for both passengers and commerce, especially after World War II. The Interstate Highway System facilitated auto transportation across the U.S., beginning in the late 1950s.

The government can do this again with space, developing cheap and reliable access to space, with an enormous payback, like the other four projects. All it has to invest its money in the right projects, and humanity, and space development, will be on its way.

3.2A The completion of the Transcontinental Railroad, where East meets West.

*3.2B The Panama Canal, after completion, where the
first ships cross from the Atlantic to the Pacific*

It cost the Apollo program a total of $20 billion (1972 dollars) to send 12 men to the Moon. Although all of it came from the American taxpayer, there were many spin-offs for society such as computer technology, satellite communications, advanced solar technology, and fire-resistant garments, just to name a few. The space program also generated jobs for scientists and engineers.

With the problem of the national debt, the government can no longer afford to pay 100 percent of the funding for a new space program. However, with the help of the private sector, national laboratories, and colleges and universities, a new movement can emerge.

There are already major corporations in the satellite launching business, such as Europe's Ariane, Russia's Proton, and America's United Launch Alliance. In these areas, the government no longer needs to get involved. All it needs is to fund R&D for advanced spacecraft, and when they are developed, turn them over to the commercial space transport industries.

The government will still have to be involved in R&D for advanced space transport, the Way Station, and transportation systems to the Moon. What is needed is a system where work on this will employ a lot of people, even unskilled laborers, thus raising the employment rate, creating a vibrant economy where many businesses and people will benefit. This can be revived up to and beyond the level of Apollo, involving a triad of universities, corporations, and the government. Universities and corporations, and even government labs like Lawrence-Livermore can do research on advanced space transportation systems and proposed lunar orbiting space stations. The government and corporations (airlines, space transports, etc.) interested in acquiring the technology for its own use can pay for it. When this technology is fully developed, the government must simply get out of the way.

Way stations can be paid for by supporting governments and all space transport companies intending to use them.

Other components these businesses can manufacture include:

- Long-term life support systems – these are needed for any habitat or facility, because people will spend long periods of time in them, up to a number of years. There must be ways to process the air they breathe, provide water, and shield from cosmic and solar radiation. Much of this is already being done on the ISS, and more advancement in this realm has yet to be accomplished.
- Mining facilities.
- Space manufacturing facilities.
- Oxygen extraction facilities.
- Propellant storage and transfer facilities
- All forms of space habitats.

Financial Incentives for Individuals to Invest

Tax breaks can be given as an incentive for companies willing to invest in space. Of course, once these companies are up and running, making profits, these tax breaks would end. Tax money from these companies would then help pay for the massive space infrastructure being built.

The Stock Market would soon come into the picture. As space develops, many space-based industries will grow, and people will be eager to buy stock from these companies.

Space bonds will be another factor. Ordinary citizens can buy bonds with five, ten, fifteen, or twenty year maturities, with progressively higher interest rates.

These interest rates would increase with higher maturities. These can be used for protection against inflation, savings, or investments for:

- Children's college funds.
- New homes.
- Retirement.

Bonds for large sums of money ($100,000; $1 million; etc.) can be sold to corporations, foreign countries, or even individuals.

Conclusions and Recommendations

NASA at present is too big and bureaucratic. It will have to be reformed, with many of its activities transferred to other administrations relevant to that activity. NASA can then pursue its traditional role as an R & D agency.

Space commercialization will have a greater role in the 21st century. The proposed Department of Space should also be a part of that role. The true role of NASA and the DoSp is to be a supporter, enabler, and catalyst of the new space movement.

The government cannot open the space frontier alone. It will be the interaction of the government, private enterprise, and individuals. With tax incentives, corporations can make initial investments in transportation systems and the needed infrastructure.

More money must be available for the space effort, and both the stock and bond markets should also get involved. In short, there are many ways to fund the space movement, even with the problem of the national debt. Also, after major space industries like mining and manufacturing are self-supporting and prosperous, they, of course, would be taxed to help pay for the infrastructure that they use.

1. **NASA's Role and Reform:**
   - Scale back NASA's scope to focus on:
     - Deep space exploration.
     - Developing advanced technologies beyond private enterprise capabilities, particularly in advanced space vehicles.
   - Transition developed technologies to private companies once complete, allowing NASA to move on to new challenges.

2. **Establishing a Department of Space:**
   - Create a dedicated department to handle complex activities that exceed NASA's scope, particularly in managing private and international collaborations.

3. **Redistribution of NASA Activities:**
   - Reassign NASA's non-exploratory functions to relevant government agencies:
     - For example, Earth Observation Systems should move to NOAA.

4. **Leveraging Private Sector Services:**
   - Have NASA and the government procure services (e.g., launches) from private companies instead of conducting them in-house.

5. **Incentives for Space Industry Development:**
   - Offer tax incentives to industries investing in space-related activities.
   - Support financing for emerging space-focused industries.

- Explore innovative financial tools, such as stocks, bonds, and other investment instruments.

6. **Gradual Space Infrastructure Development:**
   - Build space infrastructure incrementally, driven by private individuals, groups, and industries advancing at their own pace, rather than attempting rapid, comprehensive development.

The next chapter will provide more detailed analysis and plans.

Space Infrastructure

If and when the government finally exits the launch business, it will still have a major role to play in the development of space. Its role in space will grow, not diminish, and it will need the aid of other nations to begin and develop the next step.

The development of space infrastructure is essential for humanity's expansion into space, encompassing simultaneous projects such as constructing space stations, factories, solar power satellites, and habitats for workers. It also includes mining and developing the Moon and Near-Earth asteroids to support these efforts.

Eventually, after the infrastructure is complete, we will have the means to venture to Mars.

Infrastructure is needed to support these activities, and this process cannot be done alone, nor can one industry or government afford to build it alone. It has to be done on an international scale. Once completed, this infrastructure must be available for use by all countries and industries. No entity shall be prohibited from using it, except in cases where deliberate violations of international agreements or laws pose a threat to other vessels, commerce, or other individual entities.

Building the Space Infrastructure

The U.S. government, along with other governments, and with the aid of space industries, should commence building an infrastructure system in space. This should be NASA's next project. This project would generate enormous payoff, as the previously mentioned infrastructure projects have done. All we need to do is invest our money in the right projects, and humanity will be permanently settled in space.

The Space Infrastructure would consist of the following:

- Transportation Systems
- Space (Way) Stations
- Orbital Transfer Systems
- Fuel Depots
- Support System for Interplanetary Missions (eventually)
- SPS Systems (See Also Energy and the Space Infrastructure)
- Space Debris Cleanup
- Protection of Earth from Rogue Asteroids
- Law Enforcement
- An International Consortium on Land Grants

Transportation Systems

Transportation systems for space include rockets, spaceships for carrying personnel and cargo, fuel depots, and Way Stations. The first two categories are already in place, and now that private industry has stepped in, they will soon start to progress at an accelerating rate.

The governments of the U.S., Russia, Europe, India, China, and Japan have their own rockets to send satellites to Earth orbit and cargo to the ISS (U.S., Russia, and Europe at present). Now private industry is coming in with SpaceX and Blue Origin as of this writing, with other industries soon to follow.

Various passenger vehicles have been and are still being developed by SpaceX, Boeing, Sierra Nevada, and Blue Origin, from space capsules to small versions of the space shuttle (Sierra Nevada's Dream Chaser), along with designs by other companies.

Space Transportation from Earth to LEO, and later to the Moon and Near-Earth asteroids will mostly be in the private domain, with the possible exception of the first ventures to Mars, but even that may change.

Like the Federal Aviation Administration in the U.S., which regulates the safety of airplanes and airports, we need to have an "International Spacecraft Administration" to regulate all spacecraft and space stations for the protection of the public. Safety standards must be set up on all spacecraft, subject to periodic inspections for the purpose of ensuring the safety of any and all personnel who travel on these spaceships, to protect them from any possible malfunctions of the spacecraft and from the natural and man-made threats of space.

The same must be applied to space stations, for the stability and structural integrity of the stations, the shielding from radiation and any meteorites or space debris, and collisions with other ships or structures. Health must also be a concern, to prevent the spread of diseases from other personnel.

This must be an international government organization, setting up strict safety standards. It must facilitate inspections and report any safety violations, and require the parties involved fix any violation until the structure or vessel is up to par.

Private companies cannot do this. This must be government(s) run.

Way Stations - A boon to space commerce;

The present International Space Station (ISS) is a permanently manned facility, with contributions (in both cost and facilities) from Europe, Russia, Japan, Canada, and the United States.

This space facility houses up to six people, six to twelve months at a time. It serves as a permanent orbiting laboratory, utilizing the near zero gravity and vacuum of space in materials and life sciences, and some aspects of astronomy and space sciences.

The ISS is a useful tool in the sciences, and many different experiments are being performed in these fields. The results are now being used in the fields of medicine, industry, communications (for example, people testing their ham radios with the ISS), and even education. Students have proposed their own experiments on the ISS, and many of these are being performed. The ISS even hosts teaching sessions with schools back on Earth.

For space infrastructure, education of young space advocates in this concept should be encouraged, long before building the infrastructure commences. They would be taught how it will be built, why it is needed, and what benefits it offers. This could encourage young space pioneers to want to take part in building this infrastructure, and consider how they want to do so. What part could they play, what work would they want to do, where do they want to participate, be it in space or on the Moon, and how can they dedicate their lives to this project?

In materials processing, new crystals are being grown, new medicines are being created, and new alloys are being tested in zero gravity, along with new processes in manufacturing. All aspects of life, from bacteria to plants to the human body, are being tested in space, observing the effects of cosmic rays, solar radiation, and zero gravity on all these life forms and on all parts of the human body.

All the results of these experiments on the space station will supposedly be used to create new jobs, new industries, and improve the quality of life on Earth, not to mention being used in future space technology, especially in life support systems.

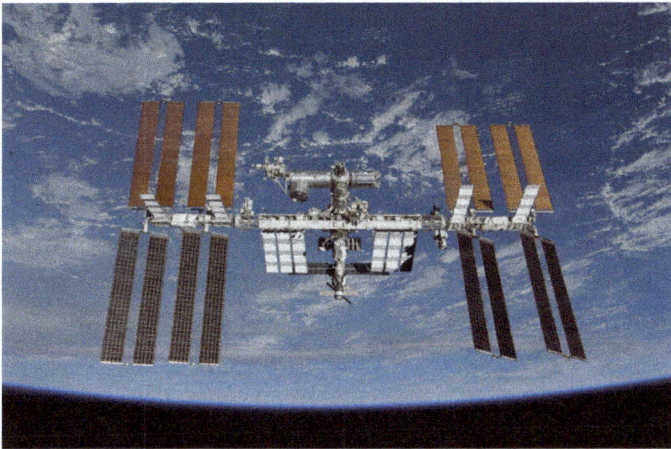

4.1 The International Space Station (NASA).

As beneficial as it is, the ISS cannot be used as a way station for ships to dock to reach other destinations. Here's why.

After leaving the Earth's surface to LEO, we will need separate transportation from LEO to the Moon, the LaGrange points, and the asteroids.

Note: Before going any further, I must briefly discuss the LaGrange Libration Points. There are five of these locations, known as L1 through L5, where the gravity fields of the Earth and the Moon cancel each other out, producing a stable orbit. An object placed at these orbits would feel equal and opposite attractions from the gravity of both the Earth and the Moon, and stay fixed at that orbit. L4 and L5 are the most stable of these orbits.

Around 1774, the French-Italian mathematician Joseph Louis LaGrange (1736-1813) used Newton's gravitational theory to explore properties of two unique points in Jupiter's orbit around the sun (L4 and L5, 60 degrees from Jupiter, both behind and ahead of the gas giant respectively). Years later, several asteroids were discovered to be trapped near the LaGrange points in permanent orbit, and these became known as "Trojan" asteroids.

In the Earth-Moon system, the stability of the L4 and L5 orbits is a lot more complex. The sun, distant as it is, greatly affects the orbits in the vicinity of Earth, a consequence of its enormous mass. This would disturb the orbits of any object at these two points.

Fortunately, there is an alternative to even this hurdle. In 1970, A. A. Kamal of Stanford University calculated that the stable regions at L4 and L5 lie in orbit of these points, 90,000 miles (144,000 kilometers) around the central libration points (see diagram). The orbit, which is around Earth, would be in an eccentric motion.

The other libration points are L1 and L2, at opposite ends of the Moon, and L3, 180 degrees from the Moon.

Earth-Moon LaGrange Libration Points

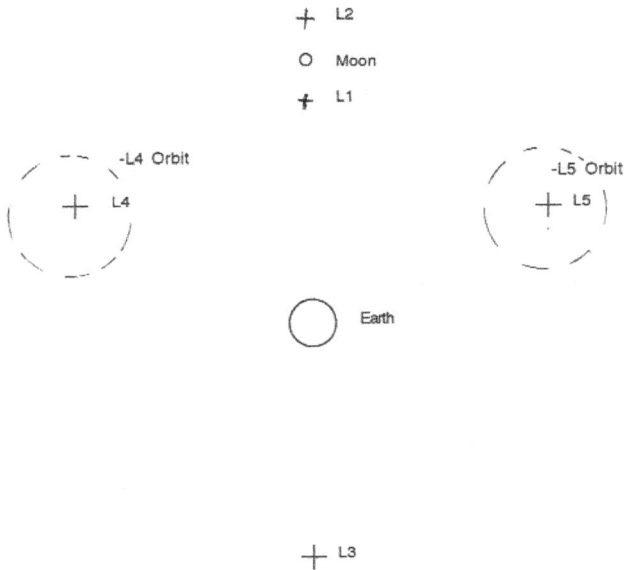

The five libration points of the Moon's orbit around Earth, where gravitational and centrifugal forces supposedly cancel each other out. (One must take in account the Sun's gravity). Objects placed at these locations tend to remain there with minimal expenditures of energy. The orbits of L4 and L5 are ideal locations to place asteroids to be mined. L1 and L2 would be ideal locations for way stations for Moonbound ships and/or mass catchers for lunar resources.

4.2 Diagram of the Earth-Moon LaGrange Points, L1 through L5. As with Jupiter, L4 and L5 lie in the Moon's orbit around Earth, sixty degrees to the Left and Right of the Moon, respectively. L3 Lies 180 degrees from the Moon in its orbit. Points L1 and L2 lie 58,000 kilometers, or 36,250 miles above the Lunar Surface. Diagram by Alastair Storm Browne. Reprinted from Cosmic Careers, used with permission.

Ships leaving Earth to LEO will still require large amounts of fuel to escape Earth's gravity field. Separate ships will be needed, or at least preferred, to travel to these libration points in space, and will not require much fuel, leaving plenty of space in these ships for cargo and personnel. They will need a point of origin from LEO, and a way station will be the key to this endeavor.

We will require ships, manufactured by private industries, to carry a range of about 50 to 100 personnel (we can start off with ten to twenty people). Ships from Earth must rendezvous with Moonbound ships, and allow the transfer of personnel and cargo. A way station will facilitate this process.

A separate way station will be needed to dock ships so they can transfer supplies to places like the Moon and other destinations, store propellant for Moonbound and space bound vehicles, and assemble spacecraft and other equipment. The ISS cannot be used for a way station because of the volume these activities will require, as well as the disruption of other activities on board, causing constant vibrations, interfering with MPS experiments, not to mention delicate the equipment used in all the presently planned activities.

To prevent disruption of other functions of the space station, it would be better to have a separate space station, for the sole purpose of serving as a transportation hub for travel to the Moon and other points in space.

This new space station (henceforth referred to as the Way Station), will require the following facilities:

1. Permanent hangers for Orbital Transfer Vehicles (OTVs) – OTVs are ferries for transporting personnel and supplies from Low Earth Orbit (LEO) to any orbital plane, all the way to the Moon, or satellites from one level of Earth orbit to another (space tugs). It is recommended that there be four or five OTVs rather than just one, for different purposes, and for spares in case any one of them needs refurbishing. One benefit of these hangers is that they can serve as protection of OTVs from space debris and micrometeorites.

2. Propellant storage and transfer facilities, for any and all space vehicles and tankers.

3. Storage facilities for payloads.

4. Gantries for preparing mission stacks of two OTVs, a lunar lander, and various manned and unmanned cargo elements.

5. Temporary storage for lunar vehicles and 20-30 tons of lunar payload.

6. Docking ports for Earth to LEO vehicles, OTVs, lunar vehicles, and spacecraft from any and all other space faring countries (Japan, Europe, Russia, etc.).

7. Transfer and integration facilities for payloads, supplies, and personnel.

8. Long duration life support systems.

9. Power units for heat rejection, cryogenic refrigeration, extra habitats, and gantries.

10. Assembly, storage, maintenance, and fueling facilities of a large variety of spacecraft in LEO. This includes literally hundreds, or even thousands, of metric tons of propellant, payload, and spacecraft per year.

The proposed Way Station is to be a single purpose station, as inexpensive as possible. To accomplish this, as much of the technology that is currently available should be utilized, with systems developed from Skylab, *Mir*, Salyut, and the International Space Station.

Eventually, it may be necessary to have more than one Way Station orbiting Earth, and at least one orbiting the Moon. The Lunar Way Station would be the same as the Earth Orbiting Way Station, with ships from Earth and the asteroids docking there to transfer personnel and cargo to and from the lunar surface.

In turn, they would be transferred to other ships bound for the Earth and other destinations.

This will save money for the next steps in advancing further on into space.

4.3A Way Station orbiting Earth, for passenger ships headed out to the Moon and other space habitats or industrial sites.

4.3B Way Station for transporting cargo, fuel, even personnel.

Fuel Depots - Why they are needed.

Imagine a bustling orbital fuel station, where spacecraft from Earth refuel before heading to the Moon or Mars. This vision could become a reality with advancements in fuel production on the Moon or in space, lower launch costs from Earth, and space tanker technology (ships that transport rocket fuel either from Earth or space, to fuel depots in Low Earth orbit).

We must have an orbital refueling station around Earth and, later, the Moon. Ships will be launched from Earth, and after expending most of the fuel escaping Earth's gravity well, dock at the orbital filling station, then refuel to continue their journeys to the Moon, Mars, asteroids, or any other space station.

The station would have docking facilities for ships to refuel with both liquid hydrogen and oxygen before continuing on to their destination.

At present, rockets require large amounts of fuel to escape Earth's gravity. These rockets continuously eject rocket stages, which become space junk, another serious problem. Heavy lift launch vehicles (HLLVs) have been proposed for use, but with the high cost of development, launch costs, fuel, and the continuing production of these rockets, all running into billions of dollars per launch, it would be a lot cheaper to use small vehicles with refueling capabilities during flight.

Fuel depots are not new concepts, but their time has come. We need to seriously take a look at them, and start building them, first in Low Earth orbit. We will have to first transport fuel from Earth via space tankers, as mentioned, but this will lead to advances in technology in new methods of producing and transporting fuel, be it on Earth or in space.

These fuel depots could revolutionize space travel, by allowing rockets to be replenished rather than discarding their stages, or sending two or three rockets on an interplanetary mission rather than one. Space trips and commerce will be faster and cheaper, just as gas stations made long distance auto travel possible.

Now to build it!

The question here is the feasibility for the near future. For now, the fueling station will need to be launched from Earth, with the fuel launched separately, then stored at sub-zero temperatures.

The proposal is to launch it in the form of water, then separate it by electrolysis into hydrogen and oxygen. The problem here is that at present, it costs $10,000 per kilogram to launch water into LEO, and it would require many launches to support the fuel depot as presently proposed. Also, how much would it cost to launch the station itself? Launching a fuel depot and fuel from Earth would not be feasible. Note: That might change if launch costs go way down, say about $22 per kilogram ($10 per pound), but it would take advanced launch systems to accomplish this feat.

The alternative would be to build a fueling station in space out of lunar and asteroidal materials.

The South Pole of the Moon, around Shackleton Crater to be exact, has been found to contain a few billion tons of water ice in permanently shadowed areas. Also, Near-Earth asteroids have been found to contain water ice, more than on the Moon (Chapter 7, Near-Earth Asteroids).

Building a fueling station from Lunar and asteroidal materials and extracting water from the Moon and asteroids can be done at a fraction of the cost. With near zero gravity from asteroids, and space factories already in place, a fuel depot can be built and placed in Earth and Lunar orbits, or at the LaGrange points, at a fraction of the cost of launching it from Earth. Extracting water from the Moon and transporting it to fuel depots will reduce the cost by a factor of ten to fourteen. Extracting water from asteroids will even be cheaper.

I feel that the best time to build a fuel depot is when we already have settlements on the Moon and space factories mining the asteroids; i.e. when there is a lot of space commerce already in existence. This is when the settlement of space will mature and become irreversible. Unless launch costs decrease exponentially, now would not be the time to build a fuel depot.

4.4 Fuel Depot, orbiting Earth, for various types of ships.

From LEO to the Moon

This segment of the infrastructure will come later, probably last, after building the infrastructure to Near-Earth Asteroids. This is because mining NEAs will probably come before returning to the Moon. Once we can mine in space, our attention will turn toward our satellite.

Orbital Transfer Vehicles – From LEO to Lunar Orbit

To make travel from Earth to the Moon routine, what is needed is a system that is reusable, saves money on fuel, and can be used spontaneously. For this process, it is best to launch the vehicle from Earth orbit rather than from Earth's surface. The ship should be composed of lightweight material free of atmospheric friction. There are to be no expendable stages, no Earth-to-orbit launch accelerations, and the ship would be able to be refurbished, refueled, and reused.

This proposed vehicle is the Orbital Transfer Vehicle (OTV). Parked at the Way Station, the OTV would be able to travel to higher Earth orbits and up to Lunar Orbit where it would dock to a Lunar Orbiting Space Station. After deploying passengers, cargo, or fuel, it could retrieve the above and return to the Way Station, drop off returned payloads or people, be refueled, and begin another errand. This OTV would have a long life and interchangeable parts, such as engines that can be immediately replaced.

4.5A. OMV Transferring Space Station to a higher orbit.

4.5B Various OTVs, Space Tugs, at a Depot.

Because of the wide range of functions for the OTV, and its continuous usage, there should be not one, but a fleet, with different types of OTVs performing different functions. There should be OTVs to perform the following tasks:

- Transferring personnel from LEO to Lunar Orbit, and back.

- Tankers, for delivering propellant from LEO to the Lunar Orbiting Station, and between the Way Station, Lunar orbit, and Lunar surface.

- Delivering payloads, such as space station parts and lunar base components.

- Towing large satellites and space stations from dangerously low orbits to higher, safer orbits (hence the name "space tug").
- Orbital Maneuvering Vehicles (OMVs), unmanned, to deliver satellites to higher orbits and to retrieve satellites for repairs.

New technologies will need to be developed for the OTV. The following are needed:

- Aerobraking systems, to slow the OTV to LEO from higher energy Earth orbits, or from lunar orbit.
- Advanced engines, for faster transportation from LEO to lunar orbit, as well as longevity.
- Lightweight structures, for lower fuel requirements and more payload.
- Automated rendezvous and docking techniques.
- Teleoperations, mostly for OMVs.
- Long-term cryogenic fluid storage and transfer (also required for hypersonic vehicles).

Lunar Orbital Space Station

In order to travel to and from the lunar surface, what is required is an OTV derived, reusable lunar landing vehicle, capable of transporting personnel, cargo, and propellant. Again, this will require different types of vehicles. Because of the propellant required to land and take-off from the lunar surface, it is suitable to permanently station these landers in lunar orbit, at a Lunar Orbiting Space Station.

A Lunar Orbiting Space Station can be built at low cost, used simply for the following purposes:

*   Docking OTVs.
*   Fuel storage and transfer.
*   Fueling OTVs and Lunar Landers.
*   Hangers for Lunar Landing Vehicles.
*   Transportation Depot – for personnel traveling to and from the lunar base.
*   Transporting payloads.

What is lacking is the means for transporting these payloads from the Lunar Landers to the OTVs. For construction of the Lunar Orbiting Space Station we need:

1. Hangers and docking ports for OTVs and Lunar Landing Vehicles.
2. Fuel storage and transfer facilities.
3. Transportation nodes for cargo from OTVs to Lunar Landers, and vice versa.
4. Personnel quarters.

4.6A and 4.6B Two different images of a Lunar Orbital Way Station taking in ships that transfer passengers and cargo to and from the Moon. Other ships are docked to transfer these passengers to cargo to go to Earth or other places in space. Note: According to NASA, the proposed Lunar Gateway itself would be in a highly elliptical orbit, coming as close as around 1,500 kilometers (930 miles) to the lunar surface at its closest point, but reaching as far as 70,000 kilometers (43,000 miles) away at its furthest point in this orbit, known as a Near-Rectilinear Halo Orbit (NRHO).

There have been several proposed locations for a Lunar Orbiting Space Station, from libration point L2 (58,000 kilometers or 36,250 miles above the lunar surface) to polar orbit. The best proposed location is polar orbit, not only for access to all locations on the Moon, but also so that base location won't be a problem for transportation. OTVs traveling from LEO to lunar orbit can maneuver their vessels to rendezvous with the lunar space station.

Recommendation: Develop an efficient, unsophisticated, inexpensive Lunar Orbiting Space Station for transport of materials and personnel to the lunar surface before building a lunar base.

Alternative: Have reusable ships travel from LEO directly to the Moon's surface for transport of materials and personnel.

Note: This is not the proposed Lunar Orbital Gateway. The Way Station comes later. In the author's opinion, it is not recommended that we build a Lunar Gateway, because all activities proposed on this station can be done on the lunar surface itself. Also, the Gateway cannot accommodate all needed activities from the proposed Way Station, which will only interfere with the Gateway's activities. This Way Station needs to be separate, and used for one purpose only, all of which are covered in this proposal. The Gateway is a totally different proposal from this proposed Way Station, and must remain separate.

Lunar Landing Vehicles

Reusable lunar landing vehicles are for transporting personnel, propellant, and consumables for the lunar base personnel. There can be several types of vehicles for these purposes.

In transporting personnel, since the first lunar base may only have six to twelve people, the lunar landing vehicles will be used first. However, in the future, a reusable personnel carrier should be developed to transport the same number, for short, two-to-four-hour trips to and from the lunar surface. In addition to transporting crew, these personnel carriers could also transport consumables, such as food, sanitation supplies, and other small necessities and luxury items, such as books, films, mail, etc.

Upon the establishment of a lunar base and the full development of the extraction of oxygen from the lunar soil to use as propellant (to be discussed in Chapter 5., Building a Lunar Civilization), a separate Lunar Propellant Carrier can then be used to transport the liquid oxygen (LOX) to the Lunar Space Station, to transfer to facilities itself, or onto OTVs for transport to the Way Station at LEO.

There should also be a Lunar Surface Transfer Vehicle, which can go from LEO to the lunar surface carrying cargo or a habitat, hover a few meters over the lunar surface, drop the cargo or habitat, and then return to LEO to be reused. Nothing is wasted placing materials on the lunar surface. Habitats can then be moved by cranes and other construction machinery to their intended locations.

4.7A Lunar Landing Vehicle for exporting propellant, from lunar surface to other points in space.

4.7B Lunar Landing Vehicle transporting cargo and habitats to the lunar surface.

Obviously, many Earth to Lunar orbit and Lunar Landing Vehicles would eventually fall into private hands. This may even be the case from the very beginning. The Lunar Orbital Space Station would be a public facility, and would be accessible to anyone who needs to use it.

Solar Power Satellites (SPS Systems)

SPS Systems, and their functions, are described in complete detail in Chapter 8, Energy and the Space Infrastructure.

"As a brief synopsis, SPS Systems are simply Solar Power Satellites, originally designed to be 10 kilometers across. They would be deployed in geosynchronous Earth orbit (GEO); that is, 22,300 miles (approximately 35 to 40 thousand kilometers) above the Earth's surface, orbiting at a fixed point on Earth at all times."

The function of an SPS system is to collect the Sun's rays in space, convert them to microwaves, and beam them down to a receiving antenna at a fixed point on Earth where they can be converted to 10 gigawatts (10 billion watts) of electricity. This would be entirely clean energy, non-polluting, and safe.

The satellite itself is way too large and expensive to build on Earth and then launch into space.

An alternative to this would be to build the satellite in Earth orbit after space factories and foundries are established, at that very point where it would operate. This SPS satellite would be built from lunar and asteroidal materials, mined from both places, to be processed into the materials needed to build this system. This will be exponentially cheaper to build in space, due to the cost of fuel and multiple launches. Originally, this will be part of the infrastructure because the first few SPS systems may be sponsored by various governments, or a combination of both government(s) and private energy companies (note the plural). This is to be expected because of the expenses involved, along with the time it takes to test for defects.

As we build more of these systems, construction costs will go down, and governments will be able to leave future construction and operations to private industry.

4.8 Solar Power Satellite beaming microwaves to Earth from GEO, to a receiving antenna (rectenna) on Earth to convert into electricity for distribution. This satellite is not drawn to scale.

Space Debris

One growing problem in Earth orbit is space debris, space garbage, or space junk. Space junk has been in existence since the launching of the first satellite, Sputnik, back in 1957. When Sputnik was released in orbit, there was not only the satellite, but its covering and the rocket stage that propelled it to orbit, meaning there wasn't one new satellite, but three.

From that point on, as more satellites and manned space missions were launched, space junk accumulated in orbit. Spent rocket bodies remained in orbit from launching these two categories of satellites and ships. Satellites went out of commission and remained in orbit, slowly falling apart, with fragments orbiting the Earth at 18,000 m.p.h. (4.3 to 5.0 miles per second), faster than a bullet.

4.9A. An image of Space Debris.

4.9B. An exaggerated image of Space Debris, but this serves as a warning. Someday, the problem may actually look like this, making it impossible to venture into space if something isn't done.

Many satellites and debris fall into the Earth's atmosphere and burn up, but other satellites, once out of commission, have been sent to higher orbits, a "graveyard orbit" thousands of miles up from LEO.

There are an estimated 900 million pieces of space debris, ranging from a few millimeters to the size of a school bus. As of January 2022, the total weight of all this junk is estimated to be about 9000 metric tons. This includes various parts, spent rocket stages, and even items lost by spacewalking astronauts.

Beyond GEO, the point where any satellite will hover over a fixed point on Earth 24 hours a day, there are over 400 dead satellites, jettisoned there in a graveyard orbit to make room for other, newer satellites. These dead satellites will remain there for centuries or more.

We don't know the exact number because different sources quote different numbers.

I would like to point out that there are millions of tiny fragments of at least one millimeter. This is one example of many, and we have a problem here.

I'm saying this here because one might not think much of a one millimeter thick piece of debris, but at high velocities, they can do plenty of damage. There was an incident in 1983 where the space shuttle *Challenger* was hit by a fleck of paint, causing a small gouge. No other damage was detected, but the entire window had to be replaced. If that piece of junk had been bigger, there might have been a major catastrophe.

In 2007, China launched a military satellite, to be used as an anti-satellite weapon. As an experiment, it was deliberately rammed into one of their defunct weather satellites, creating literally thousands of pieces of orbiting space debris.

In 2009, Iridium 33, a private communications satellite, accidentally crashed into a Russian military satellite, Kosmos-2251, destroying both satellites.

Space debris has done plenty of damage to satellites, and can be life-threatening to personnel on the ISS and to any future manned space vehicle, station, or privately owned space station. It's a wonder no lives have been lost on account of space debris crashing into an astronaut doing a space walk, or on the ISS itself.

It will only be a matter of time before a tragedy like this does happen, but if we act now, we may be able to prevent it. The solution is simple; rid Earth's orbit of space debris. Obviously, the process is a lot more complex.

As more nations and other entities participate in space exploration and development, cleaning Earth orbit will be a great priority, and all spacefaring nations, old and new, will have to take part, even if they did not contribute to the problem in the first place. This means that every entity will have to help pay for the process of cleaning up in money and/or capital; i.e. vehicles that collect space junk (space garbage trucks), devices that catch orbiting debris, and so forth.

There will be an international consortium doing this, and it will become part of space infrastructure.

One little known fact is that there is a law already on the books about collecting defunct satellites to salvage for valuable components. If one were to salvage or push a defunct satellite back into the Earth's atmosphere to burn, one must notify the satellite owners of the process.

This is one of the issues this consortium must face: space laws concerning defunct satellites.

Finally, how are we going to commence with this process? There have been many proposals about how the process of cleaning up space debris can be done. I will list a few of them here, and, if possible, come up with my own ideas.

- For tiny pieces of debris, from one millimeter and higher, such as bolts, screws and other debris, perhaps up to the size of a softball, several ideas have been proposed. Tungsten microdust, or water, can be spread in the paths of oncoming debris, decelerating it to lower orbits to burn up in the Earth's atmosphere. Lasers from Earth, or a satellite, have been proposed to target specks of debris, creating a jet stream and speeding the debris into the atmosphere. This process, however, is expensive, costing $1 million per object zapped.

- A space balloon or a large sheet could collect debris on its surface on well-traveled paths, and then fold the sail or balloon with the debris into a ship, or send it burning into the atmosphere. Debris catchers, shaped like cones, could also collect debris to recycle or burn.

- For larger debris, such as spent rocket stages and defunct satellites, there are two ways to deal with this. First, fire "spears" at the satellites and rocket parts, whether in Geosynchronous Orbit (GEO) or LEO, that guide them to burn up in the atmosphere.

- The second is a crewed space garbage ship or truck, to collect satellites and rocket parts to salvage, either for repair and reuse, or, more likely, to recycle their metals. A space station can be built for this purpose.

- Eventually, when space factories and foundries come into being, use the metals for making other products.

- A space tug can also be used to catch large, defunct satellites and spent rocket stages to tow to the Earth's atmosphere, where they would be released to burn up while plummeting to Earth.

It is feared that many of these concepts would be used for anti-satellite weapons, and this is where the international based space debris consortium intervenes. Any defunct satellite and rocket parts must be cataloged and obtain permission from their owners before being targeted for salvage or disposal, to prevent accidental damage or destruction to any satellite presently in use. Also, this technology is to be used for space clean-up only—no unlawful destruction of satellites, regardless of the country of origin, should be tolerated.

4.10A A Space "Garbage Truck" with robotic arms collecting all sorts of space junk, mostly defective satellites.

4.10B Dealing with smaller pieces of space debris, from bagging larger pieces to zapping with lasers micro-debris, one millimeter thick or under.

All operations for waste disposal are to be authorized by this consortium, and any and all activities are to be recorded and logged for any further reference, should an unfortunate event occur.

Should this activity of space clean-up come into being, I believe that this can be done in a much shorter time than one would originally imagine. This entity would remain in existence, for a lot more space debris will be generated and will need to be cleared from Earth orbit, due to the advances in space development.

Utilizing Spent Rocket Stages for Lunar Development

Spent rocket stages hold untapped potential in supporting future lunar settlements. These remnants of space missions, along with defunct satellites, are rich in materials such as copper, zinc, lead, gold, silver, platinum, and various alloys. They also often contain leftover hydrogen and oxygen— resources critical for sustaining life and operations on the Moon.

The Moon's natural resources, while abundant in some areas, lack certain essential metals required to build devices like computers and lunar rovers. Repurposing materials from spent rocket stages could bridge this gap. With the right technology, these stages could be soft-landed on the lunar surface and refurbished into habitats, laboratories, or other necessary facilities. (Refer to Chapter 5, "Building a Lunar Civilization.")

Towing spent rocket stages from low Earth orbit (LEO) to the Moon is far more economical than launching new equipment from Earth. The cost of transporting these stages down the lunar gravity well is significantly less than overcoming Earth's gravitational pull.

By leveraging space debris for lunar colonization, humanity can establish lunar infrastructure in a cost-effective, sustainable manner. This innovative approach reduces the need for constructing habitats from scratch, simultaneously addressing the growing problem of space debris in Earth's orbit.

4.11A Small OTV towing a spent rocket stage.

4.11B A "Salvage Station" salvaging a spent rocket stage, to be put to other uses; i.e. salvaging its precious metals or converting the stage into a lunar or space habitat.

Protection of Earth from Rogue Asteroids

It has been theorized, with evidence, that an asteroid impacted the Earth over 65 million years ago. This supposedly caused the extinction of the dinosaur, along with 50 percent of the other species on Earth at that time.

This is on account of not only the impact of the asteroid itself, causing worldwide earthquakes and tidal waves, but also of the enormous quantities of dust and debris thrown up into the atmosphere. An event like this could block out the sun over a period of years, even decades, killing off plant life, leaving most species to starve themselves out of existence. Acid rain is another factor here, harming any survivors.

Evidence of asteroids impacting the Earth are found in craters, such as a huge 180 kilometer wide crater at the tip of Yucatán Peninsula in Puerto Chicxulub, Mexico. Other craters include Manicouagan Lake in Quebec.

There are also craters in Arizona, Iowa, and Argentina. The crater in Argentina is supposedly the result of an asteroid slamming into Earth at a low angle and breaking apart, with its pieces skipping along Earth's surface, gouging out narrow ravines.

On February 15, 2013, an asteroid 60 feet wide exploded 18 miles (~29 kilometers) over Chelyabinsk, Russia, in the Siberian region. Though the asteroid did not hit the ground (small pieces were later found, including one in a frozen lake), the air burst produced a shock wave that caused damage to buildings in a 55 mile (90 kilometer) radius. A total of 3600 buildings had windows that were shattered. Because of this damage, 1200 people went to the hospital to be treated for injuries.

This asteroid, it was later discovered, had broken off from a bigger piece traveling near Earth's orbit. It is estimated that this broken piece fell at a velocity of 40,000 miles per hour through the Earth's atmosphere, had a brightness thirty times that of the Sun—twenty-five people reported sunburns of that cold, winter day, and ultraviolet light had been detected reflecting off the snow—and the force of the explosion equaled that of 440,000 tons of TNT, about the power of thirty atomic bombs the strength of Hiroshima.

Fortunately, no one was killed. If this asteroid had exploded at a lower altitude, over a more densely populated area, the destruction would have been far worse.

It is believed that an asteroid burst like this occurs every 100 to 200 years.

In 1908, another asteroid (some say it was a comet, possibly a piece of the comet Encke) exploded three to six miles (five to 10 kilometers) over Tunguska, Siberia, in Russia. The power was two to three times as large as the more recent Chelyabinsk, a force equivalent to five to 15 million tons of TNT, flattening 2000 square kilometers (770 square miles) of forests.

This is the largest explosive event in recorded history on Earth. Again, no human was killed because this was all forest, but if this cataclysmic event occurred over a city, it would have been a different story.

Had this asteroid/comet hit the rural U.S., 70,000 people would have been killed, with an estimated $4 billion in property damage. In an urban area, this asteroid/comet would have killed 300,000 people with an estimated $280 billion in property damage.

These two incidents show that the Earth is more vulnerable than we realize. On the average, one body with an explosive power in excess of 1000 megatons (one gigaton) will strike the Earth every 10,000 years. The probability of this magnitude occurring between the years 1000 B.C. and 3000 A.D. is 0.4 out of 1.0, or 40 percent, not a negligible threat.

Should an asteroid one kilometer wide hit the Earth, the consequences would be far more devastating. An impact on the ocean would create tidal waves that would wash out all coastal cities within its circumference. How would an asteroid, should it strike dry land, compare with nuclear weapons?

The largest nuclear device ever exploded was the 1962 Soviet nuclear test on Novaya Zemlya, under 60 megatons. That's the equivalent of 60 million tons of TNT exploding all at once. An all out nuclear exchange has been estimated to be about 20,000 megatons. One single impact of an asteroid one kilometer wide is estimated to deliver fifty times this destructive power. However, the average orbital lifetime of an NEA is approximately 30 million years. This phenomenon may not occur for about another 100,000 to one million years, but it may occur again in this century. We just don't know.

In 2009, NASA, in collaboration with JPL (Jet Propulsion Laboratory in Pasadena, California) launched an infrared space telescope called WISE (Wide-field Infrared Survey Explorer) to map out comets and asteroids close to the Earth. It ran out of coolant a few months later, but was able to extend the mission to 2011, under the name NEOWISE (Near-Earth Object Wide-field Infrared Survey Explorer) before shutting down. In 2013, it was restarted again under the Near-Earth Object Observations Program, a precursor for the agency's Planetary Defense Coordination Office, to continue the search for Near-Earth comets and asteroids. The program was then shut down in 2024, and dubbed a great success.

Shortly after Chelyabinsk, a group of astronauts, known as the Association of Space Explorers, got together and went to the U.N. urging them to form a system to respond in the event of an approaching asteroid that could impact the Earth. The International Asteroid Warning Network (IAWN) was formed.

This is truly an international body, composed of 74 nations, including the U.S., Russia, and Iran. It was agreed that not one government or space organization could deal with this threat alone. This agreement to be international came at the urging of Rusty Scheweickart, former Apollo 9 astronaut.

There are over one million asteroids in Earth's orbital neighborhood, big enough to destroy a city the size of New York, and there must be ways to not only detect oncoming NEA five to ten years in advance, but ways to deflect one should it ever become necessary. The IAWN would help coordinate a mission to launch a spacecraft to slam into the asteroid to divert it on a different path from impacting Earth, thereby saving billions of lives.

The IAWN should be (Some of these proposals are my own):

- A worldwide observing network
- Observatories on the ground
- Satellites in space (i.e. infrared satellites to track asteroids clearly)
- A system to catalog *all* asteroids and their paths, regardless of size
- A system with the ability to detect and deal with the dangers of asteroidal impact years in advance. If an asteroid is found to be on a course to collide with Earth,

there should be enough time to prepare a space vehicle to deflect it from its path, to prevent the collision with Earth.

- An equal and complete sharing of technology and expenses
- An equal and complete sharing of information on any and all asteroids
- A research effort to develop technologies for deflecting asteroids.

It is estimated that there are over one million asteroids in Earth's orbit around the Sun. These are known as Near-Earth Asteroids (NEAs) or Near-Earth Objects (NEOs). Only 10,000 of these asteroids have been tracked by NASA's NEO program.

Nine percent of these tracked NEOS are over 3000 feet long.

One half of one percent of smaller asteroids that have been found are equivalent to the one that exploded over Tunguska.

An asteroid 460 feet long is estimated to have a force of 150 to 300 megatons of TNT, and is due to hit the Earth once every 30,000 years. This asteroid has the potential to kill 50 million people and collapse the world economy for a century or two. Only 10 to 20 percent of NEAs tracked have been found to be that size.

Ninety percent of the larger NEAs are one kilometer or more. These can greatly damage human civilization as described above, but none are in danger of hitting the Earth anytime soon. It is the smaller asteroids (450 feet to 3280 feet, or 0.14 to one kilometer) that are a real threat to Earth.

With all this information about NEOs, and the newly formed IAWN, it shouldn't be so difficult, with the addition of infrared satellites, to eventually track and catalog nearly all the NEAs and their pathways, determining if and when any are likely to collide with Earth.

There is also the B612 Foundation, co-founded by shuttle astronaut Ed Lu and Apollo astronaut Rusty Schweickart. It is a private institute dedicated to searching and mapping asteroids for the purpose of locating possible killer asteroids that could be a threat to Earth, but also supporting scientific exploration, economic development, and mapping out the solar system for future reference as we progress into space.

They are backed by the University of Washington and Google Cloud.

Should they find an Earth threatening asteroid, they will warn us in advance of what could happen to Earth so we can take preventive measures.

Our first challenge may come as early as 2032. A 1345-foot wide asteroid is due to pass close to the Earth, with the distinct possibility of impact. Chances are it won't strike, but we should be prepared to deflect it if necessary. The technology to do this is already available, so we should be prepared.

We will and do have the technology to deflect asteroids, by way of rockets, solar sails, gravity tractors (a ship built for the purpose of deflecting asteroids), even nuclear devices, all of which can be launched years in advance. Using nuclear devices to destroy an asteroid isn't likely because of the debris it would generate, thereby increasing the danger by taking an asteroidal shower on Earth, causing equal or greater destruction, but the explosion could be used to nudge an asteroid if we ignite it in the right position in space.

Another scenario is that when we are settled in space, and we spot an asteroid on a path that is predicted to impact the Earth within thirty years, we would be able to mine the asteroid out of existence. This would not only eliminate the threat, but would make big money in the process, using the asteroid's minerals for constructive purposes. This would be turning the threat into wealth.

4.12 What some people see as a crisis, or even a disaster, others see as an opportunity to make big money.

Law Enforcement

As humanity advances in space, laws for everyone in space will become necessary, with a law enforcement agency to insure safety, welfare and keep order, as on Earth. Space laws are already on the books of the United Nations, and most countries have signed treaties to abide by these laws, and as we progress further out into space, more laws will be made, and others will be either abolished or updated. All laws will need to be enforced.

Space laws will apply to everyone in space, whether they go up there to visit, work for a temporary period of time, or live there permanently. When one visits a city or foreign country, that person must abide by the laws there.

Laws will be made and enforced in the fields of industry, business, property rights and protection, resources, and public safety. Public safety ranges from murder and theft, the two universal codes, to disturbing the peace, use and/or possession of weapons, and any other form of violent behavior that might pose a threat to the public.

Other forms of laws to be enforced are white collar crime such as reneging on business deals, embezzling money or resources, stealing resources from the Moon or other celestial body without filing a claim, stealing from someone else's claim (claim jumping), or dishonest business practices.

This is just a sample of the laws, but these are the general overview of what problems humanity as a whole will have to deal with on the space frontier, for as we advance, we will take our faults and weaknesses with us. Human nature will not change, and individual human beings will still have to be dealt with when bad incidents occur, and they will occur. A space law enforcement agency will be necessary to maintain order and prevent, or control, chaotic situations as migration in space accelerates.

The space police force will be an international entity composed of people from all spacefaring nations, or perhaps all nations as a whole. There would be the top echelon, doing all administrative work, stationed both in space and on Earth, and then there would be those who go out and do the actual enforcement, the space police itself. These would travel in spaceships, equivalent to our police cars and coast guard vessels, patrolling nearby inhabited space, including Earth orbit, the asteroids, and the Moon. These police should be easily accessible to all for assistance.

Any crime committed in space, be it business or murder, will have the proper court and prison facilities in space and on Earth under this international agency. For some crimes, fines will be paid to this agency through the courts. Should a long jail time be necessary, the convict could either be forced to work in an asteroidal or lunar mine, should it be a violent crime, or be incarcerated in his or her country of origin on Earth.

Would the police themselves be armed? The Outer Space Treaty prohibits all weapons, including side arms. In countries such as Britain, policemen do not carry weapons. What if extremely violent incidents occur? There may have to be a change for law enforcement personnel to carry weapons of some sort in these violent situations.

I would like to point out that this is a rough draft of proposed law enforcement, for this subject has rarely been examined, and because of this, the author took it upon himself to propose this entirely from his own ideas. There are no references for this. What finally materializes may be partly from this proposal, but the final product will be more detailed and complex than what is presented here.

An International Consortium on Land Grants

The last thing, but just as important, in forming the space infrastructure would be organizing the Moon and asteroids for settlement and industrialization.

In other words, one cannot just land on the Moon, an asteroid, or Mars, and claim it for their own, even if it is just a small plot. One has to file a claim.

This is similar to the old homestead act of 1862, on the American frontier, where one could register with the U.S. government for 160 acres of land, free, for settlement. Once it is registered, there is a residency requirement where the claimant has to settle on the land, build a home, make improvements, and farm it for a minimum of five years before said claimant can have full ownership.

During the gold rushes of 1849 in California and 1897 in the Yukon Territory in Canada, if one wanted to prospect for gold on land, or even in a river or stream, one had to file a claim with the government at the claims' office in the vicinity of the land, located in a nearby town, before doing any digging or panning.

This is how it will be to claim any land on any celestial body. The purpose is to organize the land and prevent any conflicts that could possibly lead to violent confrontations.

According to the Outer Space Treaty:

> "Outer space, including the Moon and other celestial bodies...shall be the province of all mankind."

Article II of the treaty states:

> "Outer space, including the Moon and other celestial bodies, is not subject to national appropriation by claim or sovereignty, by means of use or occupation or by any other means."

Although written in 1967, two years before the first Moon landing, this treaty is as appropriate today as when it was written, signed, and ratified. Many space advocates oppose it, but there are also laws prohibiting weapons of any kind, from nuclear weapons to a sidearm, passed for the purpose of preventing war altogether.

In this book, I shall support and abide by this treaty, proposing no changes or additions.

Paraphrased, no country or government may lay any claim to any piece of land on the Moon or any other celestial body. This means no colonies! You might think this is bad, but looking at the treaty all together will prevent war and give every person on Earth an opportunity to freely settle space if he or she so desires.

The treaty disallows colonies, but private land ownership is permitted, and that is the ticket to developing space. What is proposed is an "International Legal Regime" for managing and distributing the land.

Alan Wasser, a physicist from M.I.T. and at present head of Alan Washer Associates, is the author of the Space Settlement Initiative (or Act), which states how the Moon (along with asteroids and Mars, but for now, all reference will be mainly toward the Moon) can be parceled for land grants (see Appendix, (Draft of) AN ACT), in compliance with the Outer Space Treaty. For an already stated reason, Wasser calls the Outer Space Treaty a blessing in disguise.

The only difference between what I write here and what Alan Wasser proposes is that U.S. Congress would make the grants, while I propose that the International Legal Regime, that same regime responsible for law enforcement, consisting of representatives from different countries, would make the grants. There is no other difference.

The U.S. can and should recognize these claims. Any land granted to any entities can be subject to taxation by the receiver's country of origin.

The first land grant is proposed to be 600,000 square miles, 4 percent of the lunar surface, being the size of Alaska, to a private consortium that can commence development within seven years (my proposal). After that time, if there is no landing and development, the grant will revert to the legal regime to grant to another entity.

The purpose of such a large land grant is that transport and settlement on the Moon will cost an astronomical sum of money, in the hundreds of billions of dollars, minimum. This includes manufacturing, transporting, and setting up habitats, life support, transportation systems on the lunar surface, manufacturing facilities, and mining operations.

In paying for all this and turning a profit, the inhabitants of the first settlement will be able to sell parcels of their claim to other would-be settlers. These settlers buying the parcel would, in turn, sell their excess land to other entities.

As more people settle and set up habitats and other facilities, the technology will accelerate the ability for more people and industries to settle on the lunar surface, and costs will then decrease.

Should any settlement default, the land, along with its facilities, including ground transportation, will be put up for sale to other entities by the International Legal Regime (ILR), for a certain percentage of the original cost and investments. This is so that when it is bought, the base will continue to function.

Subsequent settlement grants should be 15 percent less in land area than any preceding grant.

Goods and services from one settlement may be sold to another settlement.

Legal business transactions shall apply.

All claims shall be mapped out and a record of them kept in a designated office of claims.

Any conflict of interest shall be settled in an international court of law.

Any manufactured goods from any entity shall be the sole property of that entity. Profits may later be subject to taxation, with proceeds going to support the space infrastructure.

As for the initial settlement, and those thereafter, there must be a transportation system already in place, ready to transport settlers, facilities, resources, and products to and from the Moon. This system must be available to all personnel and cargo, and be ready for expansion when the need arises.

Landing rights will be approved for all, provided that it is for peaceful and legal purposes.

In no uncertain terms shall any claimed land, or the enterprise claiming the land, belong to any government, either fully or partially, in any way, shape, or form.

This land is to be used for settlement, mining, and industrialization.

Portions of this grant are to be sold to other entities who wish to develop the lunar surface, as previously stated and explained.

It will be unlawful for any unauthorized entity to settle or claim a piece of land without any prior notification. Violators will be subject to a huge fine, payable to the International Legal Regime, and/or serve jail time in their country of origin. This is where the "Space Police" would participate.

Any entity from any country would have equal opportunity in land claims.

No exceptions.

On an asteroid, if the surface area is less than one million square miles, the entire asteroid will be granted to the sole entity claiming it. If the area of an asteroid is greater than one million square miles, the claim will be divided fairly among parties, or they shall develop it in collaboration. All other laws shall apply.

On Mars, the first claim shall be 3,600,000 square miles. All other laws shall apply.

All personnel in space shall be subjected to a code of ethics and proper behavior. Any violation of this code shall be subjected to disciplinary action.

Enemy Space Forces and How They Merged

I n Earth orbit, fighter ships from both China and the U.S. routinely patrolled space, keeping a watch on their space stations, factories, refueling depots, and their military satellites.

Tensions were high. The U.S. had only just made it into space as a major power, but the Chinese were on par with the U.S., determined to dominate the heavens.

The U.S., however, knew China's scheme and was not about to give up their position so easily. China has placed the U.S. on the defensive.

Then it happened. One of China's fighter ships shot at a U.S. spy satellite. The U.S. retaliated by sending their own Space Force ships to investigate, and Chinese ships fired on them. One U.S. fighter exploded, killing the pilot. Other U.S. fighters destroyed the Chinese ship, and a battle ensued.

As more military fighters from both sides converged, the first great battle in space was about to take place, not only in space but on Earth as well. The two powers sent their Navies and Air Forces over the Pacific Ocean for a face-off. China had long sought to control half the Pacific, and this was their big chance.

The war would affect not just these two countries, but their allies from both sides as well. Soon, others joined in on the confrontation.

Suddenly, there was another alert in space. At an asteroid mining colony, pirate ships, loyal to no particular country on Earth, raided it to take their minerals. At the same time, merchant ships serving the mining colonies, habitats, and the Moon were also attacked, with pirates stealing any valuable goods they could find, killing anyone that tried to stop them.

The colony was run by a Chinese company, the merchant ships were independent, but it didn't matter.

China's space force was called to deal with these pirates, aborting their present mission. Ships and planes in the Pacific were ordered to stand down.

China's space forces went out to confront these pirates, but the pirates attacked and destroyed many ships. They were fully and heavily armed, prepared to deal with any military vessel.

China needed help. They turned to the U.S., pleading for aid, vowing to drop any and all present disputes, including the recent confrontation.

The U.S. Space Force answered the call.

They first encountered the pirates in space. The pirates resisted, but both Chinese and American ships blew them up. Unfortunately, they were unable to recover any merchandise the pirates had stolen. They then came to the asteroidal mining camps, where the pirates were overwhelmed and either killed or taken prisoner.

When all was done, the pilots from both sides hugged, broke out what provisions they had, and threw a party, with plenty of booze. Both sides agreed, "We need to work together so this won't happen again."

At the U.N., the U.S. and China were no longer hostile, but cooperative. Both had representatives in their say in the conference, including many from the space confrontation.

They stated that there were separate space forces spying on and killing each other, protecting their own interests, while in deep space, there were unscrupulous "businessmen" robbing, cheating, and extorting money and goods from merchants. There were claim jumpers, staking claims on the Moon and asteroids without filing, avoiding taxes to whatever country they were from, and corrupt practices between all entities, making space a chaotic place, impossible to develop without paying some criminal organization, a space mafia, "protection money."

The power to deal with all these crime syndicates already existed but were battling each other rather than looking outward to protect all businesses in space.

It was agreed that if we are to restore order to space, we must have a law enforcement agency dedicated to patrolling all of space, from Low Earth Orbit to the Moon and beyond, as we move further out into the frontier.

The way to do this is to unite *all* the space forces into one single law enforcement agency, combining all of their assets and technologies. They would be responsible for protecting all legal entities in space, wiping out piracy and organized crime, and keeping space orderly. Anyone caught breaking the law would be prosecuted either by an international tribunal, or for lesser crimes, by their own country.

This was agreed to by all countries. Laws covering all space matters that previously did not exist were passed, and the International Space Police Force was born. There were headquarters available in all inhabited places in space, and so began the task of cracking down on all forms of criminal activity.

Building a Lunar Civilization

Humanity stands a great chance of extending its reign to a new frontier: the Moon. By building a sustainable lunar civilization, we can unlock vast scientific discoveries, forge new industries, and take the first steps toward colonizing the cosmos. This essay explores the incremental stages required to transform the Moon into a thriving outpost, taking advantage of scientific ingenuity, economic opportunity, and human resilience.

When establishing a lunar base, there has to be three main functions, for they are all dependent upon one another. One function cannot exist without the other two, and two functions cannot exist without the third.

The goals that are absolutely necessary in establishing a lunar base are scientific investigation of the Moon, and exploitation of lunar resources to later establish space-based industries. Space based industries are absolutely necessary in the development of a self-sufficient and self-supporting lunar base. This will lead to becoming the first extraterrestrial space colony. The third function, which will really be the first, will be landing on the Moon and building a self-sufficient and self-supporting base.

The exploitation of lunar resources and scientific investigation of the Moon go together. When we discover new resources, they have to be analyzed and investigated to find how they can be treated. Many minerals will be combined with other minerals and elements, as later explained in this chapter. There must be techniques to separate them before processing them for future use in industry.

All of this can be done by mining the minerals, extracting oxygen and other elements from the lunar soil, and manufacturing goods from these resources, to sell at a profit, to insure a payback of initial investments, and to pay for the expansion of the lunar base. This would then set up space industries to support the settlement of space. This process can also help fund research.

5.1 Lunar industries, using mined mineral resources.

The third proposal has been simply to build a lunar settlement, use its resources for expansion, establish an agricultural system, and, with the use of its oxygen, minerals, and food supply, make the settlement expandable and completely independent of Earth, with an ever expanding population base. This would later evolve into a city, and then a lunar civilization.

All three are interdependent. A self-sufficient lunar settlement must have an expanding industrial base to support it and make it grow. These industries, which support the lunar base, and eventually, civilization, need new ideas stemming from scientific research. Determination of the right combination requires research and development, and is to be built in several stages. The following is a detailed discussion of the three separate proposals and their benefits.

1. Self-Supporting Settlement

A lunar base built for a self supporting settlement will have many functions and benefits. The most important is the process of In-Situ Resource Utilization (ISRU), the use of resources of the Moon to create the materials to build up the settlement. This will lead to the evolution of an independent lunar society with both agriculture and new industries.

In addition, these new industries would manufacture not only the materials necessary for building the base, but other useful products that can be sold on Earth and other space settlements, creating a new economy and having the settlement pay for itself.

This is how one would create an independent society on a new world. Humans will live off the land and learn to adjust to the new space environment. Scientific communities will form doing research on the human condition on the Moon. New technologies, in all fields, will also form. Other scientists will explore the Moon itself, and a new breed of astronomers will explore the cosmos.

All these new technologies, from engineering to life sciences, will lead to supporting the exploration of Mars.

Among the factors for a self-supporting settlement are:

1. Long-term life support systems.
2. Lunar shelter technology.
3. Agricultural research and production.
4. Oxygen production plants.
5. Lunar power station.

These are the immediately crucial facilities.

Later facilities will include:

6. Mining facilities and a plant for processing lunar regolith.
7. Lunar manufacturing facility.

As we construct this base, will have to focus on:

8. Human functions and relationships.
9. Health and medicine.
10. Economic/trade system.
11. Expanding population base.

The evolution of a self-supporting lunar base would be slow. At first, everything will have to come from Earth. Over time, with the addition of mining facilities and a processing facility for lunar regolith to extract minerals and manufacture products to sell, the base will gradually become independent.

5.2 Lunar Settlement.

Setting up the Lunar Base - The Beginning

The base would start out by having cargo landers and space station derived facilities for habitation and food production, an oxygen production plant to extract oxygen from the lunar soil for replenishing the air supply, a power source for energy, and a crane, for lifting these Earth-sent facilities off the cargo landers and assembling them for the base.

Lunar Habitats

Lunar habitats can utilize technology from the International Space Station (ISS), to be modified for the Moon.

Lunar soil, about two to four meters deep, would be used to cover the habitats, for shielding against solar and cosmic radiation, especially against solar flares.

The interior of these habitats would contain the proper facilities needed for living, and can also be decorated according to the specifications of the inhabitants themselves.

Here, six to twelve people would have a setup for habitation.

Next would come the setting up of water, along with agricultural facilities. Food and water are vital for survival, anywhere.

For food supply on the Moon, we would start with growing only the most nutritious plants. Later, animals can be imported for meat, starting with rabbits and poultry.

This would be the first long-term life support system, involving the regeneration of air, water, and the production of food.

These are vital elements for survival, which are featured in the next sections.

5.3A An early example of crude lunar habitats, completely covered with regolith. This merely looks like a lump in the ground. There should be protection, yet state of the art technology should offer better shielding as we progress.

5.3B A more advanced state, but still crude.

5.3C State of the art, with tiles containing water, regolith, or lunar concrete, and thick lunar glass, all of which can protect from radiation.

Water on the Moon

Until now, it was believed that there was no water on the Moon, and therefore no hydrogen. In previous proposals, it was thought that any hydrogen or water would need to be imported, either from Earth or elsewhere.

Hydrogen is one of the main elements that would have to be imported for years to come. Note: Hydrogen does exist in the lunar soil, but, like Helium-3, it originates from the solar wind. Read further.

Water can also be obtained from asteroids composed of ice. Here we can either crash asteroids on the Moon, or we can mine the asteroid itself, melt the ice, transfer the water to a space tanker, and gently land it on the Moon.

Water can also be extracted from passing comets. Again, either crash the comet, far from any inhabited area, or extract the water by mining the comet.

Crashing either an asteroid or a comet runs the risk of major quakes, threatening any settlement that presently exists on the Moon, so this has to be given considerable thought. Most likely, such a proposition would probably be declined.

In 1998, the Lunar Prospector was launched, orbiting the Moon around its polar regions. Using a neutron spectrometer, hydrogen and hydroxyl (a chemical compound with the combination -OH) were detected in abundance, at nearly 50 parts per million (PPM), meaning 50 milligrams of water per liter (or kilogram) of lunar soil.

It was theorized that significant amounts of water ice lay in shadowed areas of craters, but when the prospector was deliberately crashed onto the lunar surface and ejected soil from the impact analyzed, no water was detected.

India sent the Chandrayaan-1 probe to lunar polar orbit in 2008, confirming the existence of hydroxyls chemically bonded to the soil.

The U.S., in 2009, launched the Lunar Reconnaissance Orbiter, set out to map the surface of the Moon. It also detected hydrates, inorganic salts containing water-bound molecules.

It has also been detected that solar wind bombards the lunar surface with protons or positively charged hydrogen atoms.

With this information, along with the existence of hydroxyls and hydrates in the lunar soil, it is proven that hydrogen is plentiful on the Moon and does not have to be imported, at least not on a permanent basis. As hydrogen is extracted from the soil, it can be bonded with oxygen, also in the soil, to produce water and fuel.

5.4 Extracting water from the lunar surface. Note the "disabled" workers. See Appendix B.

Evidence of water vapor and ice, up to this point, has not yet materialized, but more advanced probes were later sent to the Moon.

LCROSS, the Lunar Observation Crater and Sensing Satellite, was launched in 2010, and from that satellite sent a smaller probe crashing in the lunar surface. Using spectrography from both ultraviolet and infrared wavelengths, water was detected from the plumes of the lunar materials ejected from the impact.

From the Lunar Prospector, and later Clementine, it has been estimated that near pure water ice crystals are buried 40 centimeters (18 inches) beneath the lunar surface.

With this evidence, it is likely that water does exist on the Moon, if in the form of hydroxyl material, ice crystals, or ice in permanently shadowed areas.

Water ice in these areas is still yet to be fully confirmed. In these shadowed areas, mostly craters, the maximum temperature is estimated to be -170 degrees Celsius, or 100 degrees Kelvin. At night, it is much colder, and water ice might exist in these places.

It is theorized that 22 percent of Shackleton Crater, near the South Pole, is covered with water ice.

The total mass of ice on the Moon has been estimated at six trillion kilograms (6.6 billion tons).

It should be noted that the water ice on the Moon is not in the form of ice sheets, like you see in a frozen pond, either on or under the lunar surface. It is in the form of chunks mixed with the lunar regolith and some water is chemically bonded with other minerals. This will be explained further in this chapter.

In 2022, South Korea launched the lunar probe *Danuri*, to which NASA's probe ShadowCam was attached. ShadowCam is 200 times more sensitive than the Lunar Reconnaissance orbiter, in order to capture more detail in the permanently shadowed regions of the Moon, especially in places like Shackleton Crater; i.e. it can see in the dark.

No evidence of ice was found in the lunar cold traps, but there is evidence that it may exist below the lunar surface, where most ice is found anyway. Here, all they need to do is simply dig for it, and not very deep.

These are all assumptions, for nothing is definite except that water and hydrogen do exist on the Moon and are accessible.

For this essay, it is assumed that this is the case, and this proposal will be based on that assumption.

The polar regions, where water is known to exist, will be the location of the first settlement(s).

One Final Note: Water is a good fuel source BUT

It should only be used temporarily as rocket fuel. Although there is an estimate of 6.6 billion tons on the Moon (though with the latest findings, it may be less), it is still limited, and as more people migrate to the Moon, more water will be needed for drinking, agriculture, washing, and industry. The Moon cannot afford a water shortage.

Use for fuel will only waste water, because once used, it cannot be recycled. It is gone. This could result in a water shortage. The other sources of water, such as ice from asteroids and mixing oxygen and hydrogen (hydroxals) from other elements, can be used as alternatives, but only up to a point.

Water can be used as fuel until better fuel and energy sources are available, such as nuclear propulsion.

Water can be used in fuel cells, where it is split up into hydrogen and oxygen, producing energy on the Moon for the lunar night cycle when solar energy cannot be used. Then, with water as the waste product, it could be refrigerated, stored, and used again for the next night cycle, thereby preventing water from being wasted.

Water must be used conservatively and recycled from the very beginning of Moon settlement, no matter how much water the Moon has.

Sources of Food/Lunar Agriculture

In the early stages of settlement, food—like most resources—will need to be imported. However, a dedicated facility for growing food will be established, modeled after the systems used on the International Space Station (ISS). As settlers begin producing their own food, they will initially focus on plants and may gradually incorporate small animals such as rabbits and poultry for meat. Over time, larger animals like goats and sheep may be introduced, but not in the initial phases.

Plants will be cultivated using both hydroponics and processed lunar soil. Since lunar regolith contains minerals and metals that could harm plant growth, a processing system will be required to remove these unwanted elements. The processed lunar soil will then be enhanced with organic matter, including plant and human waste, to create nutrient-rich soil capable of supporting increased crop production.

There will be two ways to expand.

The first would be to set up a greenhouse to grow more crops. The greenhouse could be designed as an airtight, transparent dome anchored securely to bedrock or sintered regolith foundations. Its structure would include radiation shielding and a regulated internal environment to maintain pressure, temperature, and humidity. The greenhouse would incorporate an airlock system to minimize atmospheric loss, and deploy robotics for external and internal maintenance.

The lunar regolith would be processed to remove harmful elements and extract valuable metals for manufacturing. The remaining soil would be enriched with nutrients like nitrogen, potassium, and organic waste, creating a fertile base for crops. Advanced systems such as hydroponics or aeroponics could optimize water usage, drawing from recycled wastewater or lunar ice. Crops like wheat, potatoes, and leafy greens would form dietary staples, supplemented by herbs and spices to ensure a diverse and enjoyable menu.

In addition to plants, small animals like rabbits and poultry could be raised for meat and eggs, while sheep and goats could graze in pasture areas, contributing to soil fertilization through their waste. This integrated approach would form a self-sustaining mini-ecosystem. Advanced food preparation methods and culinary innovations would ensure variety in meals, preventing monotony. The greenhouse would not only provide sustenance but also serve as a vital psychological haven, mimicking Earth's natural environment.

This lunar agriculture system could be a model for future space settlements, demonstrating how technology and ecology can converge to sustain human life in extreme environments.

Second, the method of processing the regolith will advance to the point where the minerals separated can be used for other purposes, especially in manufacturing. Manufacturing plants and plants for processing regolith for a wide variety of minerals will then evolve.

There will also have to be a processing plant to remove oxygen from the minerals for use by the settlement.

Eventually, we will set up a huge plot of land and install a glass dome to cover it.

In the long run, we could build many such farms as the population increases.

5.5 A lunar farm, growing various crops, under a transparent dome.

Lunar Oxygen

By weight, oxygen comprises 40 percent of the lunar soil. The majority of the propellant required for the entire LEO-lunar orbit transportation system is LOX, which is approximately 85 percent. The remaining 15 percent is liquid hydrogen (LH_2). Research has been conducted in extracting oxygen from the lunar soil cheaply and in large quantities. You will read this in more detail in the next section on Oxygen Extraction.

The extraction of oxygen from lunar soil will save the trouble and expense of launching LOX from Earth to LEO and transporting it to the Moon. The energy requirements for launching LOX from the lunar surface to the lunar orbiting space station and LEO are much lower than launching from the Earth's surface because of the Moon's low gravity. This will save launch costs, and the Earth launch vehicles can be used for other purposes.

Liquid hydrogen will still need to be launched from Earth, but this will only be about 15 percent of the propellant that would otherwise be launched. Later, as lunar settlement progresses, hydrogen can be extracted from the lunar soil and asteroids containing ice water.

Oxygen Extraction

Of the lunar minerals, the easiest to process for oxygen extraction is ilmenite, also known as iron titanium oxide ($FeTiO_3$). The lunar soil contains up to 20 percent ilmenite, and there are two different proposals for extracting oxygen from this mineral: Hydrogen-reduction and the Carbothermal method.

The hydrogen-reduction reaction is

$$—\!-\!<\!-\!-\!-\!-\!-\!-\!-<\!-\!-\text{recycle}\!\leftarrow\!-\!-\!-\!-\!-\!-<\!-\!-\!-\!-\!-\!-\!-<\!-\!-\!-\!-\!-\!-\!-\!-\!-\!-\!-<\!-\!-\!-$$

$$FeTiO_3 + H_2 \;<\!-\!-\!-\!-\!-\!-\!-\!-\!->\; Fe + TiO_2 + H_2O \;\underline{electrolysis}>\; H_2 + \tfrac{1}{2}O_2$$

Ilmenite feed   solid product   oxygen product

The above process involves feeding ilmenite, with liquid hydrogen, into a thermal reactor, where it separates into iron, titanium oxide, and water vapor. Through electrolysis, the water is separated into hydrogen and oxygen, and the hydrogen is recycled for reuse.

The problem here is that the per-pass conversion of H_2 to H_2O is only 5 percent. An advanced cooling system has been proposed to increase efficiency. Nonetheless, due to the rarity of hydrogen on the Moon, the hydrogen required will have to be imported, but can also later be extracted from lunar soil as this process of extraction advances.

Note: This required element can be imported from Near-Earth asteroids, cheaper and easier than from Earth.

The second process, a carbothermal reaction, involves using carbon, which can be obtained by burning garbage. The process is as follows:

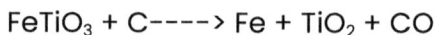

$$FeTiO_3 + C ----> Fe + TiO_2 + CO$$

Feed material is mixed with a carbonaceous reductant and heated until melting, reduction, and slag/metal separation takes place. An extra benefit to this is that the iron can be further processed to produce steel, for base expansion or export.

Other methods have been theorized using simulated lunar materials, but not adequately studied. These include (not all will be illustrated with a chemical formula):

- Heating lunar materials to high temperatures so that iron oxide decomposes to liberate oxygen gas. There are many processes to this: Pyrolysis, Vapor Phase Reduction, Ion Plasma (requires extremely high temperatures).
- Dissolving ilmenite or some other iron mineral in sulfuric acid to release oxygen.

$FeO \cdot TiO_2 + 2H_2SO_4 \text{----------} > FeSO_4 + 2H_2O + TiOSO_4$
then $FeSO_4 + H_2O \text{-------} > H_2SO_4 + Fe + O_2$
and we start all over again with the sulfuric acid.

- Using hydrofluoric acid, or fluorine, to release oxygen as the reactant. Fluorine is a very reactive gas that can liberate metal from all oxides, creating metal fluorides.

- Hydrochloric acid is another reaction.

- Using cold plasma of chlorine atoms to displace oxygen from minerals. Chlorine atoms, made by shining raw sunlight on chlorine gas, react with a metal oxide to create oxygen plus a metal chloride. The metal chloride is electrically decomposed, regenerating chlorine and providing the metal as a bonus.

- Hydrogen sulfide (H_2S) to separate iron, calcium, and magnesium from their oxides, producing oxygen and the above-mentioned metals.

Other reactions include using lithium, aluminum, and sodium reduction, to name a few.

Gasses, such as methane (CH_4), can also be combined to produce oxygen and other byproducts. Note: The heat used must be intense.

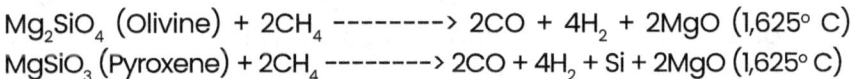

Mg_2SiO_4 (Olivine) $+ 2CH_4 \text{--------} > 2CO + 4H_2 + 2MgO$ (1,625° C)
$MgSiO_3$ (Pyroxene) $+ 2CH_4 \text{--------} > 2CO + 4H_2 + Si + 2MgO$ (1,625° C)

There are many other methods here worth mentioning:

- Bulk electrolysis

- Magma electrolysis: The melting of lunar soil in an electrolytic cell, and passing an electric current through it to release oxygen.

One variation of this process is flux electrolysis.

There are many other processes not listed here, and new ones are discovered in the lab constantly.

In any process, it has been estimated that, based on a 10 percent ilmenite content in the lunar soil, 100,000 tons of regolith can be mined to produce 1000 tons of oxygen. It has been recommended that this be done annually. Pilot plants need to be set up, with more research required for advanced processing plants.

Recommendation: Have a pilot lunar oxygen processing plant set up on the first lunar base and begin initial operations.

Note: The manufacture of LH_2/LOX propellant, used to propel ships from LEO to lunar orbit and back will be a temporary measure, from the time the Moon is settled up to the time when the Solid Core Nuclear Thermal Reactor for spaceships has proven to be feasible. This will then render the chemical propellant from LEO to lunar obsolete, though chemical fuels for lunar ascent/descent may still be used. Lunar Oxygen will still be needed for air, water, and the manufacture of lunar based goods.

As we can see, mining the Moon and processing its resources will not be like anything done on Earth. In mining the Moon, we will need equipment that can withstand the extreme temperatures in both the day and night cycles.

We will have machinery to skim the surface and then process the ore with different methods, only a few of which I have described here. There is also the task of converting the materials into useful products.

Another way to mine ore is to bore underground for the minerals where they are located, then use the space carved out to build lunar habitats, factories, or even cities. The ground itself will provide protection against the solar and cosmic rays, and against meteorites.

The processes of mining and separating the regolith and ore are not described in detail here. This is a generalized view on the entire space infrastructure itself. True, the equipment, apparatus, and processing facilities will be advanced and complex, too detailed to describe here, but there are books dedicated to covering this situation. However, living on the Moon will inspire the inhabitants with new ideas such as these.

5.6A & 5.6B Mining the Moon.

Sources of Power

A constant supply of energy is needed for life support and to run all facilities, in addition to any new facility that arrives on the lunar surface. There are three available sources to be used, and one source to be developed.

The available sources are:

- Solar (two week day cycle only)
- LOX/LH$_2$ process (for the night cycle)
- Nuclear Fission (any form presently used on Earth)
  - There is a good supply of Thorium on Mare Frigoris.

Thorium technology for nuclear fission has not yet been perfected, but we are close.

The Helium-3 fusion process, once developed, can produce vast amounts of energy with little to no nuclear waste. This has yet to be developed, but it holds great promise, and there is plenty of Helium-3 found on the lunar surface for research, development, and utilization.

A. Solar Power

Solar power in space, because of its vacuum, yields more electrical power than on Earth. A single square meter near Earth's orbit facing the sun receives over a kilowatt of power (about 1.358 kilowatts), mostly between the wavelengths of ultraviolet and infrared. High efficiency solar cells (photovoltaic cells) can turn one kilowatt of incident sunlight into 200 watts of electricity, with 800 watts of waste heat. The output could even be high enough to commence building the lunar base.

Suppose the lunar base, in its first stage, needs 100 kw/hr. to function. A solar farm of 100 solar panels can then be built to serve this purpose. As the technology improves, smaller solar panels will have the capability to absorb more of the sun's electricity and produce more power. This will take up less area as the base expands.

5.7 Solar Power on the Moon.

B. LH$_2$/LOX Reactors

The lunar night cycle is a problem. Batteries will not be able to sustain a night cycle, with the power demand far exceeding that of the day cycle. There is the possibility of using the LH$_2$/LOX reaction in fuel cells to produce power, with water as its waste. Using a refrigeration system, the wastewater can then be caught and stored to be reused. Through electrolysis, powered by solar energy during the day cycle, the water can be separated into hydrogen and oxygen, again to be used as the catalyst for spinning flywheels, powering generators, and supplying power for the night cycle.

5.8 Liquid Oxygen/Liquid Hydrogen plants on the Moon.

C. Nuclear Fission

The third option is using nuclear fission of any form presently used here on Earth. Nuclear power plants can be constructed away from any settlements. Leakage would be no problem, because the Moon is bombarded with radioactivity every second by the sun's rays. Any nuclear waste can be catapulted directly into the sun by mass drivers (discussed later in this essay).

Thorium has been found to be a good nuclear fission fuel, and it is found in the highlands to the south of Mare Frigoris, on the Moon.

5.9 Nuclear power plant on the Moon.

<u>Recommendation</u>

For power plants on the first lunar settlement, there is a choice of either the solar power/(LH_2/LOX) reaction for the day/night cycle, respectively, or the present technology of nuclear fission reactors. Both technologies can be used together, should circumstances require it.

We will also experiment with nuclear reactors using Thorium as a fuel.

Health and Medicine

Another factor is health and medicine. Humans can be observed as to how they adapt to a 1/6 gravity environment, their physical responses to it, and how they handle any illness. At least one of the personnel on the base must be a physician.

The main aspect here is one sixth gravity, and its effects on the human body. Any illness on Earth, within reason, can be treated anywhere in space, except for the fact that lower gravity can make a difference.

Understanding the effects of partial gravity environments is critical. While microgravity's detrimental impacts on human physiology have been studied extensively since the 1970s, the consequences of living under reduced gravity—such as lunar gravity at 0.16 g—remain largely unknown due to a lack of direct data. Limited lunar experience and Earth-based simulations suggest that partial gravity may provide some benefit over microgravity, but it appears insufficient to maintain normal physiological function over the long-term. Key systems such as the musculoskeletal, cardiovascular, and biomechanical systems react differently to reduced gravity, with serious implications for human health.

Bone loss is one of the most concerning effects of reduced gravity. In microgravity, astronauts lose bone mineral density at a rate of 1 percent per month. Models predict similar losses in partial gravity environments, with lunar gravity causing 0.39 percent loss per week and Martian gravity resulting in 0.22 percent loss per week. These rates are comparable to or even exceed those observed in microgravity, suggesting that partial gravity provides insufficient stimulus to maintain bone strength. Over a span of two to three years, such reductions could render bones dangerously weak, raising concerns about long-term habitation and the ability to perform physical tasks.

The cardiovascular system also experiences significant deconditioning in reduced gravity. Simulations show a strong correlation between decreased gravitational levels and reductions in heart rate, oxygen consumption, and metabolic rate. Partial gravity, like microgravity, reduces the demands on the cardiovascular system, leading to deconditioning. While this effect may be less severe than in microgravity, the decline in cardiovascular fitness remains a serious issue for individuals exposed to lunar gravity over extended periods.

Additionally, biomechanical changes occur in partial gravity due to reduced body weight and external forces. Studies show that ground reaction force, stride frequency, and work output decrease significantly, as less mechanical work is required to move in these environments. The internal work of moving arms and legs is similarly reduced, leading to a decline in overall physical exertion. While this lessens the burden on the cardiopulmonary system, it also accelerates muscle atrophy and bone density loss, as the mechanical forces necessary for maintaining these systems are diminished.

Collectively, the effects of partial gravity suggest that it is inadequate to sustain human health in the long-term.

Countermeasures such as exercise, which has limited success in microgravity, are unlikely to fully offset the negative impacts of partial gravity. Research indicates that gravitational forces below 0.4 g are insufficient to preserve musculoskeletal and cardiopulmonary systems at Earth standards.

Given these findings, artificial gravity emerges as a necessary solution for long-term habitation of the Moon. Rotating spacecraft or habitats that generate Earth-like gravity through centrifugal force may be essential to counteract the detrimental effects of partial gravity. To better understand these challenges, future research should prioritize long-term studies on partial gravity using tools such as centrifuges on the International Space Station (ISS). Experiments on animals could provide critical data on the minimum gravitational thresholds required to maintain physiological health.

While partial gravity environments may mitigate some effects of microgravity, they are insufficient to sustain human health over long durations. Bone loss, cardiovascular deconditioning, and biomechanical changes remain significant challenges for long-term habitation on the Moon and Mars. Developing artificial gravity systems and conducting further research are essential steps toward enabling humanity's future in space. Without such measures, the dream of permanent settlements on other worlds may remain out of reach.

This is a major obstacle to settling the Moon. The only solution I can think of is when one settles on the Moon, it has to be permanent, and ways of dealing with the human body's reaction to it must be discovered, probably in ways we cannot yet imagine. Keeping active may be one solution, even though the above research may contradict that. Taking chemicals like vitamins could be another, until the human body adjusts to the new gravity. Last of all comes the production of offspring, which is inevitable. Native-born bodies may naturally adjust to the environment, since they would know no other way.

This process could be useful to the handicapped and elderly whose bodies cannot function in Earth normal gravity, and they may naturally adjust to this new environment more easily than a young and healthy person from Earth could. These are just a few of the many theories I myself have just imagined.

Psychologically, human behavior can be observed in a closed environment, under stress, and how they relate with others in that same environment. How they handle two-week days and two-week nights is a very important factor here.

Work on the initial base, with expansion, may cause a lot of stress, but the work required, and observing the expansion of the base can also be therapeutic, providing satisfaction that the staff is expanding the base with their own labor.

Some people will be able to adjust easily to the new lunar environment. Others, whether physically or psychologically, may not, and they may want to return to Earth.

Further Expansion of the Base

For further expansion of the base, mining facilities would be set up, gathering material needed to manufacture components without relying on Earth. Manufacturing facilities would be sent on cargo landers to process the lunar ore, then manufacture the new lunar base components, components for satellites and space stations, and products for export to Earth. More of this will be discussed in the next section, Lunar Industries.

From here, advanced facilities in mineral and oxygen extraction would be developed. Agricultural systems can expand, along with manufacturing facilities, allowing for more personnel to arrive on the base. The oxygen processed would be available for export, for use as air on space stations and propellant for space vessels.

The manufacturing facilities could then advance to build more habitations, components for factories, and space vessels with advanced propulsion and life support systems.

An independent economic system would develop, exporting raw materials (lunar regolith for shielding, lunar ore for orbiting space factories), products, and oxygen, in exchange for either what the lunar society needs (e.g. hydrogen) or hard currency. There would then be an independent, expanding lunar society.

This cannot be done in a few years, but perhaps in a projected twenty to forty years from the establishment of the first lunar base. As soon as all this is completed, we should then journey to Mars, with the ability to make an unlimited number of trips, not just one or a few, and journey there in a short period of time. That means one or two months instead of the present projection of ten months to two years. When we do arrive on Mars, we can immediately establish a permanent base on the Martian surface, modeled after the lunar base.

2. Lunar Industry

One of the most important aspects of a self-supporting lunar base is a firm industrial base, for several different purposes.

1.   To use lunar resources to supply the needs of the base.

2. To develop these resources for mass production, supporting other space settlements, industries, and Earth. This would lead to:

3. The development of an independent economic system on the Moon, supplying goods to other settlements and Earth, in exchange for supplies unobtainable on the Moon. The alternative is hard currency.

With raw materials from the Moon, an industrial base can be developed in processing these materials into needed supplies on the Moon and elsewhere. In addition, the Moon's low gravity can help to develop purer glass, crystals, alloys, and chemical compounds.

The following can help to establish a solid, lunar industrial base:

- Lunar Oxygen
- Minerals
- Materials Processing
- Regolith, for radiation shielding
- Manufacturing Facilities

In supporting industrial development, the governments of any and all participating countries would make long-term investments, along with private corporations. Both sectors must be willing to take risks, but they would also have equitable shares of the profits.

5.10 Another Lunar Industrial Site.

There is also the "Space Settlement Act", where a large portion of land is granted to an entity, and that entity would sell off pieces of the grant to help pay the costs of settling on the Moon.

Among the categories of private corporations that might want to participate are:

- Steel Industries
- Mining Industries
- Energy Corporations
- Construction Industries
- Aerospace Industries, many of which are now relying on contracts from the Military.

Governments and corporations could invest a certain percentage of a proposed industrial project, ensuring that percentage of profits, if and when they are turned.

In establishing an industrial base on the Moon, two lunar products with potentially large markets requiring minimal processing are simple lunar regolith, used for radiation shielding, and liquid oxygen (LOX), for spacecraft propellant.

Lunar oxygen has been previously covered. It is an essential ingredient for establishing a Lunar Base for air, water, and fuel. This will carry over into the lunar industry for the same reasons, only it will be mass-produced and exported to other space colonies, space factories, and space stations, to be sold for a profit.

Lunar Regolith

Lunar regolith can be used for radiation shielding and for making lunar concrete.

Only two meters of lunar soil is required to protect a habitat from solar and cosmic radiation, occasional solar flares, and temperature extremes. This regolith can also be exported to advanced space stations for use as shielding.

Lunar rocks can be crushed to a suitable course of aggregate size, and mixed with cement paste to form lunar concrete. Reinforced with steel or glass fibers increases flexural strength and restricts the growth of microcracks. Strong in compression, the lunar concrete, with sealant on the interior surface, can be used to build lunar structures.

Lunar bases made on concrete offer the following advantages:

1. Energy ratio between aluminum alloy and concrete is 90:1, saving massive energy costs.
2. Concrete can be cast into any monolithic configuration.
3. Greater strength.

4. Greater heat resistance.

5. Excellent radiation shielding.

6. Abrasion resistance, especially against micrometeorites.

Concrete can be a major component in expansion of a lunar base and can be produced on the lunar surface. The only imported ingredient needed is hydrogen, to be used for water.

Lunar concrete can also be exported to Earth, for a high quality product to compete against Earth-made concrete.

Recommendation: Upon settlement of the first lunar base, begin research and experimentation with lunar concrete, and perhaps even build an experimental shelter.

5.11 Lunar regolith and concrete for radiation shielding.

Lunar Glass

On Earth, glass can be derived from elements in the soil, especially sand. The same process applies on the Moon. On the Moon, because of its environment, the strength of the glass can be made equal to metals and more resistant to heat due to the lack of water and air, and can hold up to a great deal of pressure.

Because of this, processed lunar glass can be used to produce

- Fibers
- Slabs
- Tubes
- Rods
- Domes

Fibers are extremely effective in reducing stress in much needed space structure components, such as bulkheads, beams, and columns. This is possible when combining fibers with lunar metals or concrete.

Lunar tunnels, naturally formed under the lunar surface, can be lined along the interior to seal in the air, protecting the tunnel from the vacuum and extreme temperatures.

Lunar glass can also be used in producing

- Satellite components
- Fiber optic cables
- Lenses
- And other needed glass components

Lunar glass is useful both in LEO and on the Moon. It will be needed especially when transparency is required, such as lunar domes which would cover settlements and farms. On O'Neill Space Colonies (Chapter 9) "windows" are needed on these habitats to let in the sun's rays for the day and night cycle.

All in all, manufacturing lunar glass for any purpose will greatly add to the lunar economy.

Recommendation: Begin research and experimentation with lunar glass, taken from the soil, at the first lunar base.

5.12 Lunar glass composing massive lunar domes, covering cities and farms.

Lunar Minerals

HELIUM-3

Helium-3 is an isotope with two protons and one neutron, as opposed to ordinary Helium, with two neutrons. Helium-3 can be both a clean and abundant energy source, releasing huge amounts of energy in a fusion reaction. However, fusion technology has not yet been perfected, and may take another fifty years before this can be achieved. Helium-3 is found to be plentiful on the lunar surface, and is replenished by a constant solar wind, so it is almost impossible for it to be depleted. Mining this element can be profitable, even more so than mining precious metals back on Earth.

Although its use in nuclear fusion is not yet possible, Helium-3 has many other valuable uses.

Among them are:

- Medical imaging in 3-D, for more precise operations on a patient.
- Detecting nuclear material, such as bombs, at an airport.

- Cryogenics
  - Freezing large amounts of food for later use, to prevent starvation.
  - Putting people in hibernation (32 to 34 degrees Celsius), to slow down their metabolism, putting them in suspended animation.

The lunar soil also consists of many different minerals:

Major elements

- Silicon (SiO_2) - Sodium (Na_2O)

- Iron $(FeO; Fe_2O_3)$ - Potassium (K_2O)

- Aluminum (Al_2O_3) - Manganese (MnO)

- Magnesium (MgO) - Chromium (Cr_2O_3)

- Titanium (TiO_2) - Calcium (CaO)

- Usable amounts of nickel-iron alloy.

Trace elements

- Hydrogen (H) - Helium (He)

- Sulphur (S) - Neon (Ne)

- Phosphorous (P) - Argon (Ar)

- Carbon (C) - Krypton (Kr)

- Nitrogen (N) - Xenon (Xe)

The trace elements can be used to produce the water, oxygen, fatty acids, vitamins, and sugars that are needed for life support systems, as well as plastics.

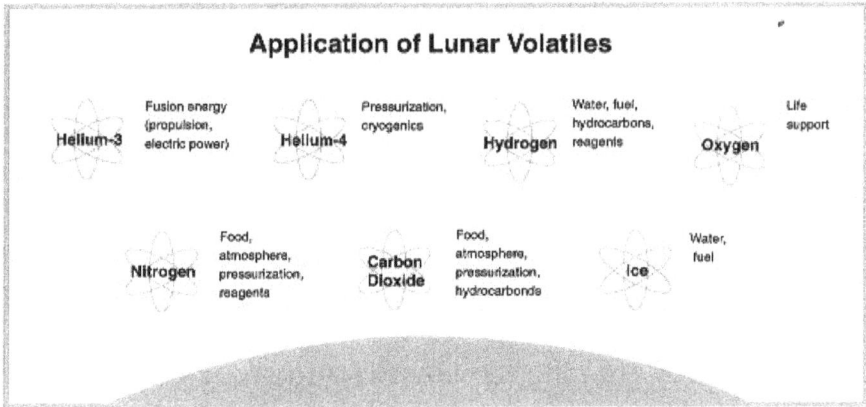

Application of Lunar Volatiles

Helium-3 Fusion energy (propulsion, electric power)	**Helium-4** Pressurization, cryogenics	**Hydrogen** Water, fuel, hydrocarbons, reagents	**Oxygen** Life support
Nitrogen Food, atmosphere, pressurization, reagents	**Carbon Dioxide** Food, atmosphere, pressurization, hydrocarbons	**Ice** Water, fuel	

5.13 Application of Lunar Volatiles. Reprinted from Cosmic Careers, used with permission.

Processing regolith would involve removing oxygen contained in the above listed major elements. It would also involve separating minerals for use in the initial production of lunar goods needed for survival and later marketing to other locations in space and on Earth.

There is an advanced form of processing elements that is used now on Earth and would be very useful on the Moon, known as sintering.

Sintering is the process of forming a solid mass of material into one, advanced form of material, out of various elements such as metal, ceramic, even plastic. This is done in the form of powders. These various materials are bonded or fused together under intense heat and pressure, without liquifying the materials in the process. The powder is compacted, the particles are bonded, and the properties are enhanced.

They do have long setting times, but the resulting products have greater strength and durability, better flexibility, and they do not deteriorate. They can also sustain a great amount of heat and pressure, which is useful on the Moon.

Other advantages include thermal and electrical conductivity, from more advanced alloys, structural integrity, and translucency. This means stronger building materials, from bricks to advanced structural components for habitats and processing facilities.

This process can be used in 3-D printing in producing complex designs, even involving mechanical movement in the process.

The process of sintering is more advantageous in a vacuum, like on the Moon, aiding in the chemical and making the product purer, stronger, less porous, and more heat resistant. Free energy is provided from the sun.

Platinum Group Metals (PGMs) are a group of rare but useful elements in the lunar soil. These include:

- Platinum	(Pt)	- Gallium	(Ga)
- Iridium	(Ir)	- Chromium	(Cr)
- Ruthenium	(Ru)	- Zinc	(Zn)
- Gold	(Au)	- Palladium	(Pd)

- Other residual elements

They are more common than the asteroids (Chapter 7) but they are useful in the fields of electronics and energy on the Moon.

Platinum Group Metals are used for many platinum products, including fuel cells, which are vital for the up-and-coming hydrogen economy. This is one of the futures of alternative energy.

A pilot plant can be set up to process lunar minerals and produce goods, starting with small components. With the Moon's low gravity, many of these products would be of better quality than if manufactured on Earth, due to gravity.

Among these products would be:

- Silicon chips, and crystals for computers
- Photovoltaic cells, for solar energy
- Finer and stronger glass
- Pure chemicals
- Purer medicines
- Alloys, for uses from superconductors to construction materials
- Fuel cells, especially for the up-and-coming hydrogen economy
- Superconductors, made from ceramics and alloys

This will require long-term investments before turning a profit, but the dividends, due to increasing demand, can be many times the initial investment.

As manufacturing on the Moon increases to make more advanced products, more and larger factories will have to be constructed. This is in order to manufacture vital products on the Moon necessary for survival. As a result, a prosperous and independent economy would commence. Some samples of what we need to produce are:

- Construction materials for advanced habitats for expansion on the moon, colonies in space, and the first settlements on Mars.

- Spaceships and their components, especially propulsion systems and space shields to protect against entering a planet's atmosphere.

- Solar Power Satellite (SPS) systems, made into separate components for assembly in space.

- Other products made from lunar resources. These can be anything, large or small. Exporting these products will add to the Moon's economy.

This entire process of research, experimentation, processing, and manufacturing would take years to mature and will require long-term investments before turning a profit. If handled properly, these investments, by both governments and private industries, will yield dividends many times the initial investment.

Recommendation: Have a facility to experiment with minerals from the lunar soil, for separation and processing, leading to small scale manufacturing, eventually progressing to bigger and more complicated products.

Note: Advancement in the technology of separation of the elements in lunar soil can apply to Earth industries as well. One example is coal ash. If we can take coal ash and separate all the lethal metals and other chemicals from the harmless ash, the ash could then be used for fertilizer on farms while the other chemicals could then be applied for some other useful purpose.

To summarize, lunar resources offer vast opportunities for up-and-coming industries for anyone willing to make the investment.

3. Scientific Research

As support for lunar science is dependent on the other two proposed lunar base functions, so are these functions equally dependent on lunar science. Lunar science is necessary for industry research and development, and is also needed for the self-supporting base for advancements in lunar agriculture, radiation shielding, and long-term life support systems.

A lunar base will create new opportunities for investigating the Moon and its environment. It can also be used as a platform for scientific investigations. The unique elements of the lunar environment include:

- Low gravity
- Absence of a planetary magnetic field
- Access to the plasma environment of the solar wind and Earth's geomagnetic tail
- No atmosphere
- Absence of water and other volatiles
- Isolation from the terrestrial biosphere
- Easily created low temperature radiative environments
- Availability of laboratory with very high thermal and seismic stability
- Easily achievable pointing stability for observations of all kinds

Because of these factors, the lunar surface is an ideal location for any experiment that suffers interference from the noise of geologic, biologic, or human origin.

Scientific research and experimentation is available in a wide range of fields:

- Lunar Geology and Geophysics
- Planetary Science
- Astronomy and Astrophysics
- Space Plasma Physics
- Life Sciences and Environmental Sciences
- Fundamental Physics
- Materials Processing
- Engineering
- Resource potential through a wide range of field investigations, sampling, and placement of instrumentation. For example, a macroparticle accelerator, an interferometer, or even a radio observatory, could be placed on the far side of the Moon.

A few of these processes will be briefly examined in the next section.

Lunar Geology

Despite the wealth of information provided by the Apollo program, the Moon remains a mystery. We don't know exactly how it evolved. This has broad implications for our understanding of the histories of other planets, including Earth.

To understand Earth and other planets, we must also understand the Moon. We must study the interior structure of the Moon, the size of the metal core, the full range and distribution of rock types, the age and nature of the oldest and youngest rocks, and the Moon's bulk composition.

An array of lunar seismic detectors, evenly distributed across the lunar surface, can detect and characterize naturally occurring moonquakes and record travel times of stress waves produced by large meteorite impacts. Heat flow and radiation measurements, which vary in different parts of the lunar interior, will also be studied.

Gas venting is a questionable activity on the Moon. If it does exist, the type of gas ejected, be it water vapor, Carbon Dioxide, or some other gas, will be investigated.

Volatile elements, known to be present in small quantities, aid in our desirability in searching for water as well as having major implications for understanding lunar origin, composition, structure, and history.

Planetary History

The Moon is the cornerstone of planetary science. From its impact history and differentiation of the core, mantle, and crust, the Moon can give us clues about the formation and history of the entire solar system, possibly even the universe.

About 65 million years ago, meteors bombarded the Earth and the Moon. This caused mass extinctions on the Earth. The craters these meteors formed wore away on Earth, but are preserved on the Moon. Studying these lunar craters and their age may hold crucial clues to how life evolved on Earth.

Cratering and volcanism has also shaped the surface of other planets, and studying these craters and the lunar interior may hold the clue to other planets' formation, history, and composition.

Astronomy

The Earth's atmosphere is a major obstacle for astronomical observations from Earth because of its distortion of the visible spectrum and absorption of the invisible spectrum, such as certain bands of radio waves, gamma rays, and galactic cosmic rays. Telescopes in Earth Orbit offer vast improvement in viewing conditions, but observatories on the Moon could be even more sensitive, since larger and more stable instruments and arrays can be emplaced.

Space astronomy from the Moon offers three potential advantages over Earth and Earth-orbital observations:

- The far side of the Moon is permanently shielded from direct terrestrial radio frequency emissions. This factor offers a potential site for a series of radio telescopes.

- The lunar surface provides a solid, seismically stable, low-gravity and high-vacuum platform for precise interferometric and astrometric observations.

- Over the next few decades, the Moon may offer the only permanently manned bases that lie beyond Earth's geocorona, also normally outside Earth's radiation belt. This will offer observations in a low-background radiation environment.

These advantages of the lunar environment suggest the development of two principle astronomical facilities on the Moon:

1. Ultrahigh (microarcsecond) astrometric positional accuracy and angular resolution with interferometric arrays at microwave, infrared, and optical wavelengths.

2. Greatly improved sensitivity for detection of faint sources of electromagnetic radiation of all wavelengths,

charged particles (cosmic rays and solar wind plasma) and gravitational radiation.

The possible astronomical observatories on the Moon are as follows:

- Optical interferometer.
- IR (infrared) submillimeter telescope - collecting area 2,500 times the infrared astronomical satellite (IRAS).
- IR/Submillimeter interferometer.
- Very large aperture EUV/X-ray telescope - reflecting area thirty times the advanced X-ray astronomy facility.
- Solar observatory.
- Cosmic ray observatory.
- Gamma ray observatory.
- Neutrino telescope.
- Gravity waves.
- Radio telescope - to be located on the far side of the Moon.

All of these observatories will be able to make new discoveries. Among these new discoveries will be:

- Detection of planets orbiting nearby stars.
- Parallax and proper motion measurements of stars all over the galaxy.
- Improvements in the Cosmic distance scale.
- More precise estimates of mass density.
- Very high resolution studies of all forms of solar activity.
- Understanding the evolution of the universe, galaxies, and individual stars.

- Properties of black holes, supernovae, neutron stars, quasars, interstellar gas, radio stars, and radio galaxies.
- The outer solar system (oort clouds, etc.).

Proposed Radio Telescope

A radio observatory has been proposed on the far side of the moon. Human tended, this observatory would consist of optical telescope arrays, stellar monitoring telescopes, and radio telescopes, allowing near complete coverage of the radio and optical spectra.

This would be built on the far side of the moon to block all radio interference from Earth, generated by signals from radio, television, and all other forms of communications and remote sensing. These, along with atmospheric activity such as lightning, generate static and interference in radio astronomy. The far side of the moon is free of an atmosphere and also blocks all forms of communications from Earth, allowing clean reception of radio frequencies. The lunar rotation also provides a monthly scan of the sky.

Very little is known of the radio sky beyond the 10 meter (m) wavelength. The long wavelength cutoff caused by the ionosphere on Earth is highly variable with so much sunspot cycle and radio frequency interference. As a result, radio sky wavelengths from 10-30 m are poorly observed, and virtually unknown for wavelengths longer than 30 m. Exploration beyond 30 m must be done from space.

To take the fullest advantage of the lunar far side, a series of radio telescopes could be built, an array that would summarily cover the entire sky the far side of the Moon faces. Only a few radio telescopes, a minimum of seven to ten, evenly spaced across the surface, will be needed, but these will be able to amass information about the universe as the Moon sweeps across the sky.

Recommendation: Have one experimental radio telescope built on the far side of the Moon as the lunar base is permanently staffed and long range exploration commences. In time, a plan to build a Moon wide array of radio telescopes can be put into place.

5.14 A radio telescope on the far side of the Moon. The far side of the Moon is chosen because all signals from Earth are blocked by the Moon, thereby enabling the telescope to pick up uninterrupted signals from the cosmos.

Space Plasma Physics

Solar winds constantly blow across the lunar surface. In addition, the Moon spends about one-fourth of its orbit in the tail of Earth's magnetosphere. Here, the Moon is shielded from the flowing solar wind plasma and its associated electric and magnetic fields and is exposed to the plasma and fields in the geomagnetic tail.

A large-scale lunar surface grid of plasma and field detectors will allow unique studies of the solar wind and magnetospheric tail not possible from single satellites. In addition, chemical releases (barium, strontium, etc.) by surface launched sounding rockets in the upstream solar wind will allow unique studies of important plasma phenomena, such as the development of micro- and macro-instabilities, anomalous ionization processes, and solar wind sweeping effects.

Life Sciences and Ecosystem Studies

There are basically two general purposes to the study of life sciences.

1. To understand how biological mechanisms function in space and lunar environments.
2. To develop life support systems that ensure human safety and mobility.

In 1/6 gravity, the study of humans, plants, and animals will identify the effects of low gravity on these mechanisms, both physically and psychologically. With this understanding, we can develop better procedures for crew health and medical care in the lunar environment. We will also develop better life support systems for long-term habitations, requiring closed ecological processes, efficient recycling procedures, food production, and a better environment in general.

This will also be good practice for a mission to Mars.

5.15 Habitats, life support systems on the Moon.
Looks like a village on the Moon.

Materials Processing and Other Research

As previously mentioned, materials processing will be an important factor. Before lunar resources can be developed for industrial use, they must be sampled and subjected to experimentation. Lunar soil must be gathered and separated to determine the properties of all the elements contained. These properties include:

- Density.
- Shear strength.
- Thermal conductivity.
- Electrical properties.

These elements must be crushed, grounded, stirred, melted into materials, and subjected to extreme temperatures.

Other research in materials processing include:

- "Clean" chemistry.
- Chemical purity.
- Bioprocessing.
- Reprocessing.
- Particle Physics.
- Chemistry and Physics based lunar materials and experiments.
- Low neutrino background on the lunar surface for less interference with experiments.
- High vacuum.
- Reduced gravity.
- Low magnetic field.
- Direct access to space.

<u>Recommendations</u>: Have an experimental facility for lunar soil along with a materials processing facility.

Conclusions

The lunar surface is an excellent location for many classes of scientific experiments, some of which could be developed for industrial use. It is recommended that a program defining the types of scientific research on the Moon be initiated to verify and extend current concepts.

Future scientific use of the lunar environment will require numerous technological developments. Among these are:

- Long range surface transportation systems.
- Communications systems.
- Techniques for construction and assembly of large instruments.

It is recommended that these techniques be researched and developed for use on the lunar base.

Evolution of the Lunar Base

A ll three scenarios described above will evolve in stages. They will start simple, with small scale experiments and operations, growing more independent as operations grow, until finally becoming an industrialized, independent, self-supporting society.

This entire process, taking an estimated two to four decades, could theoretically occur in five phases: precursor exploration; a research outpost; a permanently occupied, operational base; an advanced base; and finally, a self-supporting society.

Five Phases of Lunar Base Development

Phase I: Unmanned Satellites
(Performed simultaneously as developing the OTV and the Lunar Orbital Space Station)

- Preparatory exploration.
- Lunar orbiter explorer and mapper.
- Lunar pilot plant definition.
- Site selection.
- Automated Site preparation.

The first step in establishing a lunar base is global mapping of the Moon. This can be accomplished with a polar lunar orbiting satellite, mapping the entire surface for site selection of a lunar base. Locations of mineral deposits and metals can also be detected, selecting areas for possible mining and locations of pilot plants for oxygen and materials processing, as well as a site for scientific experimental apparatus.

Phase II: Research Outpost

- Humans return to the Moon.
- Minimum base, temporarily occupied, totally resupplied from Earth.

Science Base

- Small telescope/Geoscience module.
- Short range science sorties.
- Instrument package emplacement.

Industrial and Self Sufficiency Base

- Lunar Power Station.
- Surface mining pilot operation.
- Lunar oxygen pilot plant.
- Lunar materials' utilization research module.
- Close systems research module.
- Research on Nuclear Propulsion begins.
- Research on Helium-3 Fusion begins.

This is the point where humans will return to the Moon. Before humans return, unmanned cargo-landers will arrive, bringing an unpressurized rover and solar power generators.

Then, when humans return, there will be initial lunar landings where astronauts simply explore the lunar surface. At first, there will be one-week stays, then two-weeks, then a month, and on subsequent missions, the duration of their stays will increase. Habitats and other equipment will be delivered with each new mission, along with other survival necessities. As the number of missions increase, the base will start to take shape.

This base will be temporarily occupied and totally resupplied from Earth. Everything will be performed on an experimental level, with processing facilities for lunar soil and separation of minerals. Small scientific experiments and local geologic exploration will take place, along with the placement of a small astronomical telescope. Pilot operations for surface mining and oxygen and hydrogen/water extraction are to begin.

To achieve self-sufficiency, there will also be agricultural experiments utilizing lunar soil and recycling water, oxygen, and Carbon dioxide. A power station would utilize solar power by day, fuel cells by night, and/or use a full-time nuclear reactor.

Phase III: Operational Base

- Permanently Occupied Facility.
- Consumable production.
- Recycling pilot plant.

Science Base

- Longer range science sorties.
- Geoscience/Biomedical laboratory.

- Experimental lunar radio telescope.
- Extended surface science experiment packages.

Industrial and Self Sufficiency Base

- Expanded mining facility.
- Lunar materials pilot processing plant.
- Oxygen production plant.
- Lunar agriculture research laboratory.

Permanent occupancy begins along with the lunar industry, including the full production of lunar oxygen and concrete, and expertise in handling tools, equipment, and construction. The use of robots, performing cold welding, surface mining and drilling, and laser and electron beam welding commences.

The production of raw materials will progress to more complex forms of development. This includes:

- Powder metallurgy.
- Vapor phase metallurgy.
- Production of solar cells, computer parts, and eventually, space habitat structures, antennae, service satellite parts, reflector structures, etc.

For industry, this phase will start to generate revenue and a payback on initial investments.

Lunar agriculture will be a major source of food on the Moon, with much of it still in an advanced research phase.

For Science, there could be long-range travel on the lunar surface, for geoscience, surface geology, surface science, and an experimental radio telescope.

Life support systems will be advanced enough to support research for nuclear propulsion systems, starting with the Solid Core NTR.

Phase IV: Advanced Base

Science

- Advance consumable production.
- Satellite outposts.
- Advanced Geoscience laboratory.
- Plant research laboratory.
- Advanced Astronomical laboratories.
- Radio telescope on the far side of the Moon.
- Long range surface exploration.

Industrial Base

- Large scale oxygen production.
- Ceramics/Metals production facility.
- Locally derived consumables for industrial use.
- Industrial research facility.

Self-Supporting Research Base

- Lunar Ecology research laboratory.
- Lunar power station - 90 percent lunar materials derived.
- Agricultural production pilot plant.
- Lunar manufacturing facility.
- Lunar volatile extraction pilot plant.

All three functions—science, industry, and self-sufficiency—will become more specialized.

In science, long-range surface exploration will permit a radio telescope on the far side of the Moon, along with laboratories for advanced geoscience and plant research, with satellite outposts for astronomy.

For space travel, the Solid Core NTR systems will be developed and used. Research in Gas Core NTRs will be initialized.

For the growing industrial base, lunar materials would be the majority of the feedstock. There will be more industrial research and bigger and more complex products and assemblies. Oxygen would be produced on a large scale and some would be exported.

With high-quality, lunar made products, to be used as hard currency, a lunar economy will come into existence. The Moon will have a positive balance of trade, and from here on, further lunar expansion will be supported by the lunar economy.

Self-sufficiency will be achieved by advancements in food and energy production.

Phase V: Self Supporting Society

- Full scale production of exportable oxygen.
- Volatile production for agriculture, Moon-orbit transportation.
- Close ecological life support system.
- Lunar manufacturing facility: tools, containment systems, fabricated assemblies, etc.
- Lunar power station - 100 percent lunar materials derived.
- Expanding population base.

After twenty to forty years of an expanding lunar base, with a growing industry and population, there will be a fully developed and self-supporting society with a robust economy. There will be independent food production, energy production, full scale production of oxygen, and the manufacture of many diverse industrial goods, including fully built space vehicles.

The population base will be able to expand and new settlements will be built anywhere on the lunar surface, solely supported by the lunar economy.

Benefits to Earth from lunar development and its effects on Earth society

The establishment, growth, and full development of the Moon and its resources will demonstrate that human civilization has no limits to growth: frontiers, energy, and material resources are unlimited. Here is a partial list of the benefits of space exploration and development.

Note: Not all of these benefits listed are covered in this essay.

- Astronomy

- Biology

- Chemistry

- Ecology

- Geology (Planetary Science)

- Medical Science

- Meteorology

- Physics

- Psychology

- Sociology

Here are the advances in engineering sciences, resulting from lunar and space development:

- Biospheres
- Communications
- Computers/Electronics
- Energy Production
- Fuel Cell Technology
- Environmental Technologies
- Genetic Engineering
- Life Support Systems
- Industrial Technology
- Materials Science
- Magnetic Levitation
- Micro/Nano Technologies
- Mining Technology
- Propulsion Systems
- Robotic Systems
- Space Transportation
- Superconductivity

All this will result in improved living standards for the people of Earth.

1. Increased number and quality of jobs related to space development.
2. Expansion of business opportunities in space.
3. Low-cost access to the vast material and energy resources of space.

Quality of life will improve for the people of Earth.

1. Reduced pollution through decreased need for drilling, mining, and processing of Earth's resources.

2. Abundant, low-cost energy for the clean-up of Earth's environment.

3. Migration potential to space, acting as a "pressure valve" for population growth.

4. Enhancement/emphasis of international cooperation rather than competition.

5. Access to the engineering advances listed above.

6. More resources available to more of Earth's population. Instead of dividing the pie (Earth's resources) into smaller pieces, we can make the pie bigger.

It will be at this point in time, with advanced life support systems, propulsion systems, experience in constructing a base, and the examination of physiological and psychological factors, that we will proceed with a mission to Mars.

For now, we shall continue with our overview of space infrastructure by covering the use of Near-Earth Asteroids, which are equally as important as settling and developing the Moon.

7

Near-Earth Asteroids (NEAs)

Anecdote #2

A little over one kilometer in diameter, the asteroid soared through space. The Space Watch, a tracker of Near-Earth asteroids, calculated that Earth would be in the asteroid's path, with a collision expected in ten years time.

Should the asteroid strike land, the impact would be felt worldwide, with fifty times the destructive power of an all-out nuclear war. This would result in extremely powerful earthquakes, surpassing the Richter Scale. The fallout from the impact would blot out the sun in the equivalent of a nuclear winter. With the Sun's heat being blocked for years, a new ice age would form. The combination of disasters would destroy most life on Earth.

Should the asteroid strike the ocean, coastal cities within the impact's circumference would be wiped out by tsunamis, with the waves reaching 20 kilometers inland or more.

Billions of people would be killed, cities destroyed, the food supply would dwindle and we would not be able to grow more because of the long winter. All infrastructure, electrical grids, water lines, gas and oil pipelines, would also be destroyed. Water supplies will be poisoned.

Life on Earth could possibly revert to the Dark Ages, with humans reforming into tribes, every tribe for itself, to try and find some way to survive.

All this was predicted to happen in ten years, as was announced on the news. Already, doomsayers and religious voices were preaching the end of the world. Doom and gloom was overwhelming Earth's population, and many were turning to religion, some even to extreme cults.

7.1 An asteroid approaching Earth, with people cringing in fear.

The newly formed Ace Asteroid Mining Company saw an opportunity to stop this crisis by venturing to this asteroid and prospecting it for valuable minerals. Ace was a newly formed company, often laughed at and ridiculed for having "pie-in-the-sky" visions of "mining space" and making lots of money. "Pure fantasy," remarked any sensible individual.

Now the people working for Ace rubbed their hands gleefully, knowing that people would finally see their usefulness.

All the asteroid mining technology was available for sale, if one put up the money. Ace Mining went to several banks, telling them of the coming doom, and then offering to mine the "star of doom" out of existence, and make a lot of money in the process. This is done by mining the asteroid, shrinking it bit by bit, taking the materials and waste to be processed for valuable minerals or just plain soil, until there is no more asteroid, so it never reaches Earth.

Two banks turned them down, but one bank was willing to take the risk. "With what's about to happen, we have nothing to lose," they replied.

The money was used to buy cis-lunar orbital mining apparatus, foundries and other ore processing facilities, life support space habitats, ice refineries for extracting water, solar sails, cables 25 kilometers long or more, bags to contain the asteroid, and spaceships for transport.

The composition of this asteroid was iron, nickel platinum and related metals, and water ice. The estimation in value for all these minerals was $90 TRILLION dollars. While everyone else foresaw doom, the mining company drew pictures of a huge dollar sign heading for Earth and advertised it for their own amusement.

A new space industry was now in the making.

7.2 An asteroid approaching Earth, covered with a $ sign, and people smiling, eyeing an opportunity for big money.

While everyone anticipated and feared the impending doom, private rocket companies offered transport to Ace miners, for a share in the profits. Everything was packed, and the miners proceeded to the asteroid to commence operations.

There were still five years before the asteroid impact. It took that long to prepare. They would mine the rock and ship the materials back to the orbiting factories and processing facilities, as well as facilities on the Moon. Ace was finally ready.

The asteroid was reached after one year, and the work was about to begin with four years left to impact. The ships docked with the asteroid. Cables were connected, and the facilities were set up for mining. Work began, slowly. The ore was mined, and minerals were separated, processed and shipped to Earth orbiting space factories. Ships ferried the ore to LEO and returned repeatedly.

Water was mined and shipped both for life support and fuel. Precious metals were mined for electronics and jewelry. Despite the warning, life still went on, business as usual. There were debates as to whether the disaster would really occur, but the world knew of the mining venture by Ace.

When the asteroid finally approached Earth, it was wrapped in cables and towed by a space miner with the most powerful propulsion systems. As it approached Earth, the miner circled around the Earth to its new destination, the Earth-Moon L5 point of orbit. A song from the late 20th century blared on the airwaves with the lyrics "money money money."

The people of Earth were not amused.

This is both a worst-case and a best-case scenario, but the main point is that should another asteroid threaten to strike the Earth, disaster can be averted by mining it out of existence. The fringe benefits will be factories built and operating in space, ore to be processed in material goods, water ice for space colonies and fuel, and, of course, lots of money for the companies involved.

Note that I said *another* asteroid. There are records of asteroids striking the Earth, the last being 65 million years ago, with the above-mentioned results including the extinction of dinosaurs. Neil deGrasse Tyson, famed astrophysicist and space advocate, joked that "the dinosaurs died because they didn't have a space program."

This is better than blowing a threatening asteroid up with atomic bombs—which could make the problem worse by causing several chunks to hit the Earth, along with a meteor shower—or even just trying to divert it, postponing the day of destruction.

Although my scenario gave it ten years, asteroids can be predicted to hit the Earth thirty years in advance or more, giving us ample time to mine them, without any fear of the Earth coming to harm.

The Real Thing

This undertaking of mining Near-Earth asteroids will probably occur before we return to the Moon, and if not before, shortly thereafter.

Asteroids and comet cores (comets that have burned out and been caught in a near solar orbit), are extremely valuable sources of minerals, with the benefits of being easier to get to than the Moon and providing all the elements of life support that the Moon needs but lacks. Venturing to these asteroids and obtaining their minerals is also good practice for the Mars mission, using long-term life support systems along with navigation and operations systems on long space flights.

In addition, other needed skills for space are required that can be put into practice:

• Resource extraction and living off the land

• Radiation protection, using dirt or modern technology in manufacturing radiation shields

- Grabbing and holding large and hard to catch objects
- Moving very heavy cargo (300 metric tons or more) around the solar system.

Most asteroids orbit in the belt between Mars and Jupiter, but many NEAs have orbits that cross Earth's orbital path around the sun. These are our focus for this proposal. As of now, there are no plans to venture to the asteroid belt itself, and that may not happen until long after we have landed and settled on Mars.

There are three orbital classes of NEAs.

1. Amor – orbits completely outside Earth's orbital path. May cross paths with Mars, but only approaches Earth.
2. Apollo – crosses Earth's orbit, though its orbital period around the sun exceeds one year.
3. Aten – may cross Earth's orbit. Its distance is less than one astronomical unit (distance from Earth to the sun) and orbits the sun in less than one year.

The Apollo and Aten asteroids are our primary interests for mining.

Our knowledge of the composition of asteroids comes from three techniques.

1. Spectrophotometry – the measurement with high resolution of the dependence on wavelength of the reflection, from an asteroid, of sunlight in the visible and near infrared spectrum.
2. Polarimetry – measurement of the polarization of sunlight reflected from an asteroid.
3. Radiometry – measurement of infrared light of an asteroid.

The last two methods combine to give a measure of the diameter and average coloring, be it light or dark. The first gives a very sophisticated method, in which the spectra characteristic of particular minerals are recognized by the light reflected from an individual asteroid.

We have also learned a lot about the asteroids from the meteorites found here on Earth. A meteorite could either come from an asteroid or a piece broken off of a comet.

Pieces of both asteroids and comets are meteoroids, which travel through space. The meteoroid becomes a meteor when it enters the Earth's atmosphere. As it burns up, the meteor usually doesn't hit the ground, but if it does, the remnant becomes a meteorite.

The meteorites are found and examined, and are compared to what minerals have been detected by way of their reflections in the asteroids and extinct comet cores. The large majority of these asteroids have spectra that resemble either known classes of meteorites or mixtures of familiar meteorite minerals in somewhat different proportions than are found in actual meteorites.

The composition of these meteorites are known as chondrites.

There are five different classes of chondrites pertaining to meteorites.

1. H High iron chondrites   23 percent
2. L Low iron chondrites   16 percent
3. LL Low-Low iron chondrites   6 percent

These first three classes, known as ordinary chondrites, contain the following minerals:

- Iron
- Ferrous iron oxide in silicates
- Ferrous sulfide
- Metallic iron
- Iron sulfide (with mineral troilite)
- Feldspar - an aluminosilicate of calcium, sodium, and potassium.
- Pyroxene - silicates with one silicon atom for each atom of magnesium, iron, or calcium.
- Olivine - silicates with two iron or magnesium atoms per silicon atom.

High and Low concentrations of iron are very common in meteorites, with High iron chondrites the most similar in composition to Earth. These are the first three classes of chondrites. The two other classes of chondrites are:

4. E Enstatite chondrites
   - 31 percent metal
   - Abundance of iron free magnesium silicate $(MgSiO_3)$

5. C Carbonaceous chondrites
   - -Ferric iron
   - -Carbon
   - -Organic matter
   - -Little or no metal

Types of Carbonaceous Chondrites:
- CM (Murchison type)
  - -No metal
  - -10 percent water bound in hydrated silicates (clay minerals)

- -3 percent organic matter
- -Elemental sulfur
- -Some carbonates
- CI (Ivuna type)
  - 20 percent water in clays
  - 6 percent organic matter
  - Abundant carbonate and sulfate minerals

Ground based spectroscopic and radar studies have identified common metals and minerals composing these asteroids. In terms of their physical composition, asteroids can generally be divided into the following categories:

1. Carbonaceous (C-type)
   - Carbon rich materials
   - May hold up to 15%-20% water, along with organic chemicals
2. Silicate (S-Type)
   - Silicon compounds mixed with metals
3. Metallic (M-type)
   - rich in metals, especially nickel and iron
   - one of them analyzed, known as 1986DA, may contain a substantial amount of platinum.

Other classes of asteroids include:

4. Silicate and chondrite mixture
5. Reddish asteroids
   - probably "rusted rock"
6. Dormant or extinct comets.
   - may have been steered into Earth's vicinity by the gravitational fields of various planets

7. Unknown asteroids
    *   e.g., geologically processed materials that represent crust, mantle, and cores of minor planets

On October 29, 1991, the probe Galileo flew within 1600 kilometers of asteroid Gaspra. It is a silicate asteroid with a volume of 2508 square kilometers.

Preparation for Mining the Asteroids

Asteroids may or may not be towed into Earth's orbit. It is risky—should the asteroid be steered in the wrong direction, there is a chance that it could crash into the Earth. If they are to be towed to Earth orbit, the place to tow them, where the Earth would be safe, are to the Moon's libration points, L4 and L5.

Because of their low to near zero gravity, and their location, NEAs are the easiest places to reach in the entire solar system. The challenge will be long-term life support systems, with a crewed journey expected to last from six months to three years.

Before venturing out to an asteroid, there must be a program to map, locate, and analyze the NEAs and their compositions, especially in the Apollo category. There are over 4500 known asteroids that cross Earth's orbital path as of 2023. Between 500 and 1000 of these are over one kilometer in diameter. According to the NEO Information Centre, located in the U.K., there are literally millions of NEOs (asteroids, comets, meteors, etc.). Here is a list, in numbers according to size, measuring the diameter of NEOs.

10 meters	100 million objects
100 meters	100,000

500 meters	10,000
1 kilometer or larger	1,100 (according to NASA)

This would prove useful in both resource materials and in assessing whether they are a threat to Earth. In this category, it has been determined that asteroids that are about 30 meters in diameter or less do not pose a hazard. They would either burn up in the Earth's atmosphere, or be reduced enough to make any impact negligible, apart from the possibility of minor air blasts. This means that the vast majority of NEOs (NEAs) are not considered Potentially Hazardous Asteroids (PHAs). The vast majority, being over 100 million asteroids, are less than 30 meters.

The size of the asteroids corresponds to their weights as follows:

1+ meter	1.5 to 15 tons
3+ meters	50 to 500 tons
10+ meters	1,500 to 15,000 tons
30+ meters	50,000 to 500,000 tons

This is the maximum size where they burn up in the Earth's atmosphere without touching the planet's surface.

50+ meters	Asteroid hits Earth, creating a crater at minimum

There are several programs that observe, analyze, and map NEAs and comets. Located all around the globe, these organizations use various types of telescopes, detectors, and cameras, including charge coupled devices (CCDs) to discover and map out as many NEOs as possible, especially those greater than one kilometer. So far, as stated, over 33000 total NEOs have been discovered, out of a possible 100 million, of all sizes. Through their efforts, over 90 percent of existing NEOs over one kilometer.

So far, 878 of these asteroids have been discovered.

This project is led by NASA's Near-Earth Object Project (Spaceguard) searching for PHAs, even those less than one kilometer (but over 140 meters), and they have been very successful in tracking down these objects.

Also participating in tracking these asteroids is NASA's Jet Propulsion Laboratory at the California Institute of Technology.

There are, however, other programs aiding in this venture, both publicly and privately financed. Among them are:

1. Spacewatch - Kitt Peak, Arizona
2. Lowell Observatory Near-Earth Object Search (LONEOS) - Flagstaff, Arizona
3. Catalina Sky Surveys
4. Asiago DLR Asteroid Survey - Italy/Germany
5. Japanese Spaceguard Association (JSGA) - Japan
6. Lincoln Near-Earth Asteroid Research (LINEAR) - U.S. Air Force/M.I.T.
7. Near-Earth Asteroid Tracking (NEAT) - NASA/JPL/U.S. Air Force.
8. International Asteroid Warning Network (IAWN) - U.N.

The IAWN was formed in 2005 and is associated with some of the other programs mentioned above. IAWN is covered in great detail in Chapter 4, Space Infrastructure, in the section subtitled 'Protection of Earth from Rogue Asteroids.'

This effort will result in finding the most favorable asteroids for a rendezvous mission, and those that pose a threat to Earth.

Once the NEAs are cataloged, their mineral composition will be determined using Earth and lunar based instruments. The primary tool for surveying structure and composition will be a lunar, long baseline interferometer, as described in Chapter 5, Building a Lunar Civilization. Results will support a scientific investigation of primordial materials to determine the processes that produced the solar system. This will enable the planning for exploitation of asteroids as a resource base.

First Robotic Missions

Early robotic missions will be able to provide imagery, spectroscopy, structural information, and sample returns from exploitable Near-Earth asteroids. A multitude of small, sophisticated spacecraft can be launched simultaneously, to rendezvous with selected asteroids, one space vehicle to an asteroid. Such missions could provide scientists with the data needed to analyze the asteroids, their composition, shape, and topography, determining which one should be later visited by humans. Retrieving samples for later analysis is also probable.

An alternative or supplement to this proposal is to develop a probe with a solar sail to drift from one asteroid to another in order to analyze many NEAs to choose from for a later mission.

In getting to the destination, departure from LEO would be by way of a high thrust chemical propulsion system. Delta V (that's "vee," not "five"), the change in velocity, is needed to reach the asteroid and match the asteroid's velocity in order to land on it. This is done by burns from the rockets themselves.

- First burn from LEO to elliptical orbit will carry it out to the distance of its destination.
- Second burn is the mid-course correction maneuver at a point remote from both Earth and the asteroid.
- The third burn will occur at the time of arrival at the asteroid to match its velocity.

Departure will require a larger delta V to secure a trajectory that intersects Earth.

Any three-year period should contain roughly 300 launch windows to any kilometer sized NEA. That's about one launch opportunity every four days.

Using chemical propulsion, one typical asteroidal mission is estimated to be three years long.

Initially, the first automated missions will be to the closest NEAs. The next visits will then be to other asteroids that, based on spectral observations and data recovered from the robotic missions, differ chemically from the first asteroids observed. The next step will then be to send a human crew to a chosen asteroid.

There have been asteroid flyby missions, even one which landed on an NEA, collected a sample, and is presently on its way back to Earth.

The NEAR mission, Near-Earth Asteroid Rendezvous, was launched in 1996 and flew within 1200 kilometers of asteroid Mathilde before moving on to Eros, where it spent a year in orbit in 2000-2001.

On May 9, 2003, Muses-C, now Hayabasa, was launched in a joint U.S.-Japan collaboration. This is an asteroid sample return mission, where the probe would fly by and land on Asteroid 25143, also known as Itokawa, retrieve a sample, and return to Earth with the sample for analysis. On January 18, 2007, the probe rendezvoused with this asteroid, landed, caught a sample, and successfully returned to Earth on

June 14, 2010. The sample was 1500 grains of dust, from an S-type asteroid, whose composition matched that of an LL chondrite. It was confirmed to be extraterrestrial and has been exposed to the elements of space for eight million years.

Human Missions

Option One - Venturing out to the asteroids

The aim of human missions to asteroids would be to explore, take samples and analyze asteroids in greater detail. However, the shortest round trip times to an NEA, based on their elliptical orbit around the sun, would be approximately six to twelve months. In this situation, the two most important requirements are long-term life support and propulsion. Long-term life support system technology is at present being improvised on the International Space Station.

There is an alternative. Many asteroids naturally swing by Earth approximately every one to two years. There are already organizations such as IAWN (International Asteroid Warning Network) that track the path of asteroids passing Earth that pose a potential threat. Perhaps this can be turned into an advantage. Suppose we track the path of the asteroid, calculate when it will cross Earth's path, and then launch a space vessel from Earth on a trajectory to meet the asteroid when it does cross. How long would this take? If the speed was seven miles per second, like the Apollo spacecraft on its way to the Moon, it would take less than three days. With better propulsion systems, it may even take less than that. When the asteroid is analyzed and/or prospected or mined, the vessel would take a few days longer, depending on how fast they both are. The ship could even launch from the Moon or LEO.

Near-Earth asteroids (NEAs) present a compelling opportunity for exploration and resource extraction due to their relative accessibility compared to the Moon. While a round trip to the lunar surface requires significant energy, the best NEAs require only half the energy to reach. Their small size and low gravity further reduce the power needed for operations and return missions. Remarkably, returning from an NEA to low Earth orbit (LEO) can demand as little as 0.001 percent of the energy needed to return from the Moon. This translates to significant cost savings and operational advantages.

Beyond economic incentives, missions to NEAs provide an invaluable opportunity for deep space operational testing. These rendezvous missions would require long-duration life support systems, making them ideal "dress rehearsals" for future human missions to Mars. For example, a Mars transfer vehicle's systems—such as propulsion, environmental controls, and crew habitats—could be tested under real conditions, while crews gain experience conducting deep-space exploration. The development of long-term life support technologies, honed over decades with Skylab, Salyut, *Mir*, and now the International Space Station (ISS), provides a solid foundation for NEA missions, which will build upon and refine these advancements.

7.3 First crewed asteroidal mission.

To make these asteroid missions economically and technically feasible, a well-established facility in Earth-Moon space will be critical. This facility could act as a staging ground, supporting asteroid missions through several key functions:

Fuel and Reaction Mass: Early space manufacturing communities in Earth-Moon orbit could provide reaction mass as a by-product of industrial activities, enabling efficient propulsion for deep space missions.

Shipbuilding and Maintenance: These orbital facilities could serve as shipyards, where spacecraft are constructed, outfitted, and maintained before embarking on asteroid missions.

Resource Processing: Raw materials returned from NEAs could be processed here for use in Earth orbit, lunar industries, or on Earth itself.

7.4 Space Industrial Base for Supporting Mining of an asteroid; i.e. processing minerals mined from asteroids.

This infrastructure would form a crucial part of the broader space development strategy, laying the groundwork for sustainable deep-space exploration.

Unlike ambitious concepts of towing kilometer-sized asteroids into Earth orbit, early missions will focus on rendezvousing with NEAs as they pass close to Earth. We can mine valuable materials—such as metals or volatiles—and send them back to Earth orbit using one of two methods:

Mass Drivers: Materials could be ejected directly from the asteroid using electromagnetic mass drivers, taking advantage of the asteroid's return trajectory toward Earth.

7.5 A Mass Driver on an asteroid; most likely used for ejecting materials to Earth orbiting space factories.

Tug Transport: Alternatively, small quantities of mined material could be towed back to LEO or lunar orbit for processing and use.

Missions to NEAs represent a critical step forward in space exploration and infrastructure development. They offer opportunities to test long-duration systems, refine deep-space operations, and lay the economic foundation for broader activities in the solar system. By building facilities in Earth-Moon space, leveraging NEA trajectories, and gradually advancing resource extraction and transportation methods, humanity can create a robust infrastructure capable of supporting missions to Mars, large-scale asteroid mining, and eventually, a thriving space-based economy.

Option Two - Towing the asteroid to the Libration points, L4 and L5

Another option is to move the asteroids (by way of solar sail, space tug, or rockets) to the Moon's orbital path, 60 degrees from the Moon in either direction, to points known as L4 and L5.

As propulsion technologies advance and mining operations mature, humanity can move beyond small-scale mining and begin towing entire asteroids to strategic points such as the Earth-Moon Lagrange points. These stable positions would allow efficient processing, long-term storage, and integration of asteroid resources into broader space development activities. This shift would further reduce transportation costs and solidify a self-sustaining space economy.

It is recommended that we tow these asteroids to Lunar, or even Earth L4 and/or L5 libration points.

Libration points apply to all bodies orbiting another, larger body, in our case with the Earth orbiting the Sun as well as the Earth orbiting the Moon. The Earth-Sun libration points L4 and L5 lie sixty degrees from the Earth in its orbit path around the sun, so it is possible to place larger asteroids in these locations for mining.

In the diagram, where you see the Moon orbiting Earth, imagine the Earth representing the Sun and the Moon representing the Earth, and you have a clearer understanding of the above concept.

Earth-Moon LaGrange Libration Points

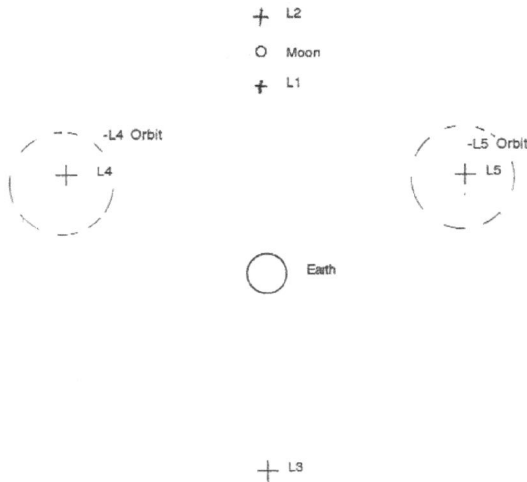

The five libration points of the Moon's orbit around Earth, where gravitational and centrifugal forces supposedly cancel each other out. (One must take in account the Sun's gravity). Objects placed at these locations tend to remain there with minimal expenditures of energy. The orbits of L4 and L5 are ideal locations to place asteroids to be mined. L1 and L2 would be ideal locations for way stations for Moonbound ships and/or mass catchers for lunar resources.

7.6 NEAs can be placed at Earth-Moon L4 and L5 points. They can also be placed at the Earth-Sun Libration points (not shown here.) Reprinted from Cosmic Careers, used with permission.

Venturing to an asteroid is not the same as traveling out to a planet. An asteroid, depending on its size, has an extremely low gravitational pull. For example, an asteroid 10 kilometers across has a force of gravity just 0.1 percent that of Earth's, with an escape velocity of nine miles per hour (four meters per second), while Earth's is seven miles per second (11.2 kilometers per second).

Due to this extremely low gravity, conventional landings are neither necessary nor practical. Instead, spacecraft will approach asteroids using docking methods, ensuring a stable connection without relying on landing gear. For emergency use only, landing gear may be included, but the crew's interactions with the asteroid will primarily involve daily visits from the mother ship via lifelines or power packs. The spacecraft would facilitate travel to and from the asteroid without ever touching the surface. As Eric Anderson, co-founder and co-chairman of Planetary Resources, explains, "You don't land on them, you dock with them."

In order to work on the surface, the astronauts would fire a bolt with a loop on it, like a mountaineer's piton, into the surface of the asteroid. The crew would then hook themselves onto the rock. Using ordinary rock climbing techniques, the crew would then explore the asteroid. An alternative would be to use a backpack propulsion system to maneuver around the body.

Human observers will be needed to work on the geology and structure of the asteroid, taking samples of minerals for analysis and researching for future operations. Core extractions from deep drilling would help define the internal structure and potential resource base. Seismic experiments would provide structural information on the stability of the asteroid. Experience gained from these activities could be used to assess the potential for robotic recovery mining missions, should the human mining of a particular asteroid not be necessary. In addition, a human mission to an asteroid would allow for the low gravity checkout for resource recovery techniques, leading to how to mine that particular asteroid along with similar ones.

How the asteroid is to be mined and how its minerals to be returned to Earth orbit and the Moon will be determined by human missions. New discoveries may also be made by humans that might be overlooked by robotic probes.

Enabling Technologies – What is Required

The following technologies are required to mine an asteroid:

1. Rendezvous techniques of large masses in highly elliptical and hyperbolic orbits.

    • Station keeping and surface operations must be developed

2. Remote sensors for robotic missions

    • Charged coupled device imaging systems

    • Mapping spectrometers to determine asteroid composition

3. Planetary surface equipment

    • Complete transportation system (except lander) should be available to fly the mission to any asteroid

    • Robotic equipment for surface exploration of an extremely low gravity object

        • Thrusters for station keeping

        • Digging holes for sampling

4. Excavation, processing, and extraction technologies should be developed

    • Some of these technologies of the lunar base include blasting, rubble collection, milling to a fine size, and heating feedstock for volatile extraction.

New Techniques in Mining Asteroids, One of Which is My Own

Various types are covered here, briefly taken from the book *Space Mining and Manufacturing; Off World Resources and Revolutionary Engineering Techniques* by Davide Sivolella. I will briefly summarize it in two general categories. The third came from my own imagination, based on what Sivolella wrote.

First, mining asteroids will be nothing like mining on the Earth or the Moon. Even with the Moon and its low gravity, there are still similarities to mining Earth's resources.

Mining any type of mineral on Earth is easy, in a sense, because of Earth's gravity. All one has to do is either dig underground and form a mine shaft, and then dig in the shaft itself and transport the mineral out, on a rail cart, like one does with coal.

The other way would simply be open pit mining, where one blasts the ground until one reaches the minerals, takes all the blasted material, and separates it from the rock, dirt, and slag to acquire the mineral itself. A pit would form as one dug deeper, but the process would be outside in the open.

Mining asteroids is a whole new concept and will require completely new techniques.

If we were to just blast and shovel, the refuse would fly out into space because of the asteroid's minuscule gravity. If one simply jumped from an asteroid, they would float out into space, forever.

However, new methods have been devised in overcoming this problem, a few of which I will mention here.

There is the possibility of placing cables around the asteroid, then placing a bag above where the asteroid would be mined, so the debris can be collected. When the bag is full, it will be transported to an orbital processing facility.

One can also use explosives, blast large chunks of the materials into bags, take the chunks to the processing facility, then crush and separate the elements.

7.7 Bagging the asteroid, as explained above, then mining it inside the bag to prevent debris from escaping.

There is also the concept of optical mining. Optical mining uses concentrated sunlight to heat a spot on an asteroid, either breaking off pieces for mining or melting elements like water ice to collect the resulting gas or liquid for condensation. Other elements like iron, nickel, and other metals would be melted into liquid, collected, separated, and then solidified at cooler temperatures.

All these are generalizations, and there are different versions of the above-mentioned concepts.

Here is my take on it.

Imagine a large mining ship approaching an asteroid. The asteroid could be any size, say 10 meters to one kilometer.

Cables are wrapped all around the asteroid, then the rock is bagged.

Then the mining operations begin inside the bag itself. The intent is to take apart that asteroid completely, and as much as possible, separate all the ores of which it is composed, even the water ice.

Other ships/factories come to collect the elements of this asteroid and take it to orbital refineries for processing.

The ice/water can be taken in a separate water tanker to be carried to the Moon or an orbiting space habitat or factory.

The rest of the metals can be refined, either at the mining ships or at supplemental ships built for that purpose, somewhere near the mining ships. Some mining ships could double as processing ships, producing perfect, separated metals ready to be sent to space factories.

With this approach, no debris would be lost to space. Any residue would be used as regolith for soil and or radiation shielding in O'Neill space habitats, space factories, or on the Moon.

In the event the asteroid is too big, we blast chunks of it off with the bag overhead to catch any debris, then assume the rest of the process. An alternative would be to have lasers cutting off pieces of the asteroid.

Taking the material after it's been mined, separating the elements, recovering water and oxygen from these elements, crushing the elements, and using the sun's heat or chemicals in pressurized vats to process the liquid and gaseous materials, would all be quite complex, more than can be written here. All this can be done on one large orbiting processing plant, say one kilometer long (a wild guess) with raw material coming in on one end, and the refined product out the other, or in separate space plants, a bit smaller. It all depends on the best way it can be done, and what the industry prefers.

The ships required would be mining ships, ore processing ships, and transport ships to ship the refined materials to space factories to manufacture whatever products desired.

Compare this to a large industrial facility along the waterfront in a major city, where, say in a steel plant somewhere along the Great Lakes, iron ore is brought in by a ship, an ore carrier. It is then moved by a "grab bucket" that scoops it up and drops it in an iron ore processing facility. By conveyor belt, it is purified and goes through a process where it is melted at high temperatures and converted into steel. This steel is shaped into anything the company desires, be it rolls or blocks, to be shipped to other factories and assembled into products.

This is how it will be in space, but more metals would be processed, the factories in space would be bigger, and the ships would be spaceships instead of sea going ore carriers. The entire processing facility would be the size of a city like Pittsburgh, or even bigger.

The next section will give a clearer picture on what these asteroids have to offer, and why we will be mining them.

Compositions of the Asteroids and their Use

Baking material from carbonaceous asteroids will contain

- 92 percent Iron (Construction materials, vessels, making steel)
- 7 percent Nickel (alloys, corrosion resistant materials)
- 1 percent Cobalt (batteries, jet engines, corrosion resistant materials)

Twenty Platinum Group Metals. These metals can be readily extracted in several ways for use as building materials, leaving behind a mixture of silicates of:

- Magnesium (heavy nutrition, remove sulfur from alloys)
- Calcium (body, especially in the bones, metal extraction)
- Aluminum (transportation, cooking, foil, construction materials)
- Sodium (food, baking soda, compounds)
- Potassium (fertilizers, glass, detergent, batteries, bones)
- Titanium (aircraft engines, medical devices)
- Other rarer elements

In other asteroidal materials, free metals necessary for construction, high technology, electronics, spacecraft, and over 1000 other uses. Rare nonmetals include:

- Germanium (electronics, infrared systems, optical devices, solar panels)
- Gallium (electronics, semiconductors, microprocessors)
- Arsenic (alloys, semiconductors, wood preservatives, metal adhesives)

The above uses in parentheses are only a fraction of their potential.

Sulfides and phosphides would also be procured.

Stony materials can shield space stations from cosmic radiation. Cobalt is used in jet engines and superalloys. Although an excellent source of raw materials, very little of it will actually be used on Earth.

Note that man's employment in space will not be so much in the mining, but using what is mined.

Platinum Group Metals (PGMs)

The following is a list of Platinum Group Metals that can be mined from the following three types of asteroids: LL Chondrite, 90 percent Nickel/Iron (Ni/Fe), and 98 percent Ni/Fe. The figures represent the estimate of grams of PGMs per ton of materials that can be extracted from these asteroids.

Metal	LL Chondrite	90% Ni/Fe	98% Ni/Fe
Germanium	1020	70	35
Gallium			87
Platinum	30.9	28.8	63.8
Ruthenium	22.2	20.7	45.9
Rhodium	4.2	3.9	8.6
Palladium	17.5	2.6	1.2
Osmium	15.2	14.1	31.3
Iridium	15.0	14.0	31.0
Gold	4.4	0.7	0.6

Most of these PGMs can be used for jewelry, electronics, chemicals, medical technologies, and even hydrogen fuel cells.

Mining these in the asteroids, instead of on Earth, will eliminate the problems of pollution and be cheaper in the long run. The concept of using these for fuel cells is explained in greater detail in Chapter 8, Energy and the Space Infrastructure..

Mining Asteroids and the Payoff

The mining of asteroids can yield more money than any of the natural resources of Earth has ever yielded. Many rare elements on Earth (i.e. Platinum Group Metals) are more common and easier to obtain in asteroids, without polluting the environment. Other metals that are becoming harder to obtain on Earth (iron, nickel, etc.) will be in plentiful supply in the asteroids, and will last for generations to come. Water is another vital element these asteroids have in the form of ice.

This is true especially as Earth's population and the demand for these minerals increases. Because of the abundance of these resources, and the convenience of not having to harm Earth's environment or pay for cleanup, there is more potential profit than there ever could be on Earth.

As we settle the Moon, there are many elements that the Moon lacks that are still needed. These asteroids can provide the necessary elements for living on the Moon.

The Moon, though rich in potential for human expansion and development, lacks some essential resources crucial for sustaining life and industry. Among these, water is particularly scarce, found only in isolated pockets at the permanently shadowed regions of the lunar poles. The Moon's barren landscape is also devoid of carbon dioxide, a critical component for plant growth and life-support systems. Nitrogen, indispensable for agriculture and atmosphere regulation, is absent as well. Finally, hydrogen, a key resource for fuel production and other industrial applications, is virtually nonexistent across most of the lunar surface. These shortages pose significant challenges for long-term lunar habitation, requiring innovative solutions to extract or import these elements to support future settlements and operations.

Asteroids contain these materials the Moon lacks. The needed elements are contained in the Carbonaceous asteroids, which compose about 50 percent of all Earth crossing asteroids. These elements are:

- Water   20 percent
- Carbon   6 percent
- Oxygen   10 percent
- Silicon   3 percent
- Nitrogen   0.1 percent

These volatiles could be readily transported to a manned space station in LEO and/or to a lunar base, as opposed to lifting them from Earth at great expense.

The resources in greatest demand for use in space are those that can be used to meet a space civilization's most massive material and energy needs. The cost of transporting these materials from Earth is so large that any material, regardless of its market price here on Earth, should be made from the resources found in space. Fortunately, the unit energy cost (kilowatt-hours/kilogram) of sending something back to Earth from any plausible mine site, whether it be from the Moon or an NEA, will be less, often much less, than the cost of launching them from Earth.

Rather than depending on Earth in any way, these volatiles can be delivered to a space station or lunar base without any net expense. Because Earth is at the bottom of a deep gravity well, it is, by nature, better suited to serve as an importer rather than an exporter of raw materials.

As a result, space and lunar settlements can become completely independent of the Earth, but Earth will buy materials from space, thus allowing space settlements to pay their own way.

Scenario - The benefits from mining a two kilometer asteroid

Is mining asteroids worth the cost? Suppose we were to mine the asteroid named 3554 Amun, the smallest known metallic asteroid. This asteroid is two kilometers in diameter with a mass of 30 billion tons. According to Dr. John S. Lewis, Professor of Planetary Science at the University of Arizona's Lunar and Planetary Laboratory, this asteroid contains the following metals, with a market value calculated in 1996, but updated by the Consumer Price Index in 2026 dollars.

1. Iron and Nickel	$24.11 trillion
2. Cobalt	$18.73 trillion
3. Platinum Group Metals	$18.7 trillion
- Platinum	
- Osmium	
- Iridium	
- Palladium	
- etc.	
TOTAL MARKET VALUE	$61.54 trillion

Therefore, one small asteroid can provide us with the potential for a space program tens of thousands of times larger in scale than anything we can afford without the use of space resources, far greater even than the Earth's present economy. With profits like these, and, after taxes, a large income for governments to do whatever is necessary for survival, this alone answers the question, "Why are we going into space when there is so much poverty here on Earth?!"

There is no "pie in the sky" however. Before undertaking a venture like this, one must determine the costs of obtaining these minerals, and determine whether the money invested is worth the outcome. What are our returns, really?

1. What is the cost of getting these same minerals from Earth's natural resources? In other words, how much would it cost to ship these same minerals from Earth to LEO or the Moon?

    - One estimate, from the above scenario, is that to ship the equivalent of the metals from 3554 Amun from Earth to LEO, at a rate of the current shuttle costs ($10 million/ton) would amount to $300 QUADRILLION, the gross global product of Earth for the next thirty thousand years!

Since the shuttle is no longer in service, it will cost less, but even 10 percent of the cost of $10 million/ton would still be $1 million/ton—not much of an improvement.

How much would it cost to export minerals from the Moon and asteroids to Earth? There has been combined research on this by NASA, SpaceX, MIT, the Colorado School of Mines, Blue Origin, and Northup-Grumman. Here is what they found.

The prospect of exporting minerals from the Moon and asteroids to Earth represents a tantalizing frontier for both science and commerce. However, it is a complex and expensive endeavor with costs that depend on various factors, including technological capabilities, the scale of operations, and the distance of the celestial body from Earth. Understanding the economics of this undertaking requires a detailed examination of the key cost components, potential innovations to reduce expenses, and the long-term feasibility of such projects.

Exporting resources from space involves significant investment across several stages:

Developing mining systems for the Moon or asteroids is a major challenge. The equipment must be tailored to harsh environments with no atmosphere and extreme temperatures. Costs depend heavily on the type of material being targeted—whether rare metals like platinum or volatiles such as water. Initial expenses for establishing such operations are likely to range from hundreds of millions to billions of dollars.

Transporting materials from space to Earth adds another layer of complexity. For the Moon, transportation costs benefit from its proximity and lower gravity, making it relatively more affordable. Using reusable launch systems, costs might decline to $10,000–$20,000 per kilogram in the near future. However, asteroid mining, which involves greater distances and complex orbital mechanics, could see costs of $20,000–$100,000 per kilogram initially.

Establishing space-based infrastructure, such as refueling stations, orbital processing hubs, and mining bases, represents a substantial upfront investment. These facilities are essential for sustainable operations and could require tens of billions of dollars to construct. This is what we need to do anyway, and what this book is about.

Maintaining mining systems, particularly robotic and autonomous equipment, will incur ongoing costs. Routine maintenance and the potential need for technological upgrades add to the financial burden.

The evolution of international space laws could introduce fees or taxes for mining operations. Additionally, ensuring compliance with regulations and addressing potential environmental concerns—both on Earth and in space—may add indirect costs.

To make space mining economically viable, significant innovations are needed to reduce costs:

By utilizing resources available at the mining site, such as extracting water from asteroids for fuel, companies can avoid the high costs of transporting supplies from Earth. ISRU could become a cornerstone of cost-efficient space mining operations.

Advances in reusable space transportation have the potential to dramatically reduce the cost of launching and returning materials to Earth. Reusable systems offer economies of scale that could make space mining more affordable.

Relying on autonomous and robotic systems minimizes the need for human presence, reducing costs associated with life-support systems and personnel. AI-driven technologies can also increase the efficiency and precision of mining operations.

At present, the costs of mining and exporting materials from space far exceed their terrestrial market value. For example, platinum-group metals might fetch approximately $30,000 per kilogram on Earth, but the cost of extraction and transport from the Moon or asteroids could initially range from $50,000 to $100,000 per kilogram. Similarly, while high-value materials such as Helium-3, platinum, or rare isotopes hold significant promise, their commercial viability hinges on achieving technological breakthroughs and economies of scale.

In the short-term, the primary focus of space mining may not be exporting materials to Earth but rather utilizing them in space. Resources like water can be converted into rocket fuel to support deep-space exploration, while metals could be used to construct habitats and other infrastructure in orbit. This in-space utilization could reduce dependency on Earth-based supply chains and open new opportunities for space-based industries.

In the long-term, as space infrastructure develops and transportation costs decrease, exporting minerals from space could become economically viable. These resources may help address Earth's dwindling supplies of rare elements while reducing the environmental impacts of terrestrial mining. Additionally, the development of a robust space mining industry could catalyze the creation of new markets, from space-based manufacturing to off-world colonization.

The journey to export minerals from the Moon and asteroids is fraught with challenges but brimming with potential. With continued innovation and investment, humanity may soon unlock the vast wealth of resources in space, propelling us into an era of unprecedented economic and technological advancement.

2. How well do the accessible resources of asteroids match the needs of a spacefaring civilization? One answer is that the asteroids contain all the elements a lunar civilization needs that are not available on the Moon.

3. What are the special interests of these asteroids?
   - Propellants
   - Life support fluids (e.g. water)
   - Metals for construction and shielding
   - PGMs for energy systems, especially fuel cells

4. What is the cost of returning materials from their sources, be it the Moon or NEAs? It is the sum of the first three factors *minus* the market value of the minerals mined and returned to Earth (minus any taxes on the market value), that will determine the profit. This is explained in the above section.

Suppose we did chart an asteroid that is predicted to hit Earth within thirty years. We could use nuclear weapons to destroy the asteroid, but that can end up being a waste of money and valuable resources.

An alternative would be to send a mining expedition there and simply mine it out of existence, averting disaster while using its minerals for lunar-orbiting, Earth-orbiting, and Earth-based industries, producing great wealth in the process.

There is little thought of performing the second option now, but as interest in mining these asteroids increases, this could very well become standard procedure.

There is one little known thought that is rarely expressed, but we need to focus our attention on it. Fortunately, this is very advantageous to the U.S. and other countries as well.

The most significant advantage of mining asteroids and the Moon is securing access to rare and precious metals, such as gallium and germanium, as opposed to obtaining them from hostile countries, many of which have these minerals. These minerals are vital for high-tech industries but scarce in the U.S. and abundant in hostile nations. Dependence on these nations creates a strategic vulnerability, as a mineral boycott could cripple U.S. industries. By sourcing these critical resources from the Moon and Near-Earth asteroids, the U.S. could eliminate this dependency, regain industrial stability, and diminish the leverage of hostile countries. Additionally, mining operations on the Moon and asteroids could generate income to further develop their industries.

Near-Earth Asteroids will definitely be a part of our space infrastructure in one form or another, and with all the space activity that will no doubt take place, there must be transport systems and law enforcement for *all* asteroidal entities, be they space factories, asteroid mines, or transport systems. These asteroids, the Moon, and cis-lunar space will be a vital part of our new space civilization before proceeding outward to Mars and beyond to the main asteroid belt.

Mining the Asteroids

Precursors
- Asteroid Search and Mapping
- Robotic Exploration

Next Operational Capability
- Expanded Exploration
- Robotic Resource Recovery

Initial Operational Capability
- 1 Piloted Flight with Crew Members
- 6-12 Month Round Trip
- Sample Collection
- Seismic Experiments

Full Operational Capability
- Asteroid Resource Utilization

Benefits
- Operational Test of Mars Transfer Vehicle
- Tests of Long Term Life Support and Propulsion Systems
- Materials for Use on Earth, Earth-Orbiting and Lunar Based Industries
- Creation of New Wealth, from the Minerals, for an Earth and Space Based Economy

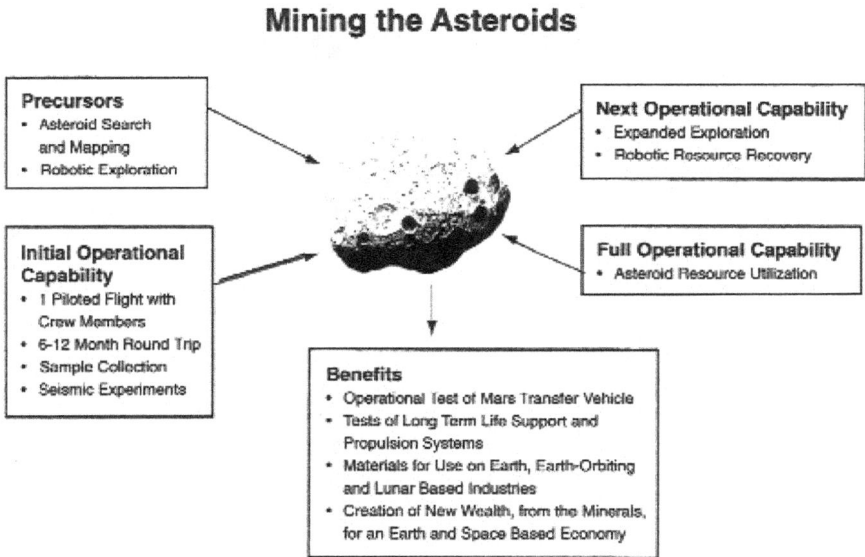

7.8 Diagram: Mining the Asteroids from the Precursors to the Benefits. Reprinted from Cosmic Careers, used with permission.

8

Energy and the Space Infrastructure

We are in another energy revolution, with the advent of clean energy. We have to be. Climate change is advancing rapidly, as a direct result of our continued reliance on fossil fuels. We can no longer afford to use them on such a large scale.

Energy revolution refers to the increasing use of energy alternatives to fossil fuels and other types of energy sources that are no longer safe for the world to keep using. Safer forms of alternative energy are being used, and more are being discovered.

Solar and wind are increasing in usage worldwide, and their output is increasing at rates we never imagined twenty years ago. Geothermal energy, the least touted of these three, is also on the rise. Other types include biomass, the burning of natural plant waste, and ocean energy, which relies on the tides moving in and out underwater. There is also bioenergy, deriving fuel from plants.

Other energy sources once deemed to be safe have been found to have downsides.

Hydropower was once thought of as a clean energy source, but dams have done unpredictable damage to the environment by blocking fish migrations, hindering needed water from flowing downstream, dwindling the water supply further down the river where it is equally as vital, and have even been known to cause earthquakes.

The following are traditional energy sources that are either depleting, found to be threatening to the environment, or both.

Coal is the most polluting fossil fuel. Mercury is one major ingredient of coal, and when burned it spreads into the air. Mercury causes permanent mental dysfunction in young children. Other toxic chemicals contained in coal include lead, cadmium, arsenic, chromium, selenium, and at least five other carcinogens. After the coal is burned and reduced to ash, these same chemicals remain in the ash, which has to be permanently stored away to protect the environment from its toxicity.

Coal is the biggest producer of energy in the world, and though the U.S. is reducing their coal burning plants, China and India continue to build more, regardless of the renewable energy sources in which they are investing. There are cases in Beijing where the air is so polluted that the residents either have to stay indoors or wear gas masks.

According to the International Energy Agency (IEA), gasoline, diesel fuel, and jet fuel are the main fuels for transportation and account for 60 percent of all oil burned. Except in countries in the Middle East that are mostly hostile to the West, the age of easy oil is gone. A surge in oil has reemerged in the form of hydraulic fracturing, or fracking, where a pipe is drilled into shale and chemically treated water is forced in, cracking it, forcing both oil and natural gas upward.

This process has been around since the early 1940s, but took off in the early 2010s, almost doubling the amount of oil on the world market and decreasing oil costs. It's beneficial to the U.S., but detrimental to the environment. The oil and gas have been known to seep into water tables, poisoning them, and there have been cases where people in areas of Pennsylvania and New York have gotten sick and subsequently relocated due to this problem.

Natural gas is being used to replace coal-fired plants, but this should be considered an intermediate step to clean energy plants. Although half as polluting as coal when burned, it still gives off climate changing gases. If released into the atmosphere unburned, the methane emitted has a more powerful effect on the atmosphere and global warming than carbon dioxide. Of course, with fracking, the natural gas released will have an adverse effect on the environment, beginning with the water tables.

Nuclear power is a clean energy source that does not produce greenhouse gasses, making it a key player in combating climate change. However, its use comes with significant risks, particularly the potential for radiation exposure in the event of a meltdown. Two major nuclear disasters highlight these dangers: Chernobyl in 1986 and Fukushima in 2011. The Chernobyl disaster resulted from a flawed reactor design and operator error during a safety test, leading to a massive explosion that released radioactive material across Europe. The nearby town of Pripyat was permanently evacuated, and the Exclusion Zone remains largely uninhabited. At Fukushima, a 9.0 magnitude earthquake triggered a tsunami that overwhelmed the plant's cooling systems, causing reactor meltdowns and the release of radiation. Though decontamination efforts continue, parts of the surrounding region remain off-limits.

In response to these disasters, the nuclear industry has made significant advancements in safety. Modern reactor designs, such as Generation III and IV, incorporate passive safety features that allow reactors to cool themselves without external power or operator intervention. Small Modular Reactors (SMRs) offer additional safety by being easier to control and less prone to catastrophic failure. Despite these improvements, public trust in nuclear power remains fragile, and issues such as long-term waste management and disaster risk must still be addressed.

Nuclear energy's potential as a low-carbon energy source is undeniable, but its future depends on balancing the risks and benefits. By investing in safer technology and transparent safety protocols, nuclear power can play a crucial role in the global transition to sustainable energy.

The flaw in that technology is the problem of ever-increasing nuclear waste, with a half life ranging from 10 to 24,000 years, or more. We cannot find a permanent place to store it. The nuclear industry is definitely on its way out, although it may be several more decades before the last nuclear power plant shuts down for good.

Clean and renewable energy, once touted as gimmicky, or believed to not be able to produce more than a small fraction of the country's, or world's energy needs, is coming into its own, and its quality is progressing at unbelievable rates. In this category, there are three main sources of renewable energy with future promise—solar, wind, and geothermal.

Solar power is making inroads beyond our wildest dreams. Photovoltaics, the concept of literally turning light into electricity, has improved in efficiency. Where electricity from a solar panel once cost $75 per watt, it now costs seven cents per watt. Because of this, a solar revolution is occurring where homes, schools, and businesses are installing solar panels on their roofs on a massive scale.

8.1 A.I. Rendition of a Solar Panel Farm. (Deviant Art)

Solar energy has become a disruptive enough technology that the utilities feel threatened by the decentralization of power production taking place, with homeowners getting off the grid permanently.

Wind power is another disruptive technology. It is now bigger than solar, generating four times the amount of electricity worldwide. The top countries deriving wind power are China, the U.S., Germany, Denmark, and the U.K. In the U.S., there are windswept plains that are ripe for wind turbines, from North Dakota to Texas, and these plains states, and California, are building turbines exponentially. The problem of them stopping when the wind stops is now becoming irrelevant, because, being hooked to the national grid, somewhere, there will be turbines producing power. The best part is that the amount of wind we use today has zero effect on the wind we use in the future, so it is inexhaustible.

8.2A. And 8.2B. Wind Turbines, on Prince Edward Island in Canada. This is a very common site in Quebec and the Maritime Provinces. Photos taken by Alastair Browne.

Geothermal energy is the third of the big three renewables. Geothermal energy is heat generated deep within the Earth's core, primarily from the radioactive decay of naturally occurring elements like uranium and thorium. Output potential is high, especially around parts of the Earth where tectonic plates meet, such as the Pacific Rim, the Continental divide in North America, Iceland, Africa, Southeast Asia, and really everywhere. Iceland derives 90 percent of space heating, and 99 percent of their energy from geothermal sources, powering the aluminum industry. China leads the world in geothermal energy, with Turkey, Japan, Iceland, India, Europe, the U.S. following.

The U.S. taps 25 percent of the world's geothermal energy in use today. The states where geothermal energy is mostly derided are California, Alaska, Idaho, Nevada, Utah, and Colorado. The amount of geothermal energy in the U.S. waiting to be tapped is 90 percent of its potential.

About 82 countries use geothermal energy directly, and about 40 countries could be completely energy independent on geothermal energy alone. These include countries in Africa, Central America, and Southeast Asia.

These are the three main sources of clean energy. The question here is, if the world is to run completely on clean energy, would solar, wind, and geothermal be enough? According to the U.S. Energy Information Administration, the total amount of renewable energy produced for the world's power supply is only 8.6 percent, as of 2022.

8.3 Nesjavellir Geothermal Power Plant in Iceland, by Gretar Ivarsson. P.D.

Should the use of renewable energy sources continue to rise, the projected rate may be higher, and it looks like it will be, but we will still need more massive sources of clean energy to satisfy the ever-growing demand in homes, transportation, and industry. Coal and nuclear power are slowly being phased out in the U.S., oil extraction is both politically dangerous and destructive to the environment, and natural gas is only a temporary fix.

China is just one country investing in renewable energy. They manufacture more solar panels than any other nation, and they are investing heavily in electric cars, building factories all over China, and in other countries as well. However, the electricity from massive coal-fired plants to power these vehicles will negate these attempts to protect the environment. One project cancels the other out.

Energy and Space Development

As we advance into space, achieving energy independence will become more attainable, as space exploration, development, and energy independence are closely interconnected.

Expanding into space will require energy sources that go beyond those currently dominant on Earth. Space-based industries will primarily rely on advanced solar and nuclear power systems.

In space, **solar power's uninterrupted availability** and the lack of an atmosphere mean that advanced solar technologies will be essential for powering spacecraft, stations, habitats, and industries. Combined with innovations like Space Based Solar Power (SBSP) and Concentrated Solar Power (CSP), solar technology in space could eventually surpass Earth's energy systems in efficiency and scalability.

Meanwhile, nuclear power systems in space will eventually progress toward fusion power, utilizing Helium-3 as a potential fuel source. This element is found in limited quantities on Earth and more abundantly on the Moon.

We can also generate a hydrogen economy here on Earth, using space based power and resources to create liquid hydrogen from water to use for transportation and power.

All this will greatly cut down, perhaps even eliminate, emissions of greenhouse gasses, which will also be discussed in this section.

One word of caution: I've mentioned nuclear power on the Moon in Chapter 5, but a meltdown on the Moon can be easily handled, because of the Moon's gravity, the vacuum on its surface, and solar and cosmic radiation bombarding the surface.

Nuclear power in space, especially in Earth orbit, is another matter. We cannot use nuclear fission, which could lead to the risk of a Chernobyl or a Fukushima in space.

A Chernobyl-style meltdown in space poses unique risks that differ significantly from terrestrial nuclear disasters. In the vacuum of space, radioactive materials released during a meltdown would not disperse through an atmosphere but could contaminate the immediate environment, threatening nearby spacecraft and astronauts. Radioactive particles might form a localized "cloud," which could pose long-term hazards to future missions, especially if debris is generated.

On Earth, the risks from a space-based meltdown are relatively minimal but not negligible. If radioactive materials from an orbital incident re-entered Earth's atmosphere, they might burn up and spread as particles. While this could lead to minor contamination, it would be highly diluted. A greater concern might arise from the creation of orbital debris, which could lead to cascading collisions (Kessler Syndrome) and disrupt satellite infrastructure, including GPS and communication systems.

Avoiding such risks involves an advanced form of engineering and design of nuclear systems for space, ensuring they have fail-safe mechanisms to prevent radiation release. Contingency plans are also essential, such as disposal trajectories to direct reactors toward the Sun or safe zones. While a meltdown in space would likely have limited impact on Earth, international cooperation and clear protocols are critical to manage and minimize potential hazards to human activities both in space and on the ground.

We cannot risk nuclear power in space, but there are other forms of space based energy that would be a lot more efficient, and safer: space solar power, the mining of Helium-3 from the Moon for nuclear fusion (which leaves no nuclear wastes), and platinum group metals from the Moon, but mostly from asteroids, to help power a hydrogen economy.

Solar Power Satellites

The energy from the sun is billions of times greater in space than it is on Earth. Because of Earth's atmosphere, Earth's infusion of the sun's power is only one in 23 billion of the Sun's output in space. This means that electric power emitted from the sun in space is 23 billion times greater than on Earth. A solar panel on a satellite up in space can absorb these Sun's rays and power the satellite as long as the panel faces the Sun.

In 1968, Peter Glaser of the Arthur D. Little Institute came up with the idea of unlimited energy from space—Solar Power Satellite (SPS) systems. Quite simply, a satellite is placed in Geosynchronous Earth Orbit (GEO). Geosynchronous Earth Orbit is a region of space, located 22,300 miles above the earth's surface, where Solar Power Satellites orbit at a fixed position relative to the Earth, allowing them to collect solar energy continuously. Panels are spread eight miles long and three miles wide, collecting the sun's rays, converting them to microwaves with a frequency of 2.45 gigahertz, and beaming them down to a receiving antenna (rectenna). This rectenna would be 10 miles long and 15 miles wide.

The **rectenna**—short for "rectifying antenna"—captures the microwaves and converts them into usable electricity. From there, the electricity can be distributed to nearby cities, powering homes, businesses, and industries. The microwaves transmitted from space are unaffected by Earth's weather. This means that rain, clouds, or fog will not disrupt the energy transmission, ensuring a continuous and reliable supply of power.

The potential power output of SPS systems is staggering. These systems are estimated to produce anywhere from five to ten *gigawatts* of energy, five to ten billion watts. Such a massive amount of energy could replace many coal, gas, and nuclear power plants, significantly reducing pollution and radiation associated with these traditional energy sources. Space-based solar power, therefore, holds the promise of delivering clean and sustainable energy on a global scale.

However, the use of microwaves in wireless power transmission (WPT) has raised concerns about safety. Some worry that microwaves could harm humans near the rectenna, birds flying through the area, or even airplanes passing through the beam. In reality, these fears are unfounded. The intensity of the microwaves used for WPT is **extremely low**—weaker than what one would experience standing next to a microwave oven with the door closed. Birds flying through the beam would not be harmed, and humans near the rectenna are completely safe. Airplanes, which are built with aluminum exteriors, are also protected since microwaves simply **bounce off** the metal hull.

Space-based solar power systems, combined with rectennas and wireless power transmission, offer a groundbreaking solution to Earth's energy challenges. By providing uninterrupted, clean power and addressing concerns about microwave safety, SPS has the potential to transform global energy production. This innovative technology could help replace polluting energy sources, paving the way for a more sustainable and energy-secure future.

An alternative to microwaves would be to beam the energy to Earth via diffuse, defocused laser beams, in the form of infrared lasers, to be received and converted to electricity on Earth.

The question with manufacturing SPS systems is whether it can be done technically and economically. What will the demand be for electricity not only in industrialized countries but in developing ones? What are the alternatives, and what effect will these alternatives (coal, oil, natural gas, nuclear fission) have on the world as a whole?

If we decide to build SPS systems, what will be the ecological effects of microwave and/or laser power beaming?

We must also develop the capability to fabricate these very large structures in space.

There is the problem of launching a 10 km satellite into GEO. One solution is to lower launch costs exponentially, but even better is to use the resources of Near-Earth asteroids and/or the Moon. An entire mining-transportation-manufacturing infrastructure can be built on the Moon, transporting the finished products to GEO, then building SPS systems on the spot.

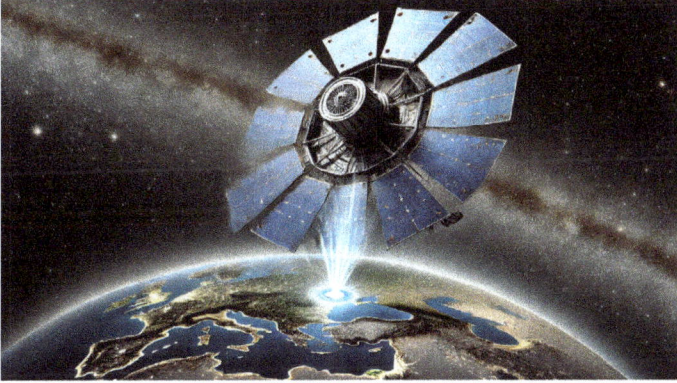

8.4A., 8.4B., 8.4C.: Three possible drawings of SPS systems, not drawn to scale, collecting the Sun's rays in GEO and beaming them down to Earth in the form of microwaves. Panels can be up to 10 kilometers long, but there are now various other designs that have been proposed, with shorter panels and at a closer distance to Earth.

8.4D. A possible Receiving Antenna (Rectenna) that can receive the microwaves and convert them back to electricity, from five to ten gigawatts.

A Pilot Plant

In order to build an SPS system, we must start with a pilot plant. This is to check the feasibility of an SPS and get the bugs out. We must also build a rectenna on the Earth's surface to check out:

- design
- environmental impact
- biological effects
- engineering and technology

A pilot plant will give us the data to evaluate risks, establish costs, and decide whether or not to proceed with a complete SPS system.

If the decision is to develop the system on Earth and launch it, things get expensive. This is where the industrial Earth orbit/lunar base system comes in.

An SPS would weigh over 50 million pounds. Would we use heavy lift launch vehicles to launch SPS parts from Earth to LEO, then tow to GEO, or use lunar and asteroidal materials, convert the raw materials to SPS parts, assemble in LEO, then tow to GEO? The latter is cheaper.

First Scenario – Manufacturing and Launching SPS systems from Earth

Manufacturing an SPS on Earth would be no problem. Launching it into space would be.

The economy of building and using an SPS must lead to a break even cost for space transportation. This means that in order to launch a solar power satellite from Earth, a space transportation system must be able to pay for itself, but preferably turn a profit.

Consider that an SPS weighs over 50 million pounds, 25,000 tons. If we used any heavy lift launch vehicle (HLLV) that could launch 100 tons, we would need 250 launches to build one solar power satellite. If the HLLV could launch 200 tons, it would require 125 launches. If the payload is 250 tons, 100 launches. Launching less than 100 tons is out of the question, because of the parts, panels, generators, etc., that are required. Even a spaceplane at $100 per pound to LEO would add up to $5 billion. The SPS would then be assembled in LEO, and if the payload was 20 tons (present payload of the shuttle) it would still need 1,250 launches. This many launches would no doubt put holes into the ionosphere, besides being too expensive.

The cost could decrease as RLVs improve, but the number of launches required would still be significant.

Second Scenario - Manufacturing and Launching SPS systems from Space

The high cost of space transportation, even from an HLLV, is a factor. Many launches are required, and there is an environmental impact to consider. One area of concern in this field is the deposit of reaction mass materials in the upper atmosphere, especially if it affects the ozone layer. There are also the sonic effects of launch and overflight.

Lunar Material

The use of lunar material would reduce 50-fold the number of launches required from the Earth to construct the SPS. If we are to use lunar material, the amount of energy required to launch these materials from Earth's moon to escape velocity would be less than one twentieth of that from Earth.

No matter how cheap launches from Earth become, the use of lunar and later, asteroidal, resources or even components manufactured on the Moon will still drastically reduce the need to use Earth materials and launches from Earth, resulting in additional cost reductions in the construction of solar power satellites

It should be noted that 100,000 tons of lunar soil must be processed to build one SPS. The best way is to process and separate the soil on the Moon. Then launch the processed soil using a mass driver. The bucket of material would be caught by a mass catcher, located at L2. The processed material will then be taken to a processing facility in Earth orbit where the materials are manufactured into the components of an SPS system. For example, aluminum can be used to manufacture trusses, and silicon to produce solar cells. These components are then assembled into an orbital SPS, where the finished satellite is then taken to its place in GEO. The SPS could also be assembled in its place in GEO. (See also Chapter 9, O'Neill Space Habitats, section on Mass Driver)

8.5 Artist's rendering of a Mass Driver on the Moon. NASA, P.D. Artist unknown.

If the SPS is built on the Moon, it can be launched with 1/6 of the Earth's gravity. If built in space, materials could be catapulted from the Moon to the construction area using a mass driver. The space factories would then process the materials. Required materials could also come from asteroids, alleviating the problem of gravity altogether.

This entire space manufacturing facility would consist of an *infrastructure* consisting of:

- Personnel transports
- Interorbital space transfer vehicle
- Location of candidate materials – the Moon and later, the asteroids.
- Excavating and mining operations.
- Transport of lunar materials into space.
- Power plants to power lunar habitations.
- Processing of lunar (and later asteroidal) materials into construction feedstocks.
- Fabrication shops – manufacturing components of the SPS
- Construction facilities – to construct the SPS in GEO
- Long-term habitation – O'Neill (or other) space habitats for construction workers and their families. The habitats would provide artificial gravity by rotation, and radiation shielding by the use of slag and other waste products of lunar or asteroidal processing, to be used as soil. Food required for inhabitants would be grown locally.

This entire *infrastructure* would be manufactured as we settle and industrialize the Moon. This would make the first SPS expensive, but once this infrastructure is set up and in place, we would be able to assemble additional SPS systems at a much cheaper rate. The manufacturing facilities (space factories) can also be used to manufacture other space made products and space factories, habitats, and stations.

It must be noted that:

1. Building the SPS system can help develop the Earth/ Moon industrial system and be used for other purposes described elsewhere.

2. If this Earth/Moon system is already being developed, it can be used to build SPS systems.

3. Building Solar Power Satellites are cheaper to build with extraterrestrial materials in space than on Earth.

4. Solar Power Satellites can replace coal, oil, and nuclear power plants; all polluting forms of energy.

5. The oil that SPS systems replace can be used for other purposes, such as the manufacture of plastics, etc.

6. Demand for electricity will decrease on Earth with industries moving out into space.

7. Two fringe benefits from lunar soil processing are the extraction of Helium-3 for nuclear fusion and platinum group metals (PGMs) for the manufacture of fuel cells for the hydrogen economy (to be discussed further in this chapter).

8. Another fringe benefit is the extraction of liquid hydrogen from water through electrolysis, using electricity from rectennas powered by SPS systems, again for the hydrogen economy.

This is how SPS systems and other space energy sources relate to the space infrastructure as a whole.

Asteroids

Asteroids, transferred to an L4 or L5 orbit, can be used to process materials for construction of an SPS.

- silicon
- carbon
- oxygen
- hydrogen
- iron
- nickel
- other elements

Platinum group metals can also be extracted from asteroids.

Asteroidal material, like lunar material, can be mined, processed and transported to manufacturing plants for conversion to SPS components. Later, they can be assembled. This would complement, not replace, using lunar materials for this process.

The proposed technology has been improved to a point where 10 kilometers of panels are not necessary. One proposal has a series of satellites 400 kilometers up, where they would beam lasers into a mirror and direct the power to Earth. When one satellite has passed, another would take its place, so the power would be constant.

These series satellites and SPS systems would complement, not replace, renewable energy sources, and would provide the massive power needed for industries and ever-growing populations that Earth solar, wind, and geothermal energy could not provide. Not only that, but remote areas in China, India, and Africa could have rectennas in places that would not normally have power, or would otherwise use polluting sources.

Number of SPS systems possible

SPS systems would be put into geosynchronous Earth orbit (GEO). The circumference of GEO is estimated to be 165,240 miles (264,384 kilometers).

With SPS systems being eight miles long, there is enough room for 23,606 SPS systems laid from end to end.

However, room is needed for other satellite systems – weather, communications, navigation, remote sensing, and others. With all that space, there could still be room for 1,000 to 5,000 SYS systems, maybe even more. One thousand SPS systems could generate five to 10 TRILLION watts of electricity, and at 5,000, 25 to 50 trillion watts, more than enough to cover the world's energy needs, in addition to other energy sources. This number of SPS systems probably would not be built, but the concept itself may be a reliable source to fulfill Earth's energy needs.

The infrastructure to build these satellites will also insure humanity's place in space.

8.6A. & 8.6B. SPS systems forming a necklace in Geosynchronous Earth Orbit. Here, supposedly they would be in equatorial orbit around the Earth, but supplying space solar power to any point on Earth. There may be other alternatives, as shown here. What SPS technology does reach fruition, it may be unknown how they will look or function. Some engineers say they do not have to be in GEO.

SPS systems can not only help deal with the world's energy problems, they can cut down on pollution and global warming by a huge percentage, and help create an infrastructure in space, both in industry and settlements. Industrializing space can help cut down on pollution even more, greening the Earth in the process.

In venturing out into space, industrializing it, and providing clean energy for Earth, SPS systems are an absolute must. It may not be THE energy solution, no one solution is, but, combined with other energy sources, SPS systems can help solve our energy dilemma.

Helium-3

The lunar soil contains ample amounts of the light isotope helium-3, constantly deposited on the surface by the solar wind.

Although extremely rare on Earth, this isotope is of interest because it is a potential fuel for use in fusion reactors not yet developed.

Helium-3 is a rare isotope of helium, differing from the more common helium-4 by one neutron (1 neutron + 2 protons), which gives it unique properties suitable for fusion.

As previously discussed under propulsion systems, the fusing of deuterium and helium-3 under superheated temperatures (over 100 million degrees Fahrenheit) in a magnetic field produces a reaction similar to the sun, releasing huge amounts of energy that can be harnessed for general use.

There is little waste of neutrons—only one to five percent of the energy released—which can be easily contained. A more advanced reaction, helium-3 to helium-3 fusion, emits no neutrons.

Deuterium can be easily obtained from Earth's oceans, but helium-3 is extremely rare.

Challenges of Mining Helium-3

While helium-3 holds immense promise, extracting this valuable resource from the Moon presents its own set of challenges, starting with the mining process itself. Mining helium-3 from the Moon requires moving approximately 200 million tons of lunar regolith for every ton of helium-3 extracted. During this process, other useful byproducts would be obtained, including:

- 500 tons of nitrogen (a vital nutrient that plants need to produce proteins and other essential compounds)
- 3,100 tons of helium-4 (abundant but not useful compared to helium-3. Can be exported to Earth, for a profit.)

- 1,600 tons of methane (a potential fuel source for future lunar settlements, allowing for the generation of electricity and powering equipment)
- 3,600 tons of carbon-oxygen compounds (Life support, especially for plants)
- 6,100 tons of hydrogen (combined with oxygen, used in producing water and fuel)

These byproducts can support both lunar colonies and Earth's industries. For example, hydrogen could be used to produce water and propellants, while nitrogen could support plant growth.

Extraction Process

To extract these volatiles, lunar soil would need to be heated to about 600°C. The solar wind gasses, weakly bound in the soil, are more concentrated in smaller particles, so sorting regolith by size could improve efficiency. The particles would be preheated by heat pipes, then fed into a solar-heated container where volatiles are extracted. Residual heat would be recovered for future use, making the process energy-efficient. This operation, however, would only be feasible during the lunar day.

Once extracted, volatiles can be separated from helium by exposing them to the cold temperatures of the lunar night. Most elements would condense, leaving helium for collection. Helium-3 can be further separated from helium-4 using well-established techniques.

Helium-3's Potential for Energy

When the fusion of helium-3 is perfected, it would serve as a clean, efficient energy source for Earth. One ton of helium-3 could power a city of 10 million people for a year. Estimates suggest that the Moon contains about one million tons of helium-3, enough to provide Earth's energy for hundreds of years. While the initial cost of extracting helium-3 is high, the long-term benefits far outweigh these expenses. At an estimated $1 billion per ton, this equates to about seven dollars per barrel of oil in today's energy costs.

Helium-3 Beyond the Moon

The atmospheres of gas giants like Jupiter, Saturn, Uranus, and Neptune contain vast amounts of helium-3, enough to supply humanity with energy for millions of years. Mercury, due to its proximity to the Sun, may also hold significant deposits of helium-3, though extreme heat presents additional challenges. Mining these distant sources would require advanced space technologies, but the energy potential is enormous.

In addition, it should be noted that 100 kg of Helium-3 can be produced from an asteroid 100 meters in diameter.

Phases of Helium-3 Fusion Development

Helium-3 fusion is performed by using heat to combine Helium-3 with one of four other elements: Tritium, Deuterium, Lithium, and another element of Helium-3. This must be done at extremely high temperatures, perhaps equal to that of the sun. For example, combining Helium-3 with Deuterium requires a temperature of 200 million degrees Celsius to fuse, releasing huge amounts of energy. Tritium requires 50 million degrees Celsius, Lithium requires tens of millions of degrees Celsius (no exact amount given), and Helium-3 with itself requires 31 million degrees Celsius.

1. <u>Helium-3/Tritium Reaction:</u> The first step in fusion technology development involves combining helium-3 with tritium, resulting in a helium-4 atom and neutrons. This reaction produces significant energy, though neutron radiation remains. Much shielding will be needed, so it is not recommended as a power source on Earth.

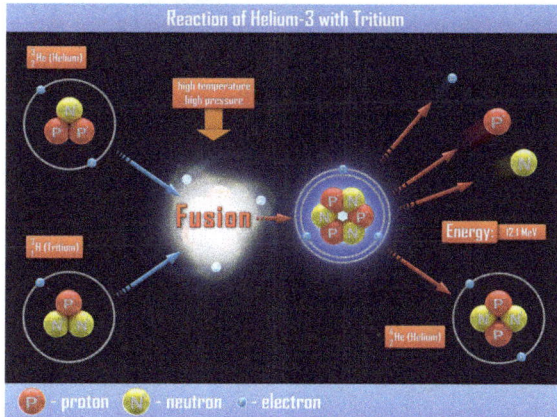

8.7 Diagram of Helium-3/Tritium Reaction.

2. <u>Helium-3/Deuterium Reaction:</u> In this phase, helium-3 is fused with deuterium, producing a proton and a helium atom. This generates even more energy with manageable low-level waste.

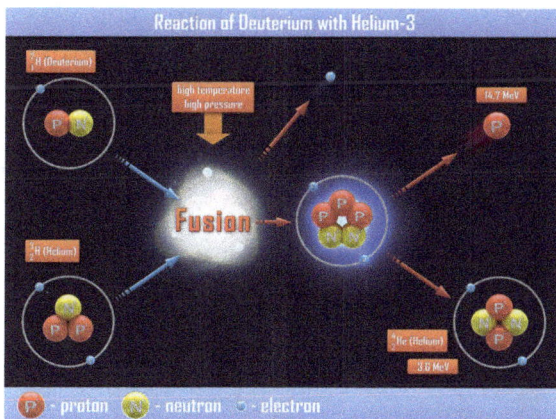

8.8 Diagram of Helium-3/Deuterium Reaction.

231

3. <u>Helium-3/Lithium Reaction:</u> Here, Helium-3 is fused with Lithium, where energy from the reaction is transferred to ionize the lithium and the combined molecule is then broken up into two helium-4 atoms along with one proton and one electron. This particular reaction is known as the Interatomic Coulombic decay.

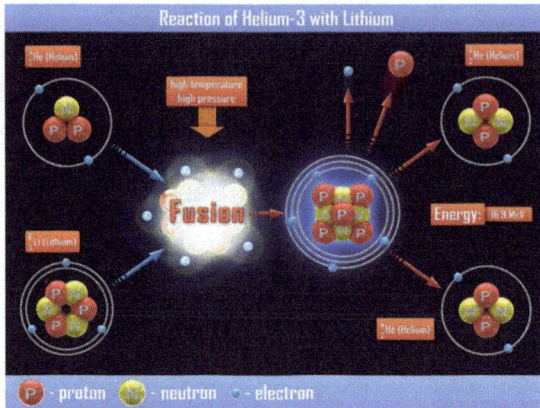

8.9 Diagram of Helium-3/Lithium Reaction.

4. <u>Helium-3/Helium-3 Reaction:</u> The most advanced stage of fusion involves fusing two helium-3 atoms, producing no neutron radiation and yielding the cleanest form of nuclear energy. This reaction results in helium-4 and protons, with electrons providing the energy source.

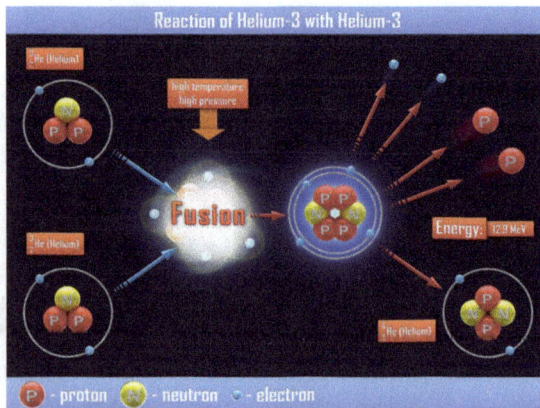

8.10 Diagram of Helium-3/Helium-3 Reaction.

Each phase of helium-3 fusion would progressively improve energy efficiency and reduce harmful byproducts.

Future of Helium-3 Fusion

Achieving sustainable helium-3 fusion requires overcoming significant technological challenges, especially in plasma confinement and energy output. Nevertheless, research on fusion has been ongoing for over sixty years, and the "break-even" point—where energy produced equals the energy expended— remains the goal. International cooperation and investment in research will be crucial to harnessing the power of helium-3.

Helium-3 holds immense potential as a clean, long-term energy source for Earth. While the initial stages of mining and fusion development are challenging and costly, the rewards of harnessing this power would be transformative, providing humanity with sustainable energy for centuries.

The Hydrogen Economy

The hydrogen economy represents a transformative vision for a cleaner, more sustainable energy future. Utilizing hydrogen as a fuel offers an alternative to fossil fuels, drastically reducing greenhouse gas emissions, conserving natural resources, and enhancing global energy independence. Key elements of this economy include electrolysis-driven fuel production, applications in transportation, and the establishment of robust infrastructure to store, distribute, and use hydrogen effectively. While challenges remain, the transition to hydrogen-based systems holds immense promise for addressing environmental, economic, and energy security concerns.

Electrolysis and Fuel Production

At the core of the hydrogen economy is electrolysis, a process that uses electricity to split water into hydrogen and oxygen. When powered by renewable energy sources—such as Solar Power Satellites (SPS)—electrolysis becomes a clean and sustainable method for producing hydrogen fuel. Unlike fossil fuel-based plants, which emit carbon dioxide, SPS provides renewable energy that aligns perfectly with the environmental goals of a hydrogen economy.

The benefits of producing hydrogen through electrolysis are far-reaching. According to the International Energy Agency (IEA), approximately 60 percent of the world's oil is used in transportation. By replacing gasoline and diesel with hydrogen, we can extend global oil reserves, reduce dependence on OPEC nations, and stabilize energy costs. Hydrogen production generates water as its only byproduct, making it environmentally benign. This positions hydrogen as a leading solution for reducing pollution and emissions, combating climate change.

Applications in Transportation

Hydrogen fuel cells are the key to transforming the transportation sector. Fuel cells operate by combining hydrogen and oxygen to produce electricity and water vapor. This clean process eliminates the harmful pollutants emitted by traditional gasoline-powered vehicles, making fuel cells an ideal solution for reducing the greenhouse effect and improving air quality.

Fuel cell vehicles can serve a dual purpose as portable power plants. With an average generating capacity of 20 kilowatts, a parked hydrogen vehicle can supply electricity to a home, business, or community. Since most vehicles remain idle approximately 90 percent of the time, owners can plug their cars into the power grid, providing electricity during periods of low demand and even selling surplus energy. This innovation not only enhances energy efficiency but also creates new opportunities for decentralized power generation.

The widespread adoption of hydrogen-powered vehicles offers numerous benefits, including:

- Zero emissions during operation, improving urban air quality.
- Enhanced energy independence by replacing fossil fuels.
- Efficient, silent operation with fewer moving parts than combustion engines.

Fuel cell vehicles represent the future of sustainable transportation, contributing to both environmental and economic progress.

Challenges and Considerations

Despite its immense potential, transitioning to a hydrogen economy requires overcoming several challenges. The most pressing is a catch-22 dilemma: hydrogen-powered vehicles and buildings need a reliable supply of hydrogen, but hydrogen producers require a strong demand for their product to justify large-scale production. Bridging this gap will require coordinated efforts to develop hydrogen infrastructure while simultaneously fostering demand for hydrogen-based technologies.

Safety is another concern. Hydrogen is highly flammable, and its storage, transportation, and use demand meticulous design and rigorous safety standards. Building public trust in the safety of hydrogen systems is essential for widespread adoption.

Lastly, for the hydrogen economy to fulfill its environmental promise, hydrogen production must rely on SPS, solar, and wind power. Using fossil fuels to produce hydrogen would undermine its benefits and exacerbate pollution.

The hydrogen economy offers a transformative solution for the challenges of energy security, climate change, and fossil fuel dependency. Through clean electrolysis, hydrogen can replace gasoline and diesel in the transportation sector, powering fuel cell vehicles that produce no emissions and even serve as portable power plants. While significant infrastructure investments are needed to support hydrogen production, storage, and distribution, technological advancements continue to address these challenges.

The transition to a hydrogen economy will not happen overnight, but with strategic planning and a focus on safety and sustainability, hydrogen can become a cornerstone of a cleaner, greener future. By embracing this opportunity, humanity can take a crucial step toward achieving energy independence and protecting the planet for generations to come.

How a Fuel Cell Works

A fuel cell chemically combines hydrogen and oxygen to make electricity. The following diagram (next page) shows how. Hydrogen is fed to one end of the cell, the anode, where it comes into contact with the catalytic surface, usually platinum (could be palladium, or a platinum-ruthenium combination).

Fuel Cell
(In General)

Heat

Flow of electrons

R

Connected to what
fuel cell powers

Anode
(- electrode)

Cathode
(+ electrode)

H_2

(May be pure hydrogen
or a hydrocarbon)

H^+
+ Ions

byproduct (pure
H_2O, or CO_2,
and/or heat)

O_2

Electrolyte

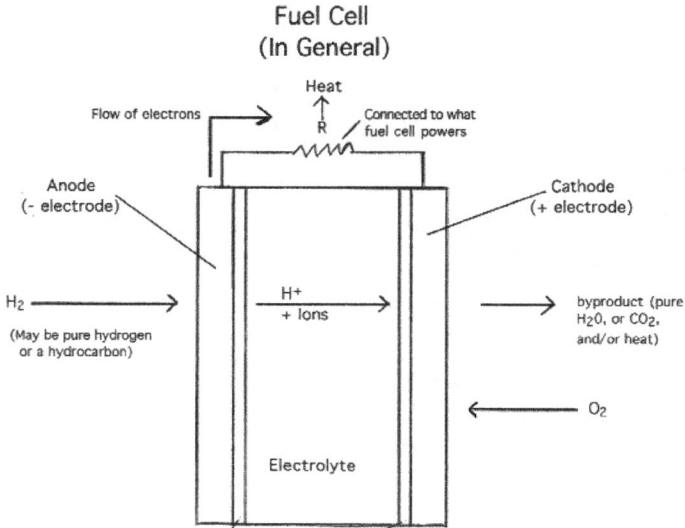

Catalytic surfaces, usually
platinum, or PGM, coated on
carbon mesh. May be
non-precious in certain types
of fuel cells (i.e. Molten Carbonate).

Electrode - Conducting material,
(anode or cathode) or pole,
where an electrical current
enters or leaves an electrolyte.

Anode - Negatively charged
electrode where electrons leave a
fuel cell.

Calalyst - Speeds reaction of
electrons.

Electrolyte - Material that
conducts ions (+ or -) across
fuel cell from one of its
electrodes to the opposite. Could
go either way.

Cathode - Positively charged
electrode where electrons return
to a fuel cell.

8.11 Diagram of Fuel Cell by Alastair Browne

The platinum acts as a catalyst, breaking down the hydrogen atom into positively charged ions and negatively charged electrons. The electrons are screened out using an electrolyte, where ions pass through, but electrons don't. Instead, the electrons flow through a wire. Here, the flow of electrons, electricity, powers whatever device the fuel cell is connected to. Heat is also generated, and can be used to heat spaces or produce more electricity.

The wire is routed from what the fuel cell powers back to the fuel cell's cathode. Here, oxygen molecules combine with the positive hydrogen ions and their wayward electrons, closing the circuit, forming water and heat. Pure water is a waste product, but is drinkable.

The entire reaction is:

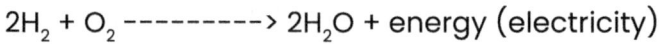

$$2H_2 + O_2 \text{--------} > 2H_2O + energy \text{ (electricity)}$$

Not all fuel cells are the same, and they don't all necessarily take in pure hydrogen. Depending on the type, they can take in a hydrocarbon, such as methane or methanol, with a byproduct of carbon dioxide. In the next section, we shall cover six different types of fuel cells.

Types of Fuel Cells

Fuel cells have been used to power the operating systems of ships since the Apollo missions. The waste product was pure water, which the astronauts drank. The water was even purer than tap water used in households. Research during the Apollo missions was invested heavily in this technology, and is still used to provide power for shuttle missions up to seventeen days.

There are many types of fuel cells using different types of chemical reactions. These types are named based on the electrolyte they use. Here are six listed below:

		Operating Temperatures ($^\circ$C)
1. Polymer Electrolyte Membrane	PEM	50-100
2. Direct Alcohol (Methanol)	DAFC (or DMFC)	50-100
3. Phosphoric Acid	PAFC	200
4. Alkaline	AFC	50-250
5. Molten Carbonate	MCFC	600
6. Solid Oxide	SOFC	500-1000

In a Polymer Electrolyte Membrane, or Proton Exchange Membrane (PEM) fuel cell, hydrogen molecules enter and pass through a platinum catalyst (or that of a platinum group metal, such as palladium). The positively charged hydrogen protons then pass through a chemical electrolyte consisting of a thin polymer sheet, also containing water, that does not allow the electrons to pass through, being an impermeable barrier to them. The electrons flow around this membrane, creating the electrical circuit.

The PEM fuel cell is about 80 degrees Centigrade or 176 degrees Fahrenheit.

The PEM is the best candidate for medium power applications, such as automobiles.

Direct Alcohol (or Methanol) cells also use a PEM along with platinum, but use 25 percent methanol (CH_3OH) in water rather than pure hydrogen. Carbon dioxide is vented while supplying hydrogen to the fuel cell. This is good for powering cell phones, laptop computers, global positioning devices, military field equipment, and lighted signs.

Phosphoric acid fuel cells use liquid phosphoric acid as an electrolyte, and also contain a platinum catalyst. Hydrogen is used and water comes out, but is more expensive. This is typically used for stationary power generators, but they can also be used to power large city buses.

Alkaline fuel cells use potassium hydroxide as an electrolyte, and again use platinum, although they can also use a variety of non-precious metals as a catalyst as well. They use pure hydrogen, but can easily be poisoned by carbon dioxide. As a result, the purification process of both hydrogen and oxygen in the fuel cell is costly.

Molten carbonate fuel cells use carbonate salts (sodium or lithium) as electrolytes, and can use hydrogen, natural gas, even gas burned from coal, as fuel. Non-precious metals can be used as catalysts. These fuel cells operate at high temperatures, so surplus heat can be used to spin steam turbines, for industrial processing, or space heating (e.g. buildings).

Solid Oxide fuel cells use a hard ceramic, porous metal oxide as the electrolyte. Anodes are composed of nickel, and cathodes are made from alloys containing metals such as lanthanum, strontium, cobalt, ferrite, magnate, or zirconium. There is no need for precious metal catalysts. This fuel cell has the potential to operate in large, stationary power plants, and waste heat can be captured and reused. They are sulfur resistant, not poisoned by carbon monoxide, and can use coal-derived gas as fuels.

Fuel cells, though imperfect at present, have the potential to power everything from light bulbs and simple computers to transportation and power plants. Many office buildings rely on fuel cells for both heat and electricity. All that is needed are the materials to build and power them.

Hydrogen and the Disadvantages of Fuel Cells

Fuel Cells have not yet been fully developed. The best fuel cells are still ten times as costly as the internal combustion engine (ICE), and may remain one step behind the gasoline engine for a long time. Gasoline, in spite of inflation, is still cheaper than liquid hydrogen by 50 percent. Gasoline is easier to produce, transport, store, and handle.

Fuel cells are ten times more expensive for power output than ICEs. A fuel cell averages $500 per kilowatt, as opposed to an ICE at $50 per kilowatt. They are also nowhere near as reliable. Vehicles powered by fuel cells can hardly run longer than 30,000 miles compared to ICE cars, which average 150,000 miles.

Fuel cell technology still needs a lot of work, requiring years or decades of further research and development, but it can be done. A new and improved membrane for the fuel cell, a hydrocarbon membrane (as opposed to the fluorocarbon membrane) could produce more electricity at half the cost. It's lighter, and can tolerate a wider range of temperatures, from 0 degrees Fahrenheit to near the boiling point (212° F). This is already being mass-produced.

This is just an example of the research that is taking place. If we continue, we can find the ideal fuel cell, at low cost, that can provide us with the power we need.

In the meantime, there could be a transition to an auto fuel economy using hybrids, biofuels, natural gas, and many other options. This is better than depending on just one fuel for autos or anything else.

Advantages of Fuel Cells over the Internal Combustion Engine

One advantage the fuel cell has over an ICE is that it can power a car three times the distance as gasoline. An ICE averages 27 miles to the gallon, while a fuel cell vehicle theoretically can average 81 miles per kilogram of hydrogen. One gallon of liquid hydrogen weighs 0.6 lbs., so 3.6 gallons of liquid hydrogen equals one kilogram. Actually, you're getting less mileage per gallon than gasoline, but it doesn't pollute the air. See below. www.wikianswers.com.

Internal combustion engines may be better than today's fuel cells, but there are also hidden costs.

- Pollution
- Health related damage (e.g. respiratory illnesses from exhaust)
- Global warming (floods, droughts, leading to crop losses, etc.)
- War in the Middle East (or at lease a military presence)
- Higher insurance premiums
- Higher taxes for defense budgets
- Military protection of oil

Will we squeeze every last drop of oil from this Earth to power our transportation needs? What happens afterward?

As an afterthought, where will we get our plastics, chemicals, medicines, and computer chips?

The age of the internal combustion engine is coming to an end. We are approaching new technologies that are coming into the mainstream of society. Note that as the need for energy increases, the technology progresses, and it gets progressively harder to produce. Look at the diagram below:

Wood———>Coal——>Oil———>Hydrogen

This represents the history and the future of energy sources. It should be noted that along with hydrogen are the equally hard to obtain technologies of Fusion and Space Solar Power. We will still have renewables, natural gas, and probably even present day nuclear power, whether we want it or not. We must rely on a variety of sources, not just one.

Fuel Cells and Platinum Group Metals

Since PEM is the best candidate for cars and transportation in general, and the transportation industry uses about 49 percent of the world's oil, we should cover this.

If hydrogen were used for cars alone, it would cut down on pollution, global warming, and greatly reduce or eliminate our dependence on foreign oil. It is estimated that by 2050, there will be three billion cars in use worldwide, so the hydrogen economy must be in existence by then.

Cars would use the PEM fuel cells. For these fuel cells that use hydrogen alone, the CO_2 output is zero.

Platinum or Platinum Group Metals (PGMs) are needed for these fuel cells, and that is where mining the Moon and asteroids come in.

One of the following Platinum Group Metals is needed for a car:

1. Platinum

2. Iridium

3. Osmium

4. Rhodium

5. Ruthenium

6. Palladium

These are extremely rare in the Earth's crust. The mines of South Africa, located at the Merensky Reef in the Bushveld Complex, have about seven to nine grams per ton of Earth ore, but the global average is about four grams per ton.

Today, the power level of a fuel cell is about 57 grams or two ounces for a catalyst for one car. This means that 14 tons of Earth ore has to be moved to provide for one automobile. Research is underway to lower the platinum loading to about 5.7 to 8.5 grams (0.2 to 0.3 ounces) per automobile.

Research is also underway to find a substitute for platinum to use as a catalyst. This may be difficult or impossible, so as of now, we have no choice but to stick to PGMs in the near future. This compounds the difficulty, for platinum has other uses that will compete with fuel cells.

- Catalytic cracking – the breaking down of heavy hydrocarbons in lighter ones in refineries
- Electronics – hard disk drives and capacitors.
- Glass – LCD screens
- Chemicals – lower energy required for chemical reactions
- Platinum fillings in teeth, spark plugs, pacemakers, catheters

- Many other items that require high temperature and corrosion resistance

Demand will soar as we move toward the hydrogen economy. Where will it come from? Before answering that question, I would like to point out the problem of mining platinum and other PGMs here on Earth.

- Strain Earth's supply
- Strain the environment
- Toxic gasses, such as chlorine, ammonia, and hydrogen chloride gas are released into the atmosphere
- Metals contain iron, zinc, nickel, and other elements not commercially viable to extract
- Makes a clean process impossible
- Takes 23.76 kilowatt-hours of electricity to product one gram of platinum and 10.45 megajoules of natural gas. As production increases, the amount of natural gas and electricity needed will increase
- Translates into 6.4 kilograms of CO_2 into the atmosphere per gram of platinum

According to the U.S. Department of Energy, should we transfer to a hydrogen economy, then five times the amount of platinum will need to be mined by 2040 than today, on a yearly basis.

The total planetary reserves of platinum and PGMs are 100 million kilograms (43 million kilograms according to South Africa). This may seem like a lot, but platinum is not easy to mine.

Suppose there is a high demand for platinum in a hydrogen economy, for fuel cells and other previously mentioned uses.

Make the total demand 1.5 million kilograms (1.5 billion grams) per year.

Estimate that there are four grams of platinum per ton. This is a conservative estimate.

Here is the environmental impact:

6.4 kg of CO_2/gram X 1.5 billion grams = 9.6 million tons CO_2/year 23.76 kw/hr electricity X 1.5 billion grams = 35,640 Gw/hr electricity (Gw = gigawatt hour or 1 billion watt-hours)

10.45 Megajoules of Natural gas X 1.5 billion grams = 15,675 Treadles (tera = 109)

4 grams platinum/ton X 1.5 billion grams = 375 million tons waste material CO_2 production will be 0.2 percent of the total 2004 CO_2 global emissions.

Natural gas will be 1 percent of total U.S. consumption.

Electricity at 23.75 kw/hr translates into four gigawatts per year, enough to demand two large nuclear power plants, or enough energy to power 2.5 million homes.

There is also the problem of toxic waste, and lots of it. Where will it be dumped?

In order to have a hydrogen economy, which is badly needed after oil, we must do it in a way that will avoid all the above-mentioned costs. It can be done. The answer for this new hydrogen economy is to obtain platinum and its group metals from the Moon and asteroids!

On the Moon, it is estimated that there are 140 to 590 billion tons of PGMs, enough to supply us for 3000 years. At 20 grams per ton times 1 billion grams per year (assume production to be 1 billion grams/year, rather than 1.5 billion grams), 50 million tons of nickel/iron asteroid from the lunar regolith will need to be processed.

This will produce palladium, osmium, iridium, ruthenium, gold, gallium, germanium, chromium, zinc, rhodium and other residual elements, in addition to platinum. These same elements can also be found in various asteroids, so Near-Earth asteroid mining will also play a large part in providing PGMs for fuel cells; i.e. if lunar production of PGMs falls short of demand, asteroid mining can make up the difference! Refer to Chapter 6, "Near-Earth Asteroids."

Suppose these PGMs were to cost $295/oz, this would mean $10.4 billion per year for platinum. The additional value of other PGMs would double this figure.

Additional benefits to mining PGMs from the Moon would be:

- 50,000 tons of cobalt
- Five to 30 million tons of nickel -20-45 million tons of iron -waste metals for shielding

Cobalt, nickel and iron would have plenty of other uses on the Moon and in space.

For fuel cells alone, platinum mining will be a large part of the lunar economy. All terrestrial production of primary metals can be shifted off planet. This would not only mean a vast lunar, asteroid, and space economy, but for this reason alone, humanity would boldly expand into space.

If there are resources on the Moon and/or Near-Earth asteroids, or products that can be derived from lunar and/or asteroid resources that can free us from our dependence on oil, that alone will justify returning to the Moon and space.

Development of PGM resources is the first step to not only reducing our dependence on foreign oil by jump-starting the hydrogen economy, but it would also reduce the pollution problem, especially global warming. As stated earlier, mining one billion grams of platinum from the Moon and NEAs will save the Earth:

- 64 million tons of Carbon dioxide
- 23,760 Gw/hr of electrical power
- 10.45 terajoules of natural gas
- 250 million ton of waste rocks

This is how going into space will save the environment here on Earth, and maintain or improve our quality of life.

There is one more factor in the hydrogen economy involving platinum and platinum group metals. These elements are rare on Earth, but are a lot more common in asteroids, and there are enough Near-Earth asteroids to provide this metal.

Platinum, for now, is needed as a catalyst to help power fuel cells.

As discussed already, there are many different types of fuel cells, using different fuels, but what will be covered here will be the Polymer Exchange Membrane Fuel Cell, which uses hydrogen.

The issue here is the platinum. With all those vehicles with fuel cells, platinum will be in high demand. The process of mining it can threaten or even destroy the environment surrounding these deposits, so we will have to look elsewhere.

There are two places to mine these metals: the Moon and Near-Earth Asteroids (NEAs). It is widely believed that platinum and platinum group metals (PGMs) might exist on the Moon. These metals, because of their scarcity compared to other metals, are known as trace elements. This list includes not only platinum, but other metals such as osmium, iridium, gold, and other related residual elements that may be of use on fuel cells. If there are metals, we can mine them from the regolith, simultaneously with other elements, including Helium-3. In order to obtain these PGMs, they would not be the metals to be mined, but other, more abundant resources, such as iron, carbon, magnesium, nickel, and these trace elements would be byproducts of the extraction of these other metals.

Whatever the supply of PGMs on the Moon, the first place these metals would be mined from are the asteroids, not the Moon.

It has been proven that asteroids have large deposits of platinum group metals, and John Lewis, author of *Space Resources* and *Mining the Sky*, explains the types of asteroids in existence and which have the PGMs. There are enough to provide metal for fuel cells to power every vehicle on Earth, and then some.

As with the Moon, the PGMs would not be the metal primarily mined as byproducts of the more common metals of nickel and iron. This process of obtaining these byproducts is known as carbonyl extraction, meaning injecting carbon monoxide in the regolith for a chemical reaction to extract the platinum. It is estimated that one can extract 31 grams per ton, with the remainder being dirt and other metals. Other PGMs range from germanium (1.02 kilograms per ton) to Rhodium and gold (a little more than four grams per ton.)

This may not seem like much, but take the asteroid name 3554 Anum as an example. It's a metallic asteroid with a diameter of two kilometers, with an estimated weight of 30 billion tons. John S. Lewis, Professor of Planetary Science at the University of Arizona's Lunar and Planetary Laboratory, estimated that, in 2024 dollars, there are $11.69 trillion worth of PGMs in the single asteroid, and that is the smallest out of the tens of thousands of mineable asteroids so far discovered.

Regardless of how rare platinum is right now, there is enough in the NEAs and on the lunar surface to satisfy the demand for platinum in fuel cells. There may be a substitute element for platinum for these hydrogen fuel cells that is more common, so the mining of so much platinum may prove unnecessary in the end.

The combination of the three clean energy sources on Earth—solar, wind, and geothermal energy—supplemented with solar power satellites, Helium-3 nuclear fusion, and fuel cells for a hydrogen economy, can create a totally clean energy economy on Earth and in space.

All this is a part of the space infrastructure, the Solar Power Satellites and their maintenance, and the mineral sources of Helium-3 and the Hydrogen Economy. These have to be protected as well as maintained, and they must be managed as close to the law as possible.

Energy is one of the dirtiest businesses there is, and as we run out of energy sources like wood (the first energy source), coal, oil, and natural gas, we have to look for other sources, requiring more advanced technologies. As we progress in energy production, the technologies get harder and more demanding, but if we are to maintain and improve our quality of life, we must go forward, not backward. We need to give up fossil fuels, though their use will be around for a long time to come, even as we advance into cleaner energy sources.

We do need advanced energy sources so as not to drown in our own poisons. Progress is possible. They are both down here on Earth, and up there in space. We need only to work and invest the money to obtain them.

9

O'Neill Space Habitats

This is an unusual chapter, in the sense that when discussing any kind of space setup or infrastructure, O'Nell space colonies or habitats might be the farthest from our minds.

This concept of the O'Neill Space Habitat is increasingly gaining attention and being taken more seriously. Space settlements will be needed, but what kind? We would want to maintain a good quality of life, a safe environment, and have many of the comforts of home, so much that those who have settled in space may never want to return to Earth. This is possible.

Of any space project imaginable, this may be the hardest to undertake, but if we succeed, it will not only be a vital part of space infrastructure, but the expansion of human civilization in ways many people have never imagined.

The late Gerard O'Neill devised the concept of building space habitats complete with Earth's outside environment—parks, forests, lakes, and rivers, with the inhabitants living in their own separate homes. From his viewpoint, why escape from one gravity well, Earth, to go down another (any moon or planet) when we have the infinity of space in which to settle?

All of this, and more, is explained in Gerard O'Neill's book, *The High Frontier - Human Colonies in Space.* There is also another book, written by T.A. Heppenheimer, dealing with the same topic, titled *Colonies in Space.* These are the only two complete volumes fully dedicated, from cover to cover, to explaining this concept. Both of these books are recommended reading, and what you find may surprise you. There are many other books that have been published since then that at least partially deal with the concept, often dedicating a chapter or two. One such book is *Settling Space* by John K. Strickland, Jr. with Sam Spencer, which includes a chapter that not only describes these space colonies but also goes into great detail on how to build one.

I will give a brief description of what these authors have written, just a brief synopsis.

I will give an overall view of these colonies and how they would function in our space infrastructure before focusing on three different types of habitats.

An Overall View

The size of these habitats vary depending on the desired population. They can comfortably fit anywhere from 10 thousand to 10 million people.

In general, the habitats would be built with an airtight shell, to be covered on the interior with dirt (slag) from the Moon and/or asteroids.

The O'Neill Space Habitat introduces a new approach, different from settling on planets like the Moon or Mars. Although the Moon is technically a satellite, for simplicity, I will refer to it as a planet.

Dr. Gerard O'Neill, who was a Physics professor at Princeton University and founded the Space Studies Institute (SSI), was not favorable toward settling either of these planets because of a lack of an atmosphere, low gravity that the human body has to adjust to, sometimes in an adverse way, exposure to solar and cosmic rays that are lethal to the human body, no oxygen, extreme temperatures, and the need to protect against all of these elements.

From O'Neill's point of view, the question is, "Why go through all this trouble to do so? Why not create our own worlds that would instantly accommodate the human being and fill all their physical (and mental) needs?"

For our next step in space, we will be working for long periods of time, and we will need space habitats in which to eat, sleep, and entertain ourselves.

The habitats originally envisioned for these workers would have been ISS like habitats, where one would sleep after a hard day's work. One would tire of it quickly, since there are nothing but walls, sleeping quarters, a kitchen, a bathroom, and a rec room. Living inside a spaceship environment for two years, possibly in zero gravity, one would not spend much time there before wanting to go home to Earth.

The space industries will be wanting for workers, even with robotic labor.

Now imagine being able to create a space colony with an Earth like environment and ample personal space.

We cannot create another planet like Earth; that's impossible.

Instead, we can use shapes like cylinders, wheels, and of course spheres, living on the interior of these shapes rather than the exterior.

They will rotate to produce the equivalent of Earth's gravity. This is known as artificial gravity. As the object rotates, everything remains on the surface of the interior.

Try this using a bottle partially filled with water. Spin it up and down in a circle. The water will remain in that bottle as long as you rotate your arm.

Now you have gravity, the first requirement for an O'Neill space habitat.

Other needs are water for farming and drinking; land, which would come from lunar and asteroid regolith, with microorganisms to keep the soil fertile; air, mostly carbon, oxygen, and nitrogen; and sunshine.

After it is processed from the removal of other minerals, the regolith would be converted into soil.

An entire ecosystem would be planted - trees, hills, exotic plants, birds, rivers, and lakes. Buildings would then go up like on Earth, and people would have their own private dwellings. The only difference is that the horizon would curve up instead of down.

These colonies would all be self-supporting, starting with producing their own food. Because of the controlled environment, there would be no pests (they would be easy to keep out, or dealt with if they did sneak in somehow) and no bad weather.

Farms to grow crops would be separated from the rest of the habitat, in their own separate compartments. These crops could be grown all year round. Nitric Oxide, a fertilizer, can be produced easily, combining excess oxygen and nitrogen from the Moon and asteroids to fertilize the plants.

9.1A Cutaway of the inside of an O'Neill Space Habitat, complete with rivers, lakes, towns, and walkways.

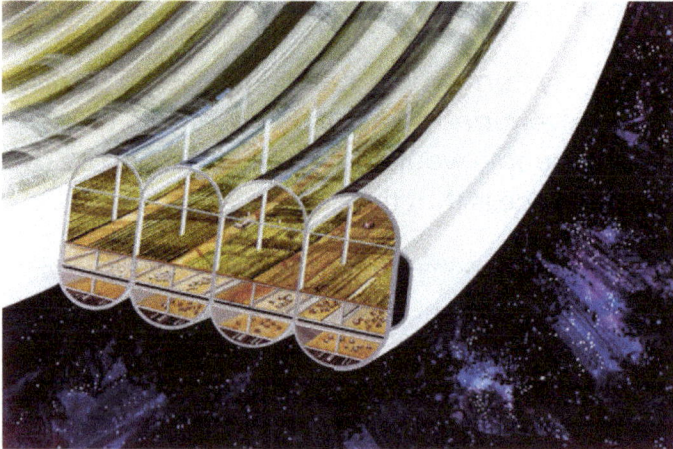

9.1B. Agricultural modules can be attached to any type of space colony.

There would be free, unlimited electricity from the sun.

Industries could be separate, floating in space but near these habitats for workers to easily commute, or better still, the industries could be connected to these habitats.

Many people would work in space factories, building solar power satellites, spaceships, or other space habitats, to name a few, and live in these habitats during their off hours. Factories and production plants would be attached to these habitats, perhaps building up an industrial section.

Goods, because of the low and zero gravity, would be made not only more cheaply, but of higher quality.

Industrial wastes, mostly toxic gasses, would be ejected into the vacuum of space, eventually just harmless atoms in the infinite void. There would be a sewer system to clean and recycle water in the closed systems of the industrial sector.

9.2 The outside of a space colony with solar panels attached (big ones), manufacturing plants, space traffic venturing around the colony.

These habitats would become new civilizations all together, an extension of humanity in space.

Permanent settlers would populate villages, communities, even small cities, with life going on as usual, as in any city or town on Earth.

Each habitat, or colony, will be its own world, with its own culture. There is the possibility of religious cults having their own habitat, but if they are happy that way, fine. They may be refugees from persecuted cultures, religions, or ethnic groups on Earth. These cultures could leave Earth and stake out their own asteroid, construct habitats, and migrate there to continue living as they please.

This will not replace or cancel out settling the Moon or Mars, only provide one more option for humanity. The Moon and Mars will still be settled and industrialized, and these new habitats will not diminish the value of that, but complement it. It will also give each individual one more choice of where to settle in space, should he or she desire to do so.

The habitats I will cover take three different forms: the Bernal Sphere, the O'Neill Cylinder, and the Stanford Torus, a sort of Ferris wheel.

Constructing the Habitats - A General View

In constructing these habitats, space industries will already have to be up and running, especially manufacturing facilities. This means foundries for the manufacture of trusses, covers of the entire habitat, and radiation shielding to protect the inhabitants, likely using regolith/dirt/soil from both the asteroids and the lunar surface.

Any habitat would have to be constructed near, or preferably on an asteroid for easy access to the necessary materials, usually minerals for processing in nearby space factories.

One necessary element will be glass windows, but not the type of glass found on Earth. As mentioned in Chapter 5, (Building a Lunar Civilization), the glass would be super strong, much stronger than the hardest metals or rocks, so that even a meteoroid would be unable to crack or dent it. The glass would be part of the habitat, able to shield radiation like regolith, and be transparent to allow the sun to shine through.

Robots will play a large part in constructing these habitats, working 24/7, but humans would also be required.

All materials would come from asteroids and the Moon. No materials would come from Earth.

A nearby asteroid would be mined for the minerals with the industries nearby to process the ore and form the needed materials for the habitat. Anything needed from the Moon would be sent from the surface by a mass driver.

9.3 Construction of a Space habitat. This could either be a Bernal Sphere or an O'Neill Cylinder.

Mass Drivers

Large scale transport of lunar material, be it regolith, oxygen, or separated metals, can be accomplished by launching small payloads with a mass driver.

The mass driver, proposed by Gerard O'Neill, is a system that uses magnetic fields to launch materials from the Moon's surface into space. This technology could significantly reduce the cost of transporting resources back to Earth.

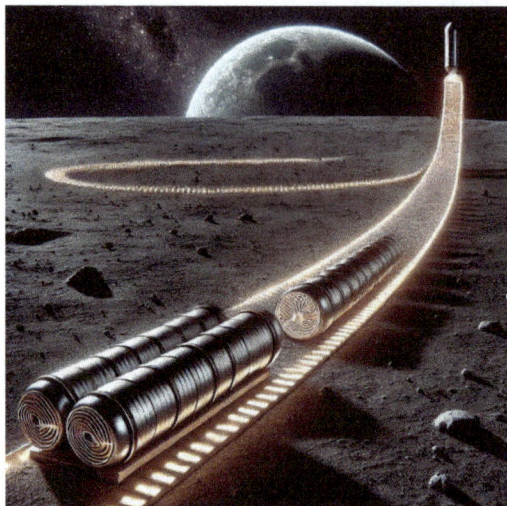

9.4A & 9.4B Two illustrations of a Mass Driver.

This process would commence upon the development of space mining and industries. The first materials to be transported could be Lunar Oxygen for the Way Station. Later, lunar regolith and raw materials for Earth orbiting processing plants would follow.

*   Other needed supplies for the habitat would be:
*   Electricity from solar energy/solar panels.

- Water sources/Plumbing facilities.
- Waste Processing, both sewage and industrial.

Everything would be recycled, and this technology would advance exponentially, subsequently applied on Earth to help clean up the environment.

Last of all, soil would be harvested from both the Moon and asteroids, serving a dual purpose.

The first is radiation shielding, to put on the "floor" of the habitat, and the second is land formation. Any environment can be created, from forests to deserts, even mountains. Independent ecosystems would be planted, to deposit only beneficial life forms, no pests. Of course, once the settlers begin to immigrate there, they would all have to be checked for these prohibited pests, and cleaned up before entering the new world.

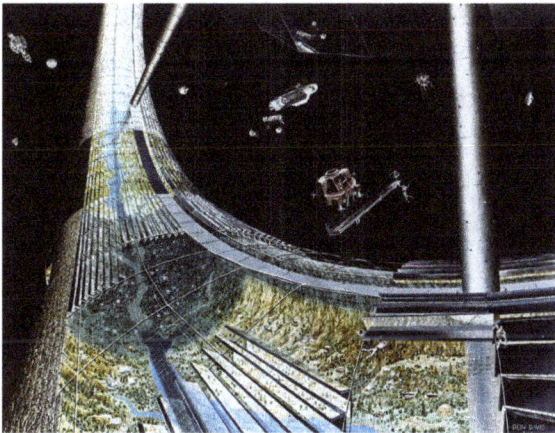

9.5 Cutaway of a Stanford Torus. Here, construction workers are applying lunar and/or asteroidal regolith to the "floor" or ground of the habitat.

Create an environment for space workers, or just those who want to settle, or both.

Create strong incentives against returning to Earth.

We will now cover the aforementioned types of space habitats: The Stanford Torus, the Bernal Sphere, and the O'Neill Cylinder. We should cover these one design at a time.

The Stanford Torus

This is the category of Werhner Von Braun's rotating wheel shaped space station envisioned in 1952, but originally proposed by Herman Potocnik in 1929. This inspired the space station in the movie 2001: A Space Odyssey. Like in the movie, this station is equipped with an outer wheel, a hub, and six spokes, and it rotates, producing artificial gravity on the interior.

Unlike the movie it is bigger, with an Earth like environment in the interior of the torus/tube with parks, cities, forests, lakes, farms, and human dwellings in all of them.

The entire wheel would be two kilometers in diameter, with a circumference of 6.28 kilometers, and the rim, or torus, would be 200 meters wide. It is calculated to have a volume of 177,472,800 cubic meters, and would fit 10,000 people comfortably.

This would allow for different environments as one would traverse the torus. The structure would be more complex, with different decks in different locations.

As one penetrates the hull from outside, there would first have to be a maintenance hull, like an engine room on a sea going vessel, with lower atmospheric pressure, by one half, and filled with nitrogen to prevent rusting and corrosion, with access to prevent or repair leaks.

This would be followed by the main floor, or ground, where the civilization is located.

Other decks above the main floor include functions for agriculture, industry, and communities meaning parks and residential areas. These decks would not dominate the entire torus, since its "world" would dominate the floor or ground of the torus. There would be city sectors, as shown in the illustrations, and they could be on different decks.

The top of the wheel section would be composed of lunar glass, thick, and dense, enough to protect from solar and cosmic radiation, as would the soil or regolith from the Moon and asteroids, three or four meters of it, covering the ground.

There would be a large, circular, and separate mirror hovering above the station at all times, perhaps connected with a cable, at a forty five degree angle. This would reflect the sunlight and help produce the day and night cycles. There would also be a double right of secondary mirrors, supported by the spokes of the wheel to control the sunlight and not let in too much light or heat. Radiators and cooling systems would also control the amount of heat to be expelled from the station.

One should note that from the viewpoint of any inhabitant of a torus, the horizon would extend up to the "sky" instead of straight, or down, like on Earth.

The six spokes of the wheel connect the hub in the center. The hub, with the top and bottom called the North and South poles, would be the docking ports for any and all ships.

The South Pole might also serve as a docking port for industrial habitats, or "construction shacks." Major industries could attach themselves to these hubs on any Stanford Torus for the process of ores and the assembling of solar power satellites, space vehicles, space factories, or space habitats. The workers would live in the torus and commute to these factories.

The spokes would have people and freight passing through for access to freighters or passenger ships to transport to other locations in the solar system.

Different Stanford Toruses means different cultures and ways of life for different people; some working at different industries, some farming, some practicing religions or other beliefs where the inhabitants can freely practice, or simply different professions, where one can work in the torus or commute outside to asteroids, space factories, or on the Moon.

There would be many different kinds of people, living different lifestyles doing whatever work suits them. Each Stanford Torus would be completely independent and self-supporting.

9.6A & 9.6B. Two illustrations of the outside of a Stanford Torus. There is a circular reflector above them, to reflect the sunlight, providing it for the inside of the habitat.

9.6C The interior of a Stanford Torus, with a park-like atmosphere.

9.6D. The interior of the same Stanford Torus, but with a
city like atmosphere. A habitat could have both.

This torus can serve as a major industrial area, where the
inhabitants work and support space infrastructure.

Bernal Spheres

The Bernal Sphere, is in reality semi-spherical, with flat ends on opposite sides. These would be the poles, with mirrors or transparent surfaces to let in the sun's rays. Encircling the poles would be belt-like cylinders with transparent glass (also known as "crystal palaces") and these would be the agricultural sectors. These farms will produce food for the population.

Manufacturing plants and ore processing facilities will be at the poles of the structure, supplying goods and other materials for the people on Earth as well as for other space colonies.

The colony itself would be built on the interior of the sphere. The diameter of the entire sphere would be 520 meters (1700 feet), the circumference in the center of the sphere, its equator, a little over a mile, or 1.6 kilometers. Its rotation would be one revolution per minute (RPM), one Earth gravity at the equator. The gravity decreases as one moves away from the equator. Near zero gravity would be at the poles There would be no habitations there, but it makes a great option for recreation or transport.

These Bernal Spheres could be built out of asteroids, providing metal and shielding on-site.

With a circumference of one mile or two kilometers, 10,000 people could easily fit.

Concerning the Elderly and handicapped

The reduced gravity regions of a Bernal Sphere, particularly those in the northern and southern zones away from its rotationally simulated Earth-like gravity equator, could revolutionize the quality of life for elderly and handicapped individuals.

For the elderly, low gravity alleviates many physical stresses. On Earth, gravity exacerbates age-related challenges such as weakened muscles, joint degradation (e.g., arthritis), and circulatory inefficiencies. In lower gravity, the strain on these systems would be significantly reduced, allowing elderly individuals to move freely and engage in physical activity. Furthermore, many aging organs—such as the heart, lungs, and kidneys—struggle to function optimally under Earth's gravitational load. Lower gravity reduces the workload on these organs, potentially stabilizing vital signs and reducing the risk of chronic conditions like hypertension or heart failure. Reduced gravity could also dramatically improve mobility for the elderly, helping them regain independence and fostering physical and emotional well-being.

For individuals with physical disabilities, reduced gravity offers transformative possibilities. On Earth, mobility impairments often limit independence and activity. In low-gravity environments, physical limitations are significantly mitigated. A person in a wheelchair could move freely with minimal effort, while prosthetics designed for reduced gravity could enable enhanced functionality. Caregivers would experience reduced strain, making it easier to assist disabled individuals and improving the quality of care.

Low gravity environments also have the potential to prevent physical deterioration. While prolonged exposure to microgravity can cause muscle atrophy and bone density loss, environments with partial gravity—such as those in a Bernal Sphere—offer a balanced solution. Elderly and handicapped individuals could maintain activity levels sufficient to mitigate these effects while still benefiting from reduced strain on their bodies.

By designing habitats like the Bernal Sphere with zones of variable gravity, we could create spaces tailored to meet the needs of diverse populations. Elderly and disabled individuals, traditionally marginalized in discussions of off-world habitation, could become pioneers in these environments. They could participate actively in research, education, artistic endeavors, or even industries like light manufacturing, transforming these challenges into opportunities to thrive and make contributions to society.

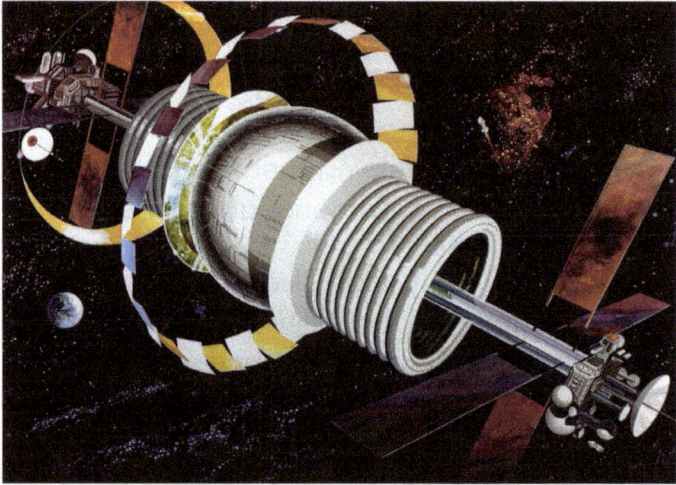

9.7A & 9.7B Two Illustrations of the outside of a Bernal Sphere.

9.7C The Interior of a Bernal Sphere with the colony on the inner wall of the sphere itself. Full gravity is at the "equator" of the sphere, but decreases in either direction, until one approaches the "poles" where there is near-zero gravity.

9.7D and 9.7E. Other approaches of a Bernal Sphere, or perhaps a saucer shaped colony. (Similar, but not covered here. Needs more research.

The O'Neill Cylinder

This structure is more advanced than the others and can be made much bigger, fitting exponentially more people than the first few habitats. Let's make the diameter four miles wide, the length 20 miles long, with a total land area of 250 square miles, discounting the solar windows. There would be six subregions, three valleys, and three arrays of windows to let the sun shine in the habitat.

In a way, this could be similar to living in a place like Silicon Valley in California. It would be as long or wide, and it would have a similar shape. People living in a long valley, with small towns, even small cities, with farms, forests, and a countryside. One could have a home in the "country" and work directly from it. The neighborhood would have a "downtown" with shops, movie theaters, restaurants, and schools, and the structure could be shaped anyway they please.

Another example is Copenhagen, Denmark. There is a beautiful city center, with everything any city would have, but it is clean. When you take a short walk out, you see parks. Very large parks, where you don't see any trace of the city. There are well-tended lawns, trees, even nature preserves. Walk along, and you run into small town sections, but with all this, you are still in Copenhagen. It's quite a place.

There would be light planar mirrors above the windows that open and close, allowing the sun to "rise" and "set," forming a day and night cycle. Each valley would be two miles wide and 20 miles long. The cylinder's axis would always point toward the sun.

All this land area, covered with soil and equipped with an ecosystem, would allow hundreds of thousands, perhaps millions, of people to live in comfort.

Above the axis, but connected, would be a regular or beaded torus, facing the sun to form an agricultural area.

Electric power would run underground from external power stations through cables laid when the community is built.

Two of these habitats could be connected by a cable, side by side, with opposite rotations.

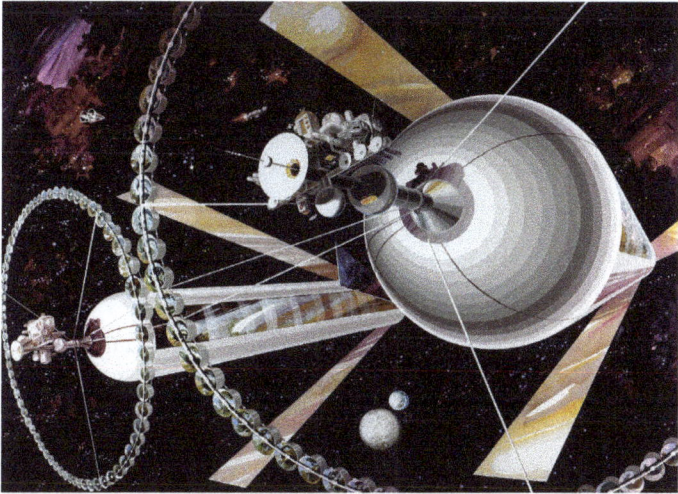

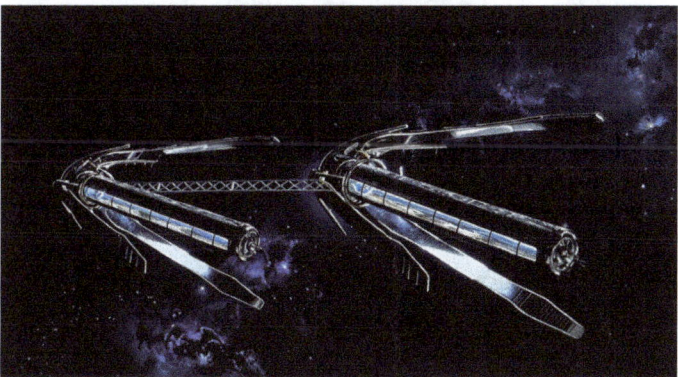

9.8A 7 9.8B Two illustrations: Two outside cylinders connected.

9.8C Inside one cylinder is vast, with farms, windows the length of the cylinder (three, evenly spaced, with the land). Only one mirror is shown but each "window" has a mirror to control the flow of sunlight.

As in the other two shapes of habitats, farms will be separate, in their own compartments, one after another in the form of a ring around the cylinder, but not attached to the surface of the cylinder.

There could be up to 10 million people living in comfort, all with their own spaces in cities and small towns.

The horizon here would point up, as with the other habitats. The difference would be three separate strips, two, from the point of view of a dweller, being way up on the sides separated by three transparent windows. Every strip of land must have a window directly above it, with a mirror panel moving up and down to reflect the sunlight and simulate the day/night cycle.

Standing on one strip, one would see the other two strips, but from the points of view of others on these two strips, they would be right side up and you would be sideways.

The rotation of the cylinder would produce Earth-like gravity. Each strip of land would have lakes, forests, rivers, parks, cities, and villages, creating an Earth-like environment to help satisfy the colonists' human needs. Living and working in space would be a normal way of life for them.

I have described three forms of habitat, but there may be many more.

Different societies and cultures will emerge in all of these habitats. Each will be a self-contained world, yet part of an expanded space infrastructure. They will help support this huge infrastructure and these industries in space while providing living quarters for these workers, but it goes further than that.

These habitats will be an alternative to Earth's gravity well, where one has to travel 4000 miles to escape. Rather than going down another, i.e. another planet, one can simply travel between these habitats using as little energy as possible.

One thing you must remember. I included the O'Nell habitats as part of this space infrastructure because I feel it would be an option for the laborers in orbiting space industries. Although these industries would be largely robotic, humans will still be needed to manage these industries, build new structures, catch and process materials from mass catchers or asteroids, and a number of other chores.

Humans will always be needed and must have a place to live in space, in comfort, with incentives for staying up there. These O'Neill habitats are the answer.

In building this space infrastructure, these habitats will come last, but they will come nonetheless.

I am going to quote John Strickland from his book Settling Space, p. 125.

- "In space, (rotating) colonies would only be built when:
- "The technology to construct them is ready.
- "Asteroidal materials are available and accessible outside a planetary gravity well.
- "When a colony can be built for less cost than the artificial 'real estate' being built can be sold. This could provide the business context for a rotating colony."

In other words, sell the land for more than it costs to build. This is for profit. (My interpretation).

Lastly, "Such colonies would probably be constructed by businesses, not governments."

These businesses would already have industries in space and on the Moon, so if they did not want to lose workers to a high turnover rate, they would have to provide for them in comfort.

One factor is that these habitats will not substitute for settling on the Moon or Mars, but simply be another option.

The Moon, and later Mars, will be settled. Civilizations will be built on both, by hardy people who can face the challenges and brave the elements in doing so.

Each habitat could also be custom-made, to be a forest or a desert, to suit the inhabitants desires. They would also have the option of choosing their own location, near or far from the sun. They could even live in seclusion or be a part of the larger space society.

New forms of government will arise, as with all new societies. Some will succeed, some will fail, but each habitat will attempt to create its own idea of heaven - or hell.

I will not attempt to describe or suggest what types of governments will arise. That is for their own choosing at their own time. There will be no utopias - that can only occur within each individual. The O'Neill space habitat is only one part of the many ways humanity will make its way to the stars.

As with individuals, some will come just to get away from Earth, for various reasons. They may just want to start fresh and reinvent themselves if they were unable to do so otherwise.

Many will want to start their own businesses. Some will succeed, others will fail.

There will be as many reasons as there are individuals, but with this new infrastructure of space, there will also be many choices.

Conclusion
The Final Infrastructure

Spaceports are located all over the world. As of this writing, they are in England, Scotland, Russia, China, Japan, the United States, Australia, New Zealand, French Guiana, and Brazil, with many more soon to be built.

The United States, Russia, and China have several spaceports. All three countries launch everything, from satellites to space stations and personnel to crew them.

French Guiana uses Ariane rockets to launch satellites for customers worldwide.

Brazil has a spaceport, Alcantara, on the equator, specializing in equatorial orbits and geosynchronous orbit.

The U.K. (England and Scotland) specializes in commercial space activities, and they are experimenting with a spaceplane known as Skylon.

Equatorial Launch Australia (ELA) operates the Arnhem Space Centre, providing spaceport infrastructure and launch services for small-medium lift rockets.

New Zealand has a spaceport located on the Māhia Peninsula, specializing in launching small satellites to orbit, with a particular focus on dedicated, frequent launch capabilities for the rapidly growing small satellite market, largely facilitated by the private company Rocket Lab, which operates the facility.

Japan has several spaceports, with activities from launching of commercial satellites to more advanced space missions like sending probes to asteroids or comets and participating in the ISS.

Space planes deliver cargo and passengers. Both types of vehicles travel to orbiting way stations for the purpose of receiving passengers and cargo, transfer them to other space vehicles for points to the Moon, space industrial plants, and space colonies.

Note that these ships will always travel in space. They will never enter the Earth's atmosphere or land on the surface.

There will be many way stations, perhaps hundreds, in Earth orbit. All would be owned privately or by certain governments, depending on the circumstances.

Now we are in Low Earth Orbit, LEO. LEO is the New York City of space, the gateway to the cosmos. Everything, crewed or not, is in LEO, from communication satellites to space laboratories, way stations to space stations built for business meetings involving space commerce, and even space police stations, all starting from LEO.

Cis-Lunar Space is the area from LEO to the Lunar orbital path around the Earth.

The Cis-Lunar Orbit region would not be just on a plane, but a sphere. Picture an imaginary sphere with a path of the Moon orbiting the Earth as the equator, with the area of the sphere around that path. This covers all orbits of the Earth, from polar to equatorial.

10.1. The Earth-Moon system, within an imaginary sphere covering cis-lunar space in three dimensions. This is all Cis-Lunar Space, from LEO to the surface of the Moon.

Space stations, industrial facilities, Near-Earth asteroids, O'Neill space colonies, all within this sphere, orbiting Earth at all angles, from every distance all the way to the Moon's orbital path. Each entity would have its own orbital path, all intersecting on the equatorial plane of Earth, but never colliding with one another. The vastness of space, even within this sphere, would make that impossible. If there was a chance of a collision of two satellites, both would have plenty of time and ample warning to avert a collision.

The asteroids, obviously, already occupy the spherical area, as they always have, but this would be a bonanza for the space foundries and prospectors.

Thousands of spaceships, liners, and taxis would travel throughout this cis-lunar sphere, with passengers and cargo from one habitat or industrial facility to another.

The space police would be active at all times because order must be maintained. Space pirates and smugglers will have to be dealt with, but the most important aspect here is maintaining space traffic.

There will be space lines for ships to travel, along with speed limits. These space line companies will no doubt have a policy of obeying speed limits and all other space laws, just like Earth-bound mass transit. There will be policemen handing out citations for any violations of space traffic laws, especially toward private individual spaceships.

All this extends to lunar orbit, with way stations there.

Anything launched from a mass driver will have to be cleared for ejection to prevent collisions with nearby spacecraft.

Cis-Lunar space will be a civilization in itself, and a base for missions to Mars and beyond.

Settling in space will diversify, with many more options on how to do so, beyond the scope of this book.

Only a small percentage of Earth's population will ever leave Earth, and overpopulation will always be a problem, but there will be a pressure valve for Earth's population for those willing to pursue the space adventure. This may not totally solve earth's overpopulation problem, but it will greatly reduce it.

On the other hand, when the technology is here and the infrastructure is built, people who can afford to will start visiting space for vacations. When they come back and share their experiences, more people will start to visit until many start making space their permanent home.

Human life will spread all over the solar system. New civilizations will be created free from the threat of Earth's destruction, should it ever occur.

A cis-Lunar infrastructure, including the O'Neill settlements, will be the best way to start.

Build a solid base here, for backup, then head for Mars, the Main Asteroid Belt between Mars and Jupiter, and eventually, the stars.

I have briefly mentioned Mars in various parts of this book, but I didn't include a chapter on it.

This was deliberate.

I don't feel we should venture to Mars just yet, without a solid base in Earth orbit and on the Moon to back it up.

I feel that going to Mars now would be another dead end, like Apollo, and a recipe for disaster.

Apollo was no doubt one of humanity's greatest achievements, but when it was done, after Apollo 17, there was nowhere else to go except in Low Earth Orbit with Skylab and the shuttle. Mars would simply be a repeat of that.

Building a space infrastructure would not only provide a base for a Mars mission, but it would lead human civilization to expand into space to the Moon, and beyond.

I feel that the first Mars mission will be done by a private expedition, like climbing Mount Everest.

As we build our infrastructure, a private expedition just might start from Earth orbit or the Moon and venture to Mars. Upon landing, they will then inform the world of their feat.

There may or may not be a few disasters leading up to this accomplishment, but some group will do it. It will not be a circus for the world to watch, as it was with Apollo 11, and it will not be done by any government.

It will be done by you! You and others like you who share your dreams for space. People from all walks of life, from any and all nations, who want to see humanity progress beyond the present problems of Earth and venture out into the cosmos to see what is out there.

Opportunities will abound. They are for people with different skills, abilities, and interests, and all of them will be needed.

Remember this, we must proceed together, and in peace. We cannot bring our wars, prejudices, and hatreds with us. All of these faults must be overcome.

We will, no doubt, bring our customs, cultures, and traditions with us. Some will form new ones, some will keep them as they are, and some will combine them in infinite combinations of diversity, but we will proceed as one human race.

We must learn from the mistakes of our history on Earth. If we can do that, we will have a giant head start on progress.

Space is our final frontier, but it will have no end, and there is room for all, no matter the number of human beings, or other species, for they, too, will come with us.

This is our hope for the future, so let's go for it!

It's there when you want it!

(Draft of) AN ACT

Recognizing the right of the first permanent settlers on the Moon or Mars to claim and trade private ownership of the real estate around them. This would create an incentive "prize" for the private entrepreneurs of Earth to risk their lives and fortunes developing affordable space travel for all, and transporting the settlers to their new home, at zero cost to US taxpayers.

Be it enacted by the Senate and House of Representatives of the United States of America in Congress assembled,

SECTION 1. SHORT TITLE

This Act may be cited as "The Space Settlement Prize Act",
or
"The Space Real Estate Act"
or
"The Land Claims Recognition Act".

SECTION 2. FINDINGS

The Congress finds that —

1. The expansion of the human habitat beyond Earth, through the establishment of a permanent Lunar settlement and a space "airline" enabling ordinary people to travel there, is a normal continuation of the age-old human drive to explore and settle unknown territory and will be of inestimable value for America and all mankind;

2. Privately financed space exploration and settlement is preferable to taxpayer financing, because the government needs to limit its own expenditures;

3. Space exploration and settlement, if financed by private companies and investors, will produce a huge boost to the economy, space industry employment for thousands, and new tax revenues for the United States;

4. A new, additional, incentive is needed because the potential short-term profit sources are currently much too small to attract the billions of dollars of private capital necessary;

5. The potential value of land on the Moon, Mars, or an asteroid can provide an additional economic incentive for privately funded space settlement at no cost to the government;

6. Prizes such as the Orteig Prize and the Ansari X Prize have an excellent record of promoting privately funded innovation, so Congress wishes to establish a "Space Settlement Prize" to promote the human settlement of the Moon and Mars.

7. At some time in the future, Congress may be in a position to add an appropriately large monetary award, but, for now at least, the tremendous economic value of land claims recognition should be more than sufficient.

8. There is currently no international law on private land ownership in space, because most major nations have

deliberately refused to ratify "The Agreement Governing the Activities of States on the Moon and Other Celestial Bodies, 1979, (hereafter called the "Moon Treaty"). The U.S. Senate's refusal to ratify means that the Moon Treaty's provisions are not "the law of the land" in U.S. courts, and therefore, do not inhibit the actions of U.S. citizens or legislators;

9. More importantly, the framers of the Moon Treaty found it necessary to attempt to write a rule forbidding private ownership of land on the Moon, clearly confirming that such an objective had not already been accomplished by "The Treaty on Principles Governing the Activities of States in the Exploration and Use of Outer Space, Including the Moon and Other Celestial Bodies", 1967, (hereafter known as the "Outer Space Treaty"), nor by U.N. resolution GA/res/1962;

10. The ratification failure of the Moon Treaty means there is no legal prohibition in force against private ownership of land on the Moon, Mars, etc., as long as the ownership is not derived from a claim of national appropriation or sovereignty (which is prohibited by the Outer Space Treaty);

11. Presumably it is only a matter of time until new treaties are negotiated, establishing a functional private property regime and granting suitable land ownership incentives for privately funded space settlements. The U.S. will, of course, abide by such new international law when it has ratified such a new treaty. But, given the urgent need for privately funded human expansion into space, as soon as possible, something must be done immediately, on a provisional basis, to correct the present inefficiencies in the international standard on property rights in space and to promote privately funded space exploration and settlement;

12. For property rights on the Moon, Mars, etc., the U.S. will have to recognize natural law's "use and occupation" standard, rather than the common law standard of "gift of the sovereign", because sovereignty itself is barred by existing international treaty;

13. U.S. courts already recognize, certify, and defend private ownership and sale of land which is not subject to U.S. national appropriation or sovereignty, such as a U.S. citizen's ownership (and right to sell to another U.S. citizen, both of whom are within the U.S.) a deed to land which is actually located in another nation. U.S. issuance of a document of recognition of a settlement's claim to land on the Moon, Mars, etc., can be done on a basis analogous to that situation;

14. This legislation concerns only the issuance of such a U.S. recognition and acceptance of a settlement's claim of private land ownership based on use and occupation, regardless of the nationality of the owner, and nothing in it, is to be considered a claim of national appropriation of, nor sovereignty over, any outer space body, or any part thereof;

15. The U.S. does not claim the right to "confer" private land ownership, and the U.S. states it is most definitely not making any claim of "national appropriation by claim of sovereignty, by means of use or occupation, or any other means" as prohibited by the Outer Space Treaty.

SECTION 3. DEFINITIONS

Space settlement: A permanently occupied facility, base, or city situated at a specific geographic location on an extraterrestrial body, such as the Moon, Mars, or an asteroid.

Private entity: A company, a consortium of companies, and/ or one or more individuals that are not controlled by any sovereign state or government. Examples of state control of a company include, but are not limited to, a government, government agency, or another government-controlled company owning or controlling an effective majority of the voting shares and/or having the ability to select the Board of Directors or executives. Merely being subject to normal government regulation, however, does not make a private company government controlled in this sense.

SECTION 4. RECOGNIZING EXTRATERRESTRIAL PRIVATE PROPERTY

1. All U.S. courts and agencies shall immediately give recognition, certification, and full legal support to land ownership claims based on use and occupation, of up to the size specified in Sections 6.1, 6.2, and 6.3 below, for any private entity which has, in fact, established a permanently inhabited settlement on the Moon, Mars, or an asteroid, with regular transportation between the settlement and the Earth open to any paying passenger.

2. For a land claim to receive such recognition and certification, the settlement must be permanently and continuously inhabited. The location and the population of the settlement may change, as long as there continues to be an inhabited settlement within the original claim.

3. Deliberate abandonment of the settlement shall be grounds for invalidating land ownership recognition derived from that settlement, but there shall be no penalty for brief unintentional absences caused by accident, emergency, or aggression.

4. Recognized ownership of land under this law shall include all rights normally associated with land ownership, including but not limited to the exclusive right to subdivide the property and sell portions to others, to mine any minerals or utilize any resources on or under the land, as long as it is done responsibly which does not cause unreasonable harm to the environment or other people;

5. If the requirements of this law continue to be met, all rights, privileges, and responsibilities shall be immediately transferable by sale, lease, or other appropriate means to other private space companies, individuals, or any other private entity. In order to facilitate that, all U.S. courts and agencies shall accept the validity of land ownership deeds issued by the settlement for portions of it's recognized land claim.

6. As long as the required conditions continue to be met, U.S. recognition documents shall remain valid for 100 years or until the U.S. ratifies a treaty that establishes an international property rights regime which gives comparable reward to privately funded settlement, whichever comes sooner;

7. The U.S. pledges to defend recognized extraterrestrial properties by imposing appropriate sanctions against aggressors, whether public or private. It pledges never to allow the sale to the U.S. Citizens of any extraterrestrial land which was seized by aggression. But it makes no pledge of military defense of recognized extraterrestrial properties.

8. If, after ten years, these limits prove to have been insufficient to get privately funded settlement efforts started, Congress, or some national or international authority it delegates, shall consider whether the maximum size of claims should be enlarged.

SECTION 5. CLAIMANTS' OBLIGATIONS

1. The claimant must commit to consistently make good faith efforts to promptly offer, or arrange for, safe and reliable transportation to and from the settlement to all, regardless of nationality, who are willing to pay a fare sufficient to cover expenses and a reasonable profit.

2. The claimant may not unreasonably deny landing rights, and the right to transport passengers and cargo, to any other safe and peaceful vehicle willing to pay a reasonable fee for such landing rights.

3. The claimant may set appropriate standards of behavior and safety, etc., for passengers and cargo and the use of its facilities, but it may not act in an anti-competitive manner.

4. If demand for transport exceeds supply, and the claimant is making a good faith effort to increase the availability of transport, it may give preference to passengers and cargo offering the largest financial inducement.

SECTION 6. RECOGNIZED CLAIM SIZE

On Earth's Moon:

1. The private entity that establishes the first such settlement on the Moon and meets the other conditions of this law shall be entitled to receive full and immediate U.S. recognition and certification of its claim of ownership of up to 600,000 square miles in a contiguous, reasonably compact shape which includes its base.

On Mars:

2. Given the greater distance, higher costs and larger amount of available land on Mars, the private entity that establishes the first such settlement on Mars shall be entitled to receive full and immediate U.S. recognition and certification of its claim of ownership of up to 3,600,000 square miles in a contiguous, reasonably compact shape which includes its base.

On Asteroids:

3. The private entity that establishes a permanently inhabited base on an asteroid shall be entitled to receive full and immediate U.S. recognition and certification of its claim of ownership of up to 600,000 square miles in a contiguous, reasonably compact shape that includes its base, or the entire asteroid if its surface area is smaller than 1,000,000 square miles.

SECTION 7. SUCCESSIVE CLAIMS

1. No entity (nor two entities which are effectively under the same control) shall receive recognition for a controlling interest in two land claims on the same body;

2. Each successive settlement on a body may receive recognition for a claim of up to fifteen percent less than the preceding one was entitled to;

3. An entity in control of one settlement may sell services, such as transport, to a genuinely independent entity which establishes a different settlement and makes a second claim on that body.

SECTION 8. CONCURRENT CLAIMS

1. In the event it cannot be established which of two settlements on the same body were established first, each may claim seven and one half percent less territory than it would have been entitled to if it were clearly the first of the two.

2. If, in such a case, the land claims of the two settlements overlap, and the claimants are unable to divide the land between them through negotiation, a U.S. court shall allocate the land between the two settlements as seems fitting, before recognizing the claims.

SECTION 9. INTERNATIONAL RELATIONS

1. The U.S. urges other countries to adopt similar laws, and the State Department is hereby instructed to try to negotiate a new multilateral treaty, or bi-lateral treaties with individual like-minded nations, making the same land claims recognition rules into international law.

2. All rights and privileges conferred by this law shall be available equally to the citizens (individual and/or corporate) of any nation which passes laws or ratifies a treaty offering similar rights to U.S. citizens.

3. If need be to secure international agreement, the State Department is authorized to agree to treaties which require that all claimants must be consortia which include companies or citizens from several different countries. It can even be required that at least one of the partners in each consortium be from a developing country.

Alan Wasser

Updated: April, 2012

For the background, purposes and answers to frequently asked questions about this law, please visit: the Space Settlement Initiative.

For a fully detailed, footnoted discussion of the many legal questions, opinions and precedents involved, as published in SMU Law School's Journal of Air Law & Commerce, the oldest and most respected law journal in its field, see: Space Settlements, Property Rights, and International Law: Could a Lunar Settlement Claim the Lunar Real Estate It Needs to Survive?.

For more on the group sponsoring this effort, please visit: The Space Settlement Institute.

Please send your comments to: contact@spacesettlement.org

APPENDIX B

Zero Gravity and the Physically Disabled

B.1. Zero Gravity and The Physically Disabled. Those sitting in wheelchairs will be able to float freely and work in the zero gravity of space without any problems.

In one of Robert Heinlein's lesser known stories, *Waldo*, there was a gifted recluse named Waldo Farthingwaite-Jones, who was born handicapped, a victim of *myasthenia-gravis*. He was also a mechanical genius, but could not adjust to society. He invented a sort of mechanical hand, the "'Waldo F. Jones' Synchronous Reduplicating Pantograph," and became a rich man from this invention.

This handicapped genius was then able to build a space habitat orbiting the Earth, serving as his home and workshop in zero-gravity. Because of the zero gravity environment, Waldo was able to fully use his entire body, his arms, legs, back, without any trouble or pain.

Things happen, and you'll have to read the rest yourself, but the concept of a handicapped person in zero-g being able to fully function is fascinating, and has been shown to work in real life.

A handicapped person on Earth, with no use of his or her arms, legs, back, regardless of what disease he's suffered or what injury he's experienced, will be able to fully function in a zero-g environment. Living with no gravity for a long period of time has serious drawbacks that are detrimental to the human body, but that will be covered, along with ways in which we can deal with this situation.

Zero gravity in space is no handicap to a physically disabled person. A person with no legs will have no problem thriving in zero-g. Amputees can have strength and dexterity, and new types of prosthetics can allow tasks beyond the powers of five fingers, as described in Heinlein's *Waldo*.

When a person is unable to move their arms, legs, or has a spinal injury, it is because their entire body is fighting against the force of Earth's gravity. They are too weak, physically, so the force of gravity holds their muscles down, rendering the entire body unable to function. There are times when the physically disabled person uses prosthetics, and is challenged to move his or her arms and stand on his legs. The brain rewires itself to adjust to these functions.

In zero gravity, everything changes. There is no gravity to hold the disabled person down. Their muscles free up, he or she is able to move about, and they can move their arms and legs to control the direction in which they are floating. They may be able to do this better than a normally functional human, for that particular human has to adjust and learn to control his or her limbs, while the disabled, fighting Earth's gravity all his life and using prosthetics, are already able to do so.

Experiments have been performed on the disabled using an airplane capable of replicating the zero-g environment.

One example of this occurred in August 2017, where the European Space Agency (ESA) sponsored a group of eight disabled kids on a parabolic airplane flight replicating the zero-g environment.

This process is common as the first step we are now taking in space tourism. Tourists board a jet where the passenger section has no seats, but are strapped to the floor. The plane takes off, and at a certain height, flies up at a steep angle. The plane then reaches a certain height and descends at the same angle, all in the form of a parabola. The passengers float around the cabin and enjoy the sensation, performing flips and other feats for thrills. The plane repeats this feat several times before the tour ends. With some people, the repetition causes them motion sickness, hence the nickname "vomit comet."

On August 24, 2017, (this is but one example; these tours occur frequently), eight handicapped children, along with six ESA astronauts and ESA Flight Director General Jan Worner got to experience this phenomenon. As the plane took off and made its parabolic curve, the children experienced zero gravity and everyone had fun, their handicaps notwithstanding. They also participated in experiments to illustrate the effects of zero-gravity on different states of matter, such as lighting a candle to see how the flame would react, mixing liquids of different densities that normally don't mix in Earth gravity, and playing games like ping pong with soap bubbles.

The ESA sponsored the initiative, Novespace organized the parabolic flight, and Reves de Gosse (Kid's Dream) arranged the project itself, culminating in the zero-g flight. You can also see the video of the flight itself at mirror.co.uk/science/esa-gives-eight-children-disabilities-11336750.

Astronauts from the International Space Station (ISS) stated "that in floating around, their legs would just get in the way" and "rookie astronauts have come onboard the ISS and started knocking things around because they don't know what to do with them (their legs)."

One disabled student asked an astronaut if a person like him needed a wheelchair in space. The answer he got was, "You have to get used to controlling your body in weightlessness, but certainly no need for a wheelchair as far as I can tell."

Even the blind can handle space, especially in bright spots a person with normal vision couldn't handle, or in the event of malfunctioning lights on a space vehicle, factory, or habitat.

When a human acquires any handicap, the brain rewires itself to adjust, as if the body had that natural function all along. The blind person is attentive to his other senses, especially to his hearing, so he can pick up sounds such as a bird flying, hearing the flapping of its wings that others would not normally notice.

According to Sheri Wells-Jensen, who has written an article in *Scientific American* titled "The Case for Disabled Astronauts," not having a disabled person on a space station/factory/habitat could be a disadvantage.

For example, let's say a blind astronaut is on a space station. An accident occurs on the station, where all the lights go out and it's totally dark, and no one can repair the life support system because they can't see. A blind astronaut, should he know the location of a flashlight, will be able to go there and directly retrieve the flashlight so work can commence on repairs. A sighted astronaut, in the dark, will have to adjust to the environment before he can find the flashlight, and even then may have trouble finding it. In a situation like a fire, as on the Russian space station *Mir* in 1997, there may not be much time to adjust and look for the lights.

The blind astronaut, because of his lack of sight, would not be bothered by the darkness, or by occluding smoke in the event of a fire. The astronaut would go directly to retrieve the flashlight and any other needed device, right away, saving valuable time.

Blind astronauts, depending on their training, will be able to work on any system in the dark in an emergency, while others will have to adjust. Only when the flashlights are retrieved will the sighted astronauts be able to repair the system. It is possible for a blind astronaut to be an expert in the field of engineering, so he will be able to fix systems in the dark, or when the sun is so bright other astronauts would not be able to see well.

There is also a case for deaf astronauts.

In 1962, an experiment was performed by the U.S. Navy on 11 men who were deaf, 10 of them due to spinal meningitis. This disease damages their inner ear, including their vestibular systems, which is mainly responsible for motion sickness.

For nearly a decade, these men were put through strenuous tests concerning the feasibility of human spaceflight.

This occurred in the 1960s, before we knew whether or not the human body could withstand a trip beyond Earth's atmosphere.

In one test, four of the men spent twelve straight days inside a 20-foot room that rotated constantly. In another experiment, they were sent out on a boat in very rough waters off the coast of Nova Scotia. The four deaf men sat around playing cards, but the researchers got seasick and had to cut the trip short so they could go home and recover. The seven other deaf men went up in the "vomit comet." In all the experiments, none of them ever got sick.

They never became astronauts but their work "made substantial contributions to the understanding of motion sickness and the adaptation of space flight," wrote Hannah Hotovy, of the NASA history division.

These students became known as the Gallaudet Eleven, after their college. One member, Harry Larson, was quoted as saying, "We were different in a way they (NASA) needed."

Adjusting to zero gravity in space is not an easy process. The body has to be maintained with diet, exercise, and the intake of vitamins and minerals, on a permanent basis.

Dr. Iddo Magen of the Davidson Institute of Science Education has written a paper on this problem, and I will quote him, along with others later noted, in the following section.

I have mentioned motion sickness when NASA has experimented with the deaf, where an astronaut can become nauseous and vomit. It has been found that it is due to the body's physiological processes, involving the ability to adapt to the sudden weightlessness in space. The internal fluids normally in balance on Earth become unbalanced in space, and the astronaut gets sick. The effects are mostly temporary, usually from a few hours to three days as the body adjusts, but there have been cases on the ISS where sickness can be long-term.

Long-term exposure to zero-g causes multiple health problems.

Fluid distribution makes up 60 percent of the body's weight and accumulates in the lower part of the body in normal Earth gravity. Our body's systems then distribute and balance the flow of blood to the heart and brain to assure just enough blood and other fluids flow to the proper parts as needed.

In the absence of gravity, these systems continue to function, but the fluids accumulate in the upper part of the body rather than the lower part, causing a person's face to puff up. There is a reduction of blood volume, red blood cell quantity, and cardiac output of blood, because of lower demands on the cardiovascular system. However, this is normal and the human body is still able to fully function in space.

There are, however, problems in balance as well as a loss of taste and smell. Vision blurs for a few days. The brain can adjust the image, and the body can adjust to the new environment, but once the astronauts return to Earth, the body again has to readjust to Earth's gravity, causing an inability to stand for more than ten minutes at a time. Fortunately, the body does readjust.

There are other adverse effects too.

Because there is no weight load on the back and leg muscles, they begin to weaken and shrink. Without exercise, astronauts may lose up to 20 percent of their muscles within five to eleven days.

Bone loss (atrophy) suffers most of all. The rate of bone loss in zero-g is 1.5 percent per month, compared to 3 percent per 10 years on Earth, and there have been situations where there was up to a 50 percent muscle mass loss on long term space missions. This loss mostly affects the lower vertebrae of the spine, the hip joint, and the femur. All in all, bones become brittle.

On Earth, there is a balance between bone builder cells and bone destroyer cells, and they complement each other. In zero-g, the increase in activity of bone destroyer cells is seen, and the bone decomposes into minerals that are dissolved in the blood and absorbed in the body.

The pelvic area carries most of the load under normal conditions, so bone destroyer activity greatly affects this area.

Elizabeth Howell in space.com stated, "Calcium in bones secretes out through urine. As the bones weaken, astronauts are more susceptible to breaking them if they slip and fall, just like people with osteoporosis." Astronauts who remain in space for three to four months do regain their bone density after a period of three to four years on Earth. On the Moon, it may be less, but that has yet to be proven.

On the ISS, muscle and bone loss is minimized by an exercise program, done by each astronaut six days a week, on three different machines: a treadmill, a bicycle, and a weightlifting machine. Each astronaut exercises for a total of two and a half hours per day.

One hour is spent lifting weights (air pressure), forty-five minutes is on the bike, and another forty-five minutes on the treadmill.

Weight setups use differential pressure by way of two evacuated cylinders. Each cylinder is a piston, and acts like a syringe, creating air pressure. These cylinders act like a simulated weight in space, pulling against the force they create.

This is known as an Advanced Resistive Exercise Device, and is capable of exercising all major muscle groups, focusing on squats, deadlifts, and calf raises, which helps the crew maintain their strength and endurance.

There is a personalized plan for each astronaut, because of their different physical make-ups.

The Combined Operational Load Bearing External Resistance Treadmill (COLBERT - Yes, it's named after Stephen Colbert) requires that the astronaut be harnessed and connected to the exercise machine, with the help of bungee cords.

The astronaut is weighted down as he runs in place on the treadmill. This is good for both the legs and the cardiovascular system.

The Russians also have a treadmill in their own separate module on the ISS, as well as a bicycle (VELO Ergometer Bike (VB-3)), Cycle Ergometer with Vibration Isolation System (CEVIS).

The "bicycle" is similar to an actual bicycle or an exercise bike, but is mounted to the wall and has no seat. The device is harnessed to the wall and the astronaut stands while pedaling. The astronaut then pedals for about forty-five minutes.

This exercise keeps the legs in shape so astronauts can walk when they return to Earth. It also helps maintain heart rate and the circulatory system.

Mark Springel, a research assistant of the Department of Pathology at Boston's Children's Hospital writes, "All human organ systems are affected by gravity's absence. The body is highly adaptive and can acclimatize to a change in gravitation environment, but the physiological adaptations may have pathological consequences, or lead to a reduction in fitness that challenges a space traveler's ability to function normally upon return to Earth. An astronaut does recover, but depending on their time in space, it can take up to four years to recover on Earth.

In this paper, we are covering spending a lifetime in space, including dying there. What would the overall effects of the body be? Some of it has been discussed. Is a human able to spend a lifetime in zero-g, dealing with the adverse effects? What would he or she have to do to keep their body safe from harm?

There are ways around all this; diet, exercise, protection from radiation, and development of new technologies that can accommodate zero-g workers.

For diet, the main problem of bone loss is a decrease of calcium. There is plenty of calcium available. Whenever zero-g workers eat, calcium can be added to their food, rather than taking it in pill form, which can and should be available. Other necessary vitamins can be supplemented as well, some occurring naturally in the food they eat. On Earth, sugar is added to almost all processed foods today, and though it is not a good thing to do, this very concept can be applied to vitamins in space food.

Exposure to an environment in space with microgravity and ionizing radiation can perturb the cardiovascular, excretory, immune, musculoskeletal, and nervous systems. Astronauts on the ISS are mostly protected by the station's shielding, along with Earth's magnetic field. This will have to change as we proceed further out into space. Antioxidants like Vitamins A and C can also absorb radiation before it causes harm to the human body.

Cosmic rays from space are constant, originating from supernovae tens of thousands of light years away. Local solar flares will occur, but one can be inside an asteroid mine or a space habitat with an efficient radiation shield for protection.

The Earth's magnetic field is a big plus in protecting astronauts from radiation in cis-lunar space. The magnetic field protects the entire globe from cosmic and solar radiation. This field forms a bullet shaped bubble, and extends into space about 60,000 kilometers (37,500 miles) toward the sun, and 300,000 kilometers (187,500 miles) away from it, toward deep space. Any space habitat within the range of 60,000 kilometers of the Earth, which is beyond Geosynchronous Earth Orbit (37,280 kilometers or 23,300 miles) would be safe most of the time, though shielding will still be required.

Beyond the safe zone, denser shielding will be required, but resources from the Moon and near Earth asteroids could be obtained to achieve this.

The human body at work will solve a lot of problems, be it in a space factory, a mine in an asteroid (moving rocks and other heavy objects, which is easy in zero-g) or moving segments of habitats, asteroids, or any heavy object by hand rather than by mechanical arm.

In habitats, there will be exercise machines, as on the ISS, as well as sports and other activities for workers during their spare time. There will also be rotating shifts of perhaps four months at a time.

In order to ensure a long life and protect the worker from the adverse effects of zero gravity and radiation, the worker would work four months, spend four months on the Moon or a rotating space habitat with gravity, and then four months on again at work in zero gravity.

They would spend their free time on the Moon rather than Earth because 1) the laborer would revert to being disabled under gravity and 2) it would take up to four years for a normal astronaut to recover, never mind the disabled worker.

The Moon has only one sixth of the Earth's gravity, and that worker will be able to function in a much lighter gravitational environment. The Moon's habitats, protected by regolith, also provide shielding against radiation.

What sort of jobs will be available in zero-gravity space, or on the Moon, for the Earth disabled (phrase mine)? The answer is simply any job that the non-disabled could do. There will be no limitations for anyone. A non-disabled person, unless that person intends to settle in space permanently, and many of them will, may want to return to Earth after a few years, and someone else will have to be trained to take his place, which costs time and money.

A disabled person may not want to return to Earth because its gravity will revert him back into the wheelchair, something he will not want to do.

In space, the disabled working in near-zero gravity won't be disabled, for they will be able to use every function of their bodies. This would build up their self-confidence and benefit not only themselves, but society as a whole to have more productive workers, and do more projects.

How can this benefit the laborer, and society as a whole?

Let's go over the list.

1. Labor jobs will be available. Jobs such as mining the Moon and asteroids, holding drills and other equipment, moving rocks and minerals.

2. Construction workers, constructing new habitats in space, be they passenger terminals, space factories, space stations, space living quarters, and doing repairs on them, especially when the repairs require that worker to go out in space to perform it.

3. Helping to assemble these habitats by hand and making the proper connections.

4. Operation of heavy equipment in space, on an asteroid, or on the Moon.

5. Working in space factories where zero gravity is essential in manufacturing a product. This could be metals, crystals, chemicals, medicines, alloys, or anything else. These workers would be professionals with a college education, up to a doctorate.

6. Being a scientist, experimenting with new materials in zero gravity.

7. Life sciences, working with human and other biological organisms, and observing how they function in zero-g, and how many adverse effects of zero-g on humans can be resolved. This is very important—with more of the human population coming into space, there must be applications for their bodies to remain healthy.

8. Piloting spaceships around space for long periods of time.

Space is the perfect place for the disabled. These individuals would only be considered disabled on Earth, making disability nearly a thing of the past.

With a broken spine or missing limbs, these people will simply be different, but equally important in helping to maintain stability, be it economic, technical, or otherwise, in this new spacefaring civilization.

Space will offer a lot of opportunities for the physically disabled from Earth. It has been proven that zero gravity can allow a person's body to function fully, as demonstrated in this paper.

Should a handicapped person decide to spend the rest of their lives in space, be it in labor or working with computers, life will be demanding, still having to keep their bodies in shape against zero-g, but if they are willing to adjust to the demands and self-discipline required, they will have productive and fulfilling lives.

Written by Alastair Browne

Edited by ChatGPT

Space and Earth's Environment – A Collaborative Solution

(C1.) A factory in space, leading to (C2.) A clean environment on Earth. This is possible. By putting more or more of our industrial activity, pollution on Earth will decrease exponentially, thereby giving humanity a chance to clean up the Earth and restore our natural environment. It is not too late to do so.}

The environmental and space movements, often seen as separate spheres of influence, have the potential to form a powerful partnership to address some of the most pressing global challenges. By merging their goals and leveraging space technologies, humanity can mitigate environmental harm, achieve sustainable energy solutions, and foster economic growth. This essay explores how space development can complement environmental efforts to restore Earth's ecosystems while advancing industrial and technological progress.

The Environmental Crisis

Pollution and climate change remain among the most critical challenges of our time. Factories and power plants spew harmful emissions such as carbon dioxide, methane, and mercury, leading to rising global temperatures, melting ice caps, severe weather disruptions, and poisoned ecosystems. Similarly, mining practices for minerals—from coal and iron to gold and platinum—ravage landscapes, pollute waterways, and contribute to biodiversity loss. For instance, mountain-top removal for coal mining renders entire regions uninhabitable, while chemical-intensive extraction processes poison rivers and soils.

At the same time, societies rely on these industries to power homes, factories, and transportation systems, driving economic growth and maintaining quality of life. The challenge is clear: how can humanity balance industrial needs with environmental sustainability? The solution may lie beyond Earth.

Space as the Key to Sustainability

The development of space-based industries offers a transformative approach to resolving the environmental crisis. By shifting key industrial activities—such as manufacturing, energy production, and mining—to space, humanity can significantly reduce the environmental burden on Earth.

Space Manufacturing

Space-based manufacturing could replace many Earth-based factories that rely on coal and oil for energy. Factories in orbit can use solar power—a virtually limitless and clean energy source—to process metals and create advanced materials. Zero-gravity conditions in space allow for the development of new alloys and products that are impossible to produce on Earth. Moreover, space manufacturing would eliminate the emission of toxic gases and liquids into Earth's atmosphere and waterways. While solid waste must be managed to avoid contributing to space debris, materials can be reused efficiently in orbit.

Clean Energy

Space technologies offer innovative solutions to the global energy crisis. Solar power satellites could beam clean energy directly to Earth, providing a renewable alternative to fossil fuels. Additionally, Helium-3, a rare isotope found on the Moon, holds promise for nuclear fusion energy, a clean and nearly limitless power source. Platinum mined from asteroids and the Moon could also be used in hydrogen fuel cells, supporting the transition to a hydrogen-based economy. These advancements would reduce greenhouse gas emissions and help phase out fossil fuels, creating a cleaner and more sustainable energy landscape.

Space Mining

Mining asteroids and celestial bodies like the Moon could supply critical materials without degrading Earth's landscapes. Asteroids are rich in metals such as iron, nickel, and platinum, which are essential for advanced technologies. By sourcing these materials from space, humanity can reduce the need for destructive mining practices on Earth. With fewer mines, damaged ecosystems could be restored, and land previously exploited for resources could be repurposed for conservation and reforestation efforts.

Environmental Benefits and Restoration

Transitioning industrial activities to space would have profound environmental benefits. Pollution from factories and power plants would decrease dramatically, as space-based facilities take on the burden of manufacturing and energy production. Restored landscapes and cleaner air and water would improve biodiversity and human health. The reduction of greenhouse gas emissions would slow climate change, offering hope for a more stable future.

Additionally, land restoration science is advancing, providing tools to rehabilitate degraded ecosystems. Forests and jungles could be replanted in areas previously cleared for mining and industry, gradually reversing the effects of deforestation and climate change. With time, Earth could begin to recover its natural beauty and ecological balance.

Challenges and Considerations

Despite its promise, the transition to space-based industries poses significant challenges. As factories and mines migrate to space, many Earth-based jobs will be lost, potentially causing widespread unemployment and economic disruption. This "outsourcing to space" may spark global objections and require careful management to ensure economic stability.

Furthermore, certain Earth-specific materials, such as petroleum for plastics, cannot be sourced from space. Limited production of these materials will need to continue on Earth, though on a much smaller scale. Finally, developing space infrastructure will require substantial investment and international cooperation, as well as solutions for managing space debris and ensuring ethical practices in space.

Conclusion

The partnership between the space movement and the environmental movement offers a visionary path forward. By harnessing space technologies, humanity can reduce pollution, transition to clean energy, and restore Earth's ecosystems. While challenges remain, the potential benefits far outweigh the obstacles. A cleaner, healthier planet is within reach, and space development can play a pivotal role in achieving this goal. With determination and innovation, the Earth of tomorrow could become a global park, a testament to human ingenuity and a sanctuary for future generations.

Written by Alastair Browne

Edited by ChatGPT

Ethics and Morals in the Space Movement

In this appendix, I am deviating away from the normal discussions about space development to pointing out that some leaders in this movement lack a moral compass. What they do and how they behave affects all of us, especially those of us dedicated to the settling and industrialization of space

Now is the time to discuss ethics and morals because they need to be covered in the space movement - badly!

Without a moral compass and a code of ethics, the space movement cannot survive as a whole. Many of these leaders who own industries covering space represent the future of the space movement. They also represent all of us who support it, write about it, and try to urge the general public to support it and take part in it.

If they, or any other space industrialist, exhibit any kind of bad behavior, big or small, and many of them are doing this now, they will give all of us a bad name.

This is exactly what is happening right now.

Let me reiterate. I am an author. When I signed my contract with HarperCollins for my first book, I noticed a section where the author, anytime he or she mingles with the public, and this means everywhere, at all times, he or she must always exhibit good behavior. This means no trouble, no vandalism, stealing, no creating an unnecessary and unpleasant scene in public, such as sexual or racial incidents, fights, or doing anything else that can result in disturbing the peace. i.e. No yelling "fire" in a crowded theater. I think you get the message here, and I am in complete agreement.

I'll give you another example. One woman in Central Park, New York, ran into a black man and she, not the man, gave him a lot of racial flack that brought in the police. This made the papers, and national news, and the woman was fired from her job. The company she worked for had nothing to do with this incident, but they, meaning the company, simply could not have someone like her representing them. She was an embarrassment, so they fired her.

What is happening with many of these CEOs in the space movement is a thousand times worse, and they are ruining it for all of us.

The space movement cannot support any industrialist or politician who supports space, but also corruption in the government and industry. The space movement cannot ignore human rights, woman's equality, racial discrimination, thievery, destroying our Constitution, or stealing money from the poor, sick, disabled and helpless. This means taking away Social Security, Medicare and Medicaid, or defunding money for the prevention of future pandemics, simply to use the money to fund cutting taxes for the rich. This is what is happening right now, and it's just the tip of the iceberg.

THIS IS NOT WHAT WE STAND FOR, AND WE WON'T PUT UP WITH IT.

We, as space advocates, who support humanity's advancement into space, cannot and will not stand for the support of making the U.S. or any other country into a Kleptocracy. We will not favor the rich if they are guilty of scandal and corruption, or pose a threat to society, even if they fully support the space movement. We will not ignore or disregard the poor or any other people different from ourselves. We will not tolerate any forms of criminal activity, and we will not tolerate racial or any other form of discrimination.

We also cannot venture into space and ignore the problems here on Earth. The space movement must contribute to help solve Earth's problems, not ignore them.

Settling and developing space means the advancement of ALL humanity - regardless of race, creed, color, religion, national origin, and, (the following is my own) wealth, or the lack of it.

I once read about a case where a single migrant worker was walking alone on a road in Texas looking for work. Looking up in the night sky, this migrant dreamed of being in a spaceship, traveling and working in space. He was poor, broke, and probably hungry, but people like him matter - they matter just as much as the wealthy industrialists building space factories in Earth orbit.

Should that migrant ever realize his dream, who knows what he could accomplish in space.

To the opposite end, I once saw a movie, Elysium, where there was one space station, an O'Neill space colony in the shape of a Stanford Torus, that was the perfect utopia in space, for the wealthy and privileged.

Meanwhile, back on Earth, there was war, poverty, destruction, total chaos, a worldwide oblivion, and nowhere was safe. All civilization had collapsed and people were killing each other.

There are many that say that this is the world the rich are trying to create, if not in space, then some isolated place on Earth.

No! The answer is no! We cannot and will not have that!

First, we are not going into space to escape, but to help improve the quality of life on Earth. If we industrialize space, we will then want to clean up Earth, because pollution will greatly decrease, perhaps even be eliminated. We can then restore the natural environment on Earth and make it a better place to live.

Second, I liked the O'Neill space habitat in the the movie, but there should be hundreds of them, or even thousands, all over the solar system, for people of all cultures, lifestyles, religions, vocations, meaning doing different types of work like asteroid mining or working in industrial plants, or for any other purposes one can imagine. The inhabitants would live all kinds of lives from all backgrounds.

To put it bluntly, the movie Elysium sucks!

We need to go into space. The people who lead us into space need the highest set of morals and ethics, not be racial, and willing to take with them all people with the necessary qualifications.

All of these morals and ethics need to be practiced on Earth by the very people who will lead us into space. We are in an age where we are losing all of this, and we need to get it back.

I am not a socialist, but I don't believe in unethical or dishonest behavior. I certainly don't believe we should cut back, or abolish, the rights of women and minorities, because they will also participate in the space movement and we need their skills. We better treat them as our equals, or we, as Americans will be left out in the cold.

Nor can we establish a new feudal system like we had in the Middle Ages, where we had the very rich living opulent lifestyles, and the very poor working for them, living in squalid conditions, forever in debt and poverty. We need a well to do middle class, and opportunities for all to advance according to their talents and abilities. It was like this once, we need to return to it.

Here is where I stand. (Note that I am referring to the up and coming industrialization of space here, but this applies everywhere, in any and all working environments. You could call this a Code of Ethics).

ALL morals and ethics must be practiced equally on Earth as in space. It is the only way to keep our civilization stable. Without this, we will collapse, possibly into savagery. They must also be practiced by all people, no matter who or what they are.

We will have major industries in space, and many industries and industrialists will stand out and make money in the trillions. That's all right, because that will propel us into space. It is not a sin to be rich. It is how you acquire it and what you do with it that matters.

It's all right to make a trillion dollars, as long as it's honorable and is at no one else's expense, or detriment.

It's not all right to acquire this same amount of money at other people's expense. By this, I mean taking away their Social Security, the healthcare benefits, or making them pay higher taxes, for the benefit of the trillionaire.

It's all right to hire a large number of laborers to work in your industries, be it construction, mining, or performing any dangerous job with, for example, exposure to radiation or other deadly elements. These laborers must be paid at least a living wage, or more, but not less and they must be protected from these deadly elements; by this, I mean 100 percent protection, no less.

It's not all right to exploit these workers, to leave them unprotected to the dangers of space, ignore them if they become ill or injured from these dangers, or pay them meager wages and have them live in adverse living conditions. If these workers are going to do the menial labor that is required for the industrialist to make a handsome profit, they must be paid a living wage and be provided decent meals and comfortable (I didn't say luxurious) shelter, especially from the ravages of space. The industrialist must earn their loyalty to him, other laborers, and the company. This industrialist will still have plenty of profits for him (or her) self. In fact, they may even earn more, and they will have the fierce loyalty of their workers.

The industrialist must also pay his or her fair share of the taxes. When a space infrastructure is built, they will no doubt use it every day. One must pay for its construction and its continued maintenance, like everybody else. No exceptions!

Again, this will not affect the profits of any industry in space.

The problem here is greed. The sad thing is, greed isn't necessary. With the profits many CEOs are earning today, they cannot even begin to spend the money that they have, even after taxes. Why do they want more, especially at other people's expense?

It's all right to live in a luxury home, or even have several of them in different places.

It's not all right to live in a luxury home and have all your laborers live in squalid conditions. This is not the feudal system of the Middle Ages. This is the era of space development, and it's time we all start living and treating each other like human beings. This is the only way we are going to survive and prosper up there.

It's all right to be the head/CEO of a space industry. It's all right to be on top, be in the lead, and make the most profits.

It's not all right to destroy your competitors, steal their business, or deny up and coming space businesses their opportunity to grow, develop, and prosper.

It's all right to greatly and ambitiously expand into space, form private space industries, greatly expand them, make massive fortunes, and then venture into the infinite void of space.

It's not all right to do all this at the expense of people's lives, rights, freedoms, security, or to steal their life savings they have and need to live on, nor is it all right to help place a country under a dictatorship to achieve the goals they desire, even if these goals are noble.

It's not all right to ignore the people back on Earth.

It's not all right to destroy the environment.

It's all right to fiercely compete.

It's not all right to destroy each other.

In order to prosper in space, one must be honest, ethical and have a moral compass, and apply these equally on Earth as well as in space.

This is the only way we can prosper and be free as we venture into space.

(No help from ChatGPT. Again, it's all in my own words, because I have to speak my mind!)

GLOSSARY OF ACRONYMS

AI – Artificial Intelligence

ATV – Automatic Transfer Vehicle

BEAM – Bigelow Activity Expendable Module

CAS – Center for Aerospace Sciences (located at UND)

CCD – Charge Coupled Device

COLBERT –Combined Operational Load Bearing External Resistance Treadmill

CEVIS – Cycle Ergometer with Vibration Isolation System

COTS – Commercial Orbital Transport Services

CSP – Concentrated Solar Power

DoSp – Department of Space

ELV – Expendable Launch Vehicles

ESA – European Space Agency

G (g) – Grams

GEO – Geosynchronous Earth Orbit (22,300 miles up)

HLLV – Heavy Lift Launch Vehicle

HTV – HII (H two) Transfer Vehicle (Japan)

IAWN – International Asteroid Warning Network

ICE – Internal Combustion Engine

IEA – International Energy Agency

ISDC – International Space Development Conference

ISRU – In Situ Resource Utilization

ISS – International Space Station

JAXA – Japan Aerospace Exploration Agency

JPL – Jet Propulsion Laboratory (Pasadena, California)

Kg – Kilograms

LCROSS – Lunar Observation Crater and Sensing Satellite.

LEO – Low Earth Orbit (about 200-500 miles up)

LH_2 – Liquid Hydrogen

LOX – Liquid Oxygen

NASA – National Aeronautics and Space Administration

NEA – Near Earth Asteroid

NEO – Near Earth Object

NOAA – National Oceanic and Atmospheric Administration

NSC – National Space Council

NSF – National Science Foundation

NSS – National Space Society

OMV - Orbital Maneuvering Vehicle

OTV - Orbital Transfer Vehicle

PEM - Polymer Electrolyte Membrane or Proton Exchange Membrane

PPM - Parts Per Million

PGM - Platinum Group Metals

PD - Public Domain

PHAs - Potentially Hazardous Asteroids

R & D - Research and Development

SBSP - Space Based Solar Power

SEI - Space Exploration Initiative

SLS - Space Launch System or Senate Launch System

SMRs - Small Module Reactors

SPS - Solar Power Satellite

U.K. - United Kingdom (Great Britain)

U.N. - United Nations

UND - University of North Dakota

U.S. - United States

WISE - Wide-field Infrared Survey Explorer

WPT - Wireless Power Transmission

Zero-g - Zero Gravity

BIBLIOGRAPHY

Introduction

1. The Coming of Private Enterprise

1. Carter, Jamie; "Despite SpaceX Success NASA Will Pay Russia $90 Million To Take U.S. Astronaut To The ISS," Forbes, Jun 3, 2020; Updated Jul 27, 2020; https://www.forbes.com/sites/jamiecartereurope/2020/06/03/despite-spacex-success-nasa-will-pay-russia-90-million-to-take-us-astronaut-to-the-iss/.

2. June 1989 — Apollo Program Benefits. https://castle.eiu.edu/~scienced/3290/science/moon/benefits.html#:~:text=The Apollo program increased our,both Earth and the sun.

3. Klerkx, Greg; *Lost in Space - The Fall of NASA and the Dream of a New Space Age*; Pantheon Books, New York, 2004, pp. 211.

4. Krukin, Jeff; "Unaffordable and Unsustainable? Signs of Failure in NASA's Earth-to-orbit Transportation Strategy;" Space Frontier Foundation; 25 July 2006; 18 pp.

5.   Kuhr, Jack; "Starliner by the Numbers: Payload Research." May 8, 2024; https://payloadspace.com/starliner-by-the-numbers-payload-research/#:~:text=Dragon and Starliner seat cost,extension increased to $65M.

6.   National Security Technology Accelerator (NSTXL); Reducing the Cost of Space Travel with Reusable Launch Vehicles; February 12, 2024; https://nstxl.org/reducing-the-cost-of-space-travel-with-reusable-launch-vehicles/#:~:text=The cost of a space launch, over $2 billion per launch.

2. A Call for Private Leadership in Space Development

3. The New Role of NASA, the Government, and a Proposed Department of Space

1.   Barnes-Svarney, Patricia; "Staking a Claim," *Ad Astra*, November/December 1992, p. 26.

2.   Berger, E. (2022). SpaceX's Starship could save NASA billions on lunar missions. Ars Technica. Retrieved from https://arstechnica.com.

3.   Congressional Budget Office. (2021). The cost of NASA's Artemis program. CBO Report.

4.   Drake, Nadia, "The 'Program Is Precarious': Lori Garver on NASA's Artemis I Moonshot," *Scientific American*, August 25, 2022, https://www.scientificamerican.com/article/the-lsquo-program-is-precarious-rsquo-lori-garver-on-nasa-rsquo-s-artemis-i-moonshot/.

5.   Extravehicular Activity, https://en.wikipedia.org/wiki/Extravehicular_activity

6.   Foust, Jeff; "The Long Goodbye: Transitioning from the ISS to Commercial Space Stations will take time," *Space News*, March 27, 2017, p. 14

7. Leone, Dan; "NASA, NOAA Prepare for Procurements on Signature Programs," *Space News*, January 27, 2014, p. 11.

8. Lucchesi, Emile Le Beau; "Looking back at the space shuttle Challenger disaster;" Published: October 25, 2021 | Last updated on May 18, 2023; https://www.astronomy.com/space-exploration/looking-back-at-the-space-shuttle-challenger-disaster/.

9. Lunar Gateway; https://en.wikipedia.org/wiki/Lunar_Gateway. (See Criticism)

10. Lynch, Timothy B.; "Space-The Final Department?" *Ad Astra*, March, 1990, p. 48.

11. NASA Office of Inspector General. (2022). NASA's management of Space Launch System program costs and contracts. NASA OIG. Retrieved from https://oig.nasa.gov.

12. NASA. (2020). Artemis Plan: NASA's lunar exploration program overview. NASA. Retrieved from https://www.nasa.gov

13. The Planetary Society, "Your Guide to NASA's Budget," https://www.planetary.org/space-policy/nasa-budget.

14. Polaris Dawn, https://en.wikipedia.org/wiki/Polaris_Dawn.

15. Reiley, Jennifer; "How The Columbia Shuttle Disaster Changed Space Travel;" *Texas A&M Today*; Texas A&M University College of Engineering; February 1, 2023; https://today.tamu.edu/2023/02/01/how-the-columbia-shuttle-disaster-changed-space-travel/

16. SpaceX Updates. (2023). Elon Musk's vision for cost-efficient spaceflight.

17. Thangavelu, Madhu; "A U.S. Department of Space?" *Space News*, July 2, 2012, pp. 19, 21.

4. Space Infrastructure

1. Babb, G.R.; Davis, H.P.; Phillips, P.G.; Stump, W.R.; "Impact of Lunar and Planetary Missions on the Space Station," *Lunar Bases and Space Activities of the 21st Century*, W.W. Mendell, Editor; Lunar and Planetary Institute, Houston, 1985, pp. 125-139.

2. Chang, Kenneth; "More Asteroid Strikes Are Likely, Scientists Say," *The New York Times*, November 7, 2013, p. A11.

3. Choi, Charles Q., "Earth at Higher Risk of Asteroid Impact, Russian Meteor Explosion Reveals," November 06, 2013, http://www.space.com/23487-asteroid-threat-earth-russian-meteor-explosion.html?cmpid=514630_20131107_14120644

4. Gabrynowicz, Joanne I.; "Space Law: A Case for the Cosmos," *Space World*, December, 1988, pp. 7-9.

5. Godwin, Richard; "Why Do We Have a Space Program Anyway?" Apogee Books, *Yuri's Night*, Chicago, 2004.

6. Gray, Richard; "United Nations to lead efforts to defend Earth from Aster-oids," *The Telegraph*, 30 October 2013, http://www.telegraph.co.uk/science/space.

7. Horz, Friedrich; "Mass Extinction and Cosmic Collisions: A Lunar Test," *Lunar Bases and Space Activities of the 21st Century*, pp. 349-358.

8. Kramer, Miriam; Incredible Technology: How to Clean Up Dangerous Space Junk; www.space.com/22969-space-junk-clean-up-ideas-incredible-technology.html; September 30, 2010.

9. Markham, Derek; 9 Concepts for Cleaning up Space Junk; www.treehugger.com/clean-technology/9-concepts-cleaning-space-junk.html; April 26, 2012.

10. Moore, Amanda Lee; "Legal Responses for Lunar Bases and Space Activities of the 21st Century," *Lunar Bases and Space Activities of the 21st Century*, pp. 735-739.

11. Moskowitz, Clara; "United Nations to Adopt Asteroid Defense Plan," *Scientific American*, October 28, 2013, http://www.scientificamerican.com/article.cfm?id=un-asteroid-defense-plan.

12. National Aeronautics and Space Administration (NASA), "Near Earth Object Program," http://neo.jpl.nasa.gov.

13. Near Earth Objects Information Centre, (The Spaceguard Centre) http://www.nearearthobjects.co.uk.

14. Pike, John, "Project Chicken Little," *Ad Astra*, November/December 1992, pp. 33-35.

15. Platt, John; "United Nations takes aim at asteroids," Mother Nature Network, October 29, 2013, http://www.mnn.com/earth-matters/space/stories/united-nations-takes-aimat-asteroids

16. Simberg, Rand; "Homesteading the Final Frontier: A Practical Proposal for Securing Property Rights in Space;" http://www.space-settlement-institute.org/support-files/space-homesteadingsimberg-report.pdf; April 2012; pp. 11-14.

17. Spahr, Timothy; Director, Minor Planet Center; "NEO Threat Detection and Warning: Plans for an International Asteroid Warning Network," UN COPUOS Scientific & Technical Subcommittee, Smithsonian Astrophysical Observatory, 18 February 2013.

18. Tunguska event, http://en.wikipedia.orgwiki.Tunguska_event

19. Wasser, Alan; "An Act to Promote Privately Funded Space Settlement;" http://www.spacesettlement.org/law/

20. Yu, Alan; "Space Agencies of the World, Unite: The U.N.'s Asteroid Defense Plan," NPR News, http://www.npr.

org/2013/11/03/242353389/space-agencies-of-the-world unite-the-u-n-'-s-asteroid-defense-plan.

5. Building a Lunar Civilization and
6. Evolution of the Lunar Base

1. Arnold, William H.; Bowen, Stuart; Fine, Kevin; Kaplan, David; Kole, Margaret; Kolm, Henry; Newman, Jonathan; O'Neill, Gerard K.; and Snow, William R.; "Mass Drivers I: Electrical Design," Space Resources and Space Settlements, NASA, Scientific and Technical Information Branch, NASA SP-428, Washington, D.C., 1979, pp. 87-100.

2. Blacic, James D.; "Mechanical Properties of Lunar Materials Under Anhydrous, Hard Vacuum Conditions: Applications of Lunar Glass Structural Components," *Lunar Bases and Space Activities of the 21st Century*, pp. 487-495.

2A. Browne, Alastair Storm and Maryann Karinch; *Cosmic Careers - Exploring the Universe of Opportunities in the Space Industries,* HarperCollins Leadership, 2021, pp. 168, 170-174.

3. Criswell, David R.; "Powder Metallurgy in Space Manufacturing," Space Manufacturing 4, *American Institute of Aeronautics and Astronautics,* New York, 1981, pp. 389-398.

4. Cutler, Andrew Hall and Krag, Peter; "A Carbothermal Scheme for Lunar Oxygen Production," *Lunar Bases and Space Activities of the 21st Century*, pp. 559-569.

5. Danuri, https://en.wikipedia.org/wiki/Danuri

6. Duke, Michael B.; Mendell, Wendell W.; Keaton, Paul W.; Report of the Lunar Base Working Group, April 23-27, 1984, Los Alamos National Laboratory, Los Alamos, New Mexico, LALP-84-43, Issued August, 1984, 41 pp.

7. Duke, Michael B.; Mendell, Wendell W.; Roberts, Barney B.; "Strategies for a Permanent Lunar Base," *Lunar Bases and Space Activities of the 21st Century*, pp. 57-68.

8. Ehricke, Krafft A.; "Lunar Industrialization and Settlement- Birth of Poly-global Civilization," *Lunar Bases and Space Activities of the 21st Century*, pp. 827-855.

9. Friesen, Larry Jay; "Search for Volatiles and Geologic Activity From a Lunar Base," *Lunar Bases and Space Activities of the 21st Century*, pp. 239-244.

10. Gibson, Michael A. and Knudsen, Christian W.; "Lunar Oxygen production From Ilmenite," *Lunar Bases and Space Activities of the 21st Century*, pp. 543-550.

11. Granath, Bob; "Lunar, Martian Greenhouses Designed to Mimic Those on Earth," NASA's Kennedy Space Center, Florida, April 24, 2017. https://www.nasa.gov/science-research/lunar-martian-greenhouses-designed-to-mimic-those-on-earth/?utm_source=chatgpt.com.

12. Haskin, Larry A.; "Spartan Scenario for the Use of Lunar Materials," *Lunar Bases and Space Activities of the 21st Century*, pp. 435-443.

13. Heppenheimer, T.A.; "Achromatic Trajectories and the Industrial Scale Transport of Lunar Resources," *Lunar Bases and Space Activities of the 21st Century*, pp. 155-167.

14. Jones, Harry W.; "The Partial Gravity of the Moon and Mars Appears Insufficient to Maintain Human Health;" NASA Ames Research Center, Moffett Field, CA, 94035-0001; 50th International Conference on Environmental Systems 12-15 July 2021; https://ntrs.nasa.gov/api/citations/20210019591/downloads/ICES-2021-142.pdf.

15. Kokh, Peter, *A Pioneer's Guide to Living on the Moon*, Luna City Press, October 1, 2018, 727 pages.14. Lin, T.D., "Concrete for Lunar Base Construction," Lunar Bases and Space Activities of the 21st Century, pp. 381-390.

16. Lunar Water, https://en.wikipedia.org/wiki/Lunar_water.

17. Lin, T.D., "Concrete for Lunar Base Construction," *Lunar Bases and Space Activities of the 21st Century*, pp. 381-390.

18. Lunar Water; en.wikipedia.org/wiki/Lunar_water;

19. NASA Office of Public Affairs, Washington, D.C., "Global Exploration Strategy and Lunar Architecture," Speakers Shana Dale, Doug Cooke, Scott Horowitz, Moderated by Dean Acosta, NASA Press Secretary, Malloy Transcription Service, Johnson Space Center, December 4, 2006, 49 pp.

20. National Aeronautics and Space Administration (NASA), *Beyond Earth's Boundaries-Human Exploration of the Solar System in the 21st Century*, Annual Report to the Administrator, The Office of Exploration, Washington, D.C., 1988, 51 pp.

21. Schrunk, David; Sharpe, Burton; Cooper, Bonnie; and Thangavelu, Madhu; The Moon: Resources, Future Development and Colonization; John Wiley and Sons; Chichester, New York, Brisbane, Toronto, Singapore; Published in association with Praxis Publishing, Chichester; 1999; pp. 52, 53, 216, 245-275, 302, 303, 347, 348.

22. Synthesis Group, The; *America At The Threshold: America's Space Exploration Initiative*; Superintendent of Documents, U.S. Government Printing Office, Washington, D.C., 20402; 1991; pp. A34.

23. Taylor, G. Jeffrey; "The Need For a Lunar Base: Answering Basic Questions About Planetary Science," *Lunar Bases and Space Activities of the 21st Century*, pp. 189-197.

24. Thompson, Andrea; " 'Significant Amount' of Water Found on Moon"; www.space.com/7530-significant-amount-water-moon.html; November 13, 2009.

25. Thompson, Andrea; "It's Official: Water Found on Moon" www.space.com/7328-official-water-moon.html; September 23, 2009.

26. Tucker, D.S.; Vaniman, D.T.; Anderson, J.L.; Clinard, F.W., Jr.; Feber, R.C., Jr.; Frost, H.M.; Meek, T.T.; and Wallace, T.C.; "Hydrogen Recovery from Extra-terrestrial Materials Using Microwave Energy," *Lunar Bases and Space Activities of the 21st Century*, pp. 583-589.

27. Williams, David R.; "Ice on the Moon -A Summary of Clementine and Lunar Prospector Results; NASA Goddard Space Flight Center, Greenbelt, MD; nssdc.gsfc.nasa.gov/planetary/Ice/ice_moon.html; December 10, 2012.

28. Wingo, Dennis; *Moonrush - Improving Life on Earth with the Moon's Resources*, Apogee Books; Burlington, Ontario, Canada; 2004; pp. 9, 10, 17, 21, 32, 59, 60, 77, 78, 81, 82, 83, 86, 89, 195, 196, 200, 201.

7. Near-Earth Asteroids (NEAs)

1. Barnes-Svarney, Patricia; "Grabbing a Piece of the Rock," *Ad Astra,* October, 1990, pp. 7-13.

2. Berger, Brian; "Obama Proposes $17.7B NASA Budget, Asteroid Retrieval Mission," *Space News*, April 15, 2013, p. 5.

3. Bormanis, Andre; "Rocks of Ages Past," *Ad Astra,* November/December, 1992, pp. 21-24.

4. Boyle, Alan; "Luxembourg sets its sights on space resources, with Seattle as launch pad; April 10, 2017; https://www.geekwire.com/2017/luxembourg-asteroid-space-resources-seattle.

4A. Browne, Alastair Storm and Maryann Karinch; *Cosmic Careers - Exploring the Universe of Opportunities in the Space Industries,* HarperCollins Leadership, 2021, pp. 131, 133, 134.

5. Federal Reserve Bank of Minneapolis - Consumer Price Index; Economic Research & Data; What is a dollar worth? (CPI Calculator); http://minneapolis.org/research/data.us/calc.

6. Foust, Jeff; "Commercial Space Entrepreneurs Embrace NASA Asteroid Retrieval Plans," *Space News*, April 15, 2013, p.14.

7. geo.libretexts.org/Bookshelves/Geography_(Physical)/ Physical_Geography_and_Natural_Disasters_ (Dastrup)/02:_Universe_and_Solar_System/2.07:_ Other_Objects_in_the_Solar_System

8. Hein, Andreas M.. et al. (2018): "A Techno-Economic Analysis of Asteroid Mining" This study evaluates the economic viability of asteroid mining, emphasizing factors like spacecraft reuse and throughput rate. It provides a framework for assessing the return of high-value resources, such as platinum, to Earth while identifying technological hurdles for cost reduction.

9. Jet Propulsion Laboratory, California Institute of Technology; Twenty Years of Tracking Near-Earth Objects; July 23, 2018; https://www.jpl.nasa.gov/news/ twenty-years-of-tracking-near-earth-objects/.

10. Keck Institute for Space Studies (KISS): Explores asteroid retrieval missions, focusing on the technical and logistical challenges of transporting materials. Learn more.

11. Klotz, Irene; "Commercial Firms Push Alternative Approaches for NASA Asteroid Initiative," *Space News*, October 7, 2013, p. 6.

12. Leone, Dan; "NASA, Slowly Amassing List of Potential Targets for Asteroid Retrieval Mission," *Space News*, January 13, 2014, p. 9.

13. Lewis, John S.; *Mining the Sky*; Helix Books, Addison Wesley Publishing Company; Reading, Massachusetts, etc.; 1996; pp. 67-114, 126, 127, 135-138, 160, 161, 168.

14. Lewis, John S. and Ruth A. Lewis; *SPACE RESOURCES Breaking the Bonds of Earth*, Columbia University Press, New York, 1987, pp. 242-269, 293, 327.

15. Lewis, Ruth A.; "The Horn of Plenty Renewed -A Look at Space Resources," *L5 News*, pp 4-6.

16. Luxembourg Space Agency, Space Resources, www.spaceresources.public.lu.

17. Moskowitz, Clara; "NASA's Vision to Lasso Asteroid: New Concept Art Revealed (Video); http://www.space.com/22492-nasa-asteroid-capture-concept-images-video.html.

18. Robertson, Donald F.; "What is Wrong With Retrieving an Asteroid?"*Space News*, January 13, 2014, pp. 19, 21. http://DonaldFRobertson.com

19. Sivolella, David; *Space Mining and Manufacturing - Off-World Resources and Revolutionary Engineering Techniques;* Springer/Praxis, Praxis Publishing, Chichester, U.K., 2019, pp. 67-71.

20. SpringerLink - Asteroid Prospecting and Space Mining: Discusses the classification of extractable materials and their economic implications, focusing on reducing costs through in-situ processing. Access the study.

21. Synthesis Group, The; *America At The Threshold: America's Space Exploration Initiative*; Superintendent of Documents, U.S. Government Printing Office, Washington, D.C., 20402; 1991; pp. A37, A38.

8. Energy and the Space Infrastructure

1. Bauer, Wolfgang and Gary D. Westfall; University Physics with Modern Physics, Chapter 40, Problem 47, "Estimate the temperature that would be needed to initiate the fusion reaction (Helium-3/Helium-3);" Vaia; https://www.vaia.com/en-us/textbooks/physics/university-physics-with-modern-physics-2-edition/chapter-40/problem-47-estimate-the-temperature-that-would-be-needed-to-/#:~:text=Question: Estimate the temperature needed to make, nuclei to occur is approximately 3.1×107 K.

2. Cohen, Aaron; "Human exploration of space and power development," *Solar Power Satellites-A Space Energy System for Earth*, Peter E. Glaser, Frank P. Davidson, Katinka Csigi Editors; John Wiley and Sons; Chichester, New York, Brisbane, Toronto, Singapore; Published in association with Praxis Publishing, Chichester; 1998; p. 229.

3. Diagrams of Helium-3/Deuterium, Helium-3/Tritium, Helium-3/Lithium, and Helium-3/Helium-3 reactions courtesy of Adobe Stock. Extended Licenses used to reprint these illustrations in this book have been purchased from Adobe Stock. Used by permission.

4. Diagram of Fuel Cell by Alastair Browne.

5. Encyclopedia Britannica; Nuclear Accident, Soviet Union [1986]. https://www.britannica.com/event/Chernobyl-disaster?utm_source=chatgpt.com. November 23, 2024

6. Fuel Cell Works, "Types of Fuel Cells," http://fuelcellsworks.com/Typesoffuelcells.htmp, October 20, 2004, pp. 1-4.

7. International Atomic Energy Agency (IAEA) - Guidelines and research on nuclear safety, including space-based applications: IAEA Publications: "Use of Nuclear Power Sources in Outer Space" (https://www.iaea.org).

8. Kirtley, Dr. David, CEO; "Explaining Helion's Fusion Fuel, D-He-3;" HELION; https://www.helionenergy.com/articles/explaining-helions-fuel-choice-d-he-3/#:~:text=D-He-3 fusion requires more energy into the system.

9. Kulcinski, Gerald L. and Schmitt, Harrison H.; "Nuclear Power Without Radioactive Waste-The Promise of Lunar Helium-3; *Return To The Moon II Proceedings of the 2000 Lunar Development Conference;* Space Front Press, a division of the Space Frontier Foundation; 2000; pp. 272-276.

10. Latyshev, L.; and Semashko, N.; Global Space Power Plant Industry Set (GSPPIS); *Solar Power Satellites-A Space Energy System for Earth*; Peter E. Glaser, Frank P. Davidson, and Katinka Csigi; Praxis Publishing; Chichester; 1998; pp. 408, 409.

11. Lewis, John S.; *Mining the Sky*; Helix Books, Addison-Wesley Publishing Company; Reading, Massachusetts, etc.; 1996; pp. 112.

12. Maryniak, Gregg E. and O'Neill, Gerard K.; Nonterrestrial resource for solar power satellite construction; *Solar Power Satellites-*A Space Energy System for Earth; Peter E. Glaser, Frank P. Davidson, and Katinka Csigi; Praxis Publishing; Chichester; 1998; pp. 579-596.

13. McMurray, Clifford R., "In One Giant Leap: Shackleton Energy Company's Strategic Vision," *Ad Astra*, Winter 2013, pp. 26, 27.

14. Minnesota Office of Environmental Assistance, "Common Types of Fuel Cells," http://www.moea.state.mn.us/p2/fuelcells-types.cfm, October 20, 2004, pp. 1-5.

15. New Mexico Solar Energy Association, "Explore Fuel Cells," http://www.nmsea.org/Curriculum/7_12/Fuel_Cells/fuel_cells.htm, October 13, 2004, pp. 1-5.

16. International Atomic Energy Agency (IAEA) - Guidelines and research on nuclear safety, including space-based applications: IAEA Publications: "Use of Nuclear Power Sources in Outer Space" (https://www.iaea.org).

17. National Academies of Sciences, Engineering, and Medicine - Reports on planetary protection and nuclear propulsion systems: "Nuclear Power and Propulsion in Space: Assessing Potential Benefits and Risks" (https://www.nap.edu).

18. National Aeronautics and Space Administration (NASA) - Technical reports on space nuclear power systems and safety protocols: NASA Glenn Research Center: "Nuclear Power Systems for Space Exploration" (https://www.grc.nasa.gov).

19. National Space Society, "Space Solar Power - The Way Forward for Clean, Limitless Energy." (https://nss.org/space solar power).

20. Peterson, Russell W.; The state of global ecology and the search for benign energy systems; *Solar Power Satellites-A Space Energy System for Earth*; Peter E. Glaser, Frank P. Davidson, and Katinka Csigi; Praxis Publishing; Chichester; 1998; pp. 125-132.14. Roberts, Paul; *The End of Oil - On the Edge of a Perilous New World*; Houghton Mifflin, Boston, New York, 2004, pp. 2, 3, 5, 7, 26, 45-49, 64, 87-89, 120-123, 130, 131, 145, 146, 215-217, 242, 274, 275, 295, 313.

21. Roberts, Paul; "Over a Barrel," *Mother Jones*, December, 2004, pp. 68, 69.

22. Rocky Mountain Institute, "Energy - Types of Fuel Cells," http://www.rmi.org/sitepages/pid556.php, October 20, 2004, p. 1.

23. Sundyne, "How do Hydrogen Fuel Cells Work," (https://www.sundyne.com/how-does-a-hydrogen-fuel-cell-work/).

24. Synthesis Group, The; *America At The Threshold: America's Space Exploration Initiative*; Superintendent of Documents, U.S. Government Printing Office, Washington, D.C., 20402; 1991; pp. A32, A33.

25. U.S. Department of Energy (DOE), "Space Based Solar Power." (http://www.energy.gov/space-based-solar-power.)

26. U.S. Nuclear Regulatory Commission (USNRC). "Backgrounder on Radioactive Waste; (http://www.nrc.gov/reading-rm/doc-collections/fact-sheets/radwaste.html;)

27. Wald, Matthew L.; "Cheaper Part for Fuel Cells To Be Announced Today - New Membrane Said to Be Half as Costly," *The New York Times*, October 5, 2004, p. C8.

28. World Nuclear Association. Fukushima Daiichi Accident UPDATED MONDAY, 29 APRIL 2024 https://world-nuclear.org/information-library/safety-and-security/safety-of-plants/fukushima-daiichi-accident?utm_source=chatgpt.com

29. Yeomans, Matthew; *Oil - Anatomy of an Industry*; The New Press, New York, London, 2004, pp. 205-207, 217.

30. Zielinski, Sarah; "Natural Gas Really Is Better Than Coal - If too much methane leaks during production, though, the benefits will be lost" Smithsonian Magazine; February 13, 2014; https://www.smithsonianmag.com/science-nature/natural-gas-really-better-coal-180949739/?no-ist

9. O'Neill Space Habitats

1. Browne, Alastair Storm and Maryann Karinch; *Cosmic Careers - Exploring the Universe of Opportunities in the Space Industries*, HarperCollins Leadership, 2021, pp. 143-146.

1A. Heppenheimer, T.A.; Colonies in Space, Warner Books, 1978, pp. 144, 145, 153-161.

2. International Academy of Astronautics (IAA): Artificial Gravity Research and Development in Space Habitats. This technical report reviews the design of artificial gravity environments like the Bernal Sphere and their potential impact on human health. Reference: IAA Study Group. (2019). Artificial Gravity Research. International Academy of Astronautics.

3. NASA Human Research Roadmap: https://humanresearchroadmap.nasa.gov

4. O'Neill, Gerard, *The High Frontier-Human Colonies in Space, Anchor Books*, Anchor Press/Doubleday, Garden City, New York, 1982, pp. 223-231.

5. O'Neill, Gerard, *The High Frontier-Human Colonies in Space,* 3rd. Edition, Apogee Books, Space Studies Institute, 2000, pp. 14, 37-44, 57, 62, 63.

6. Sagan, Carl. *Pale Blue Dot: A Vision of the Human Future in Space.* Ballantine Books, 1997, 384 pages. This book explores the potential for humanity to adapt and thrive in space, touching on how unique environments like low gravity could expand human potential.

7. Strickland, John with Sam Spencer; Settling Space - Human Settlements in the Solar System and Beyond; Apogee Books; Burlington, Ontario, Canada; 2021; pp. 125, 128, 130, 133, 134, 145, 147, 158.

Appendix A - (Draft of) An Act

1. Wasser, Alan, *An Act to Promote Privately Funded Space Settlement*, http://www.spacesettlement.org/law.

Appendix B - Zero Gravity and the Physically Disabled

1. Cofield, Cara; "Kids with Disabilities Float Like Astronauts in Gleeful Flight," www.space.com, August 25, 2017.

2. "Disabled Student Inspired by Astronaut Tim Peake" www.bbc.com/news/uk-england-wiltshire-33323870; June 30, 2015.

3. "Disability Can be a Superpower in Space. https://space.nss.org/disability-can-be-a-superpower-in-space/, ISDC, NSS Press Release, May 16, 2018.

4. Eveleth, Rose; "It's Time to Rethink Who's Best Suited for Space Travel," Wired, January 27, 2019, wired.com/story/its-time-to-rethink-whos-best-suited-for-space-travel/.

5. Grush,Loren;"HowDoAstronautsExerciseinSpace?"TheVerge, December 23, 2019, the verge.com/2017/8/29/16217348/nasa-iss-how-do-astronauts-exercise-in-space/.

6. Howell, Elizabeth, "Weightlessness and Its Effect on Astronauts," www.space.com/23017.weightlessness.html, December 16, 2017.

7. Magen, Dr. Iddo, "The Dangers of Zero Gravity," Davidson Institute of Science Education, https://davidson.weizmann.ac.it/sciencepanorama/dangers-zero-gravity, February 27, 2017.

8. O'Neill, Gerard, The High Frontier- Human Colonies in Space, 3rd. Edition, Apogee Books, Space Studies Institute, 2000, p 259.

9. Springel, Mark; "The Human Body in Space: Distinguishing Fact from Fiction," Harvard University, The Graduate School of Arts and Sciences, SITN-Science in the News; sitn.hms.harvard.edu/flash/2013/space-human-body/, July 20, 2013.

10. Wells-Jensen, Sheri; *Scientific American*, blogs. scientificamerican.com/observations/the-case-for-disabled-astronauts/, May 30, 2018.

11. "The International Space Station Advanced Restive Exercise Device;" NASA Technology Transfer Program, technology.nasa.gov/patent/MSC-TOPS-59/

12. NASA; "Exercising in Space," nasa.tumbler.com/post/136706596374/exercisinginspace.

13. "Cycling on the International Space Station with Astronaut Doug Wheelock;" YouTube; May 11, 2013.

AUTHOR BIO

ALASTAIR S BROWNE is a writer and lives in Durham, North Carolina. He is the author of *Cosmic Careers*, a book on future jobs in the coming space movement, published internationally. His other writings include topics pertaining to different problems this world is facing today and how they can be resolved for the benefit of all.

Alastair attended North Carolina State University in Raleigh, and earned a B.S. degree in Statistics, and the University of North Dakota, in Grand Forks, where he obtained an M.S. degree in Space Studies.

Besides his passion for reading books and writing essays, Alastair likes to play music with friends and likes to travel, especially in northern regions of the world.